The Market Research Society

With over 8,000 members in more than 50 countries, The Market Research Society (MRS) is the world's largest international membership organization for professional researchers and others engaged in (or interested in) marketing, social or opinion research.

It has a diverse membership of individual researchers within agencies, independent consultancies, client-side organizations, and the academic community, and from all levels of seniority and job functions.

All MRS members agree to comply with the MRS Code of Conduct (see Appendix 2), which is supported by the Codeline advisory service and a range of specialist guidelines on best practice.

MRS offers various qualifications and membership grades, as well as training and professional development resources to support these. It is the official awarding body in the UK for vocational qualifications in market research.

MRS is a major supplier of publications and information services, conferences and seminars and many other meeting and networking opportunities for researchers.

MRS is 'the voice of the profession' in its media relations and public affairs activities on behalf of professional research practitioners, and aims to achieve the most favourable climate of opinions and legislative environment for research.

The Market Research Society (Limited by Guarantee) Company Number 518685

Company Information: Registered office and business address:
15 Northburgh Street, London EC1V 0JR
Telephone: 44 20 7490 4911
Fax: 44 20 7490 0608
e-mail: info@marketresearch.org.uk
website: www.mrs.org.uk

MARKET RESEARCH IN PRACTICE SERIES

**Published in association with The Market Research Society
Consultant Editors: David Barr and Robin J Birn**

Kogan Page has joined forces with The Market Research Society (MRS) to publish this unique series of books designed to cover the latest developments in market research thinking and practice.

The series provides up-to-date knowledge on the techniques of market research and customer insight and best practice in implementing them. It also shows the contribution market research and customer information management techniques can make to helping organisations of all kinds in shaping their strategy, structure, customer focus and value creation.

The series consists of several essential guides that focus on the core skills developed in the MRS training and qualifications programmes (www.mrs.org.uk). It provides practical advice and case studies on how to plan, use, act on and follow-up research, and on how to combine it with other sources of information to develop deep insights into customers.

Fully international in scope of content, its readership is also from all over the world. The series is designed not only for specialist market researchers, but also for all those involved in developing and using deeper insights into their customers – marketers in all disciplines, including planning, communications, brand management, and inter-active marketers.

Other titles in the series:

Business to Business Market Research, Ruth McNeil
Consumer Insight, Merlin Stone
The Effective Use of Market Research, Robin J Birn
Market Intelligence: How and why organizations use market research, Martin Callingham
Market Research in Practice: A guide to the basics, Paul Hague, Nick Hague & Carol-Ann Morgan
Questionnaire Design, Ian Brace

Kogan Page Ltd
120 Pentonville Road
London N1 9JN
Tel: 020 7278 0433
www.kogan-page.co.uk

MRS. MARKET RESEARCH IN PRACTICE

RESEARCHING CUSTOMER SATISFACTION & LOYALTY

HOW TO FIND OUT WHAT PEOPLE REALLY THINK

PAUL SZWARC

KOGAN PAGE

London and Philadelphia

Publisher's note

Every possible effort has been made to ensure that the information contained in this book is accurate at the time of going to press, and the publishers and authors cannot accept responsibility for any errors or omissions, however caused. No responsibility for loss or damage occasioned to any person acting, or refraining from action, as a result of the material in this publication can be accepted by the editor, the publisher or the author.

First published in Great Britain and the United States in 2005 by Kogan Page Limited

120 Pentonville Road
London N1 9JN
United Kingdom
www.kogan-page.co.uk

525 South 4th Street, #241
Philadelphia PA 19147
USA

© Paul Szwarc, 2005

ISBN-10   0 7494 4336 7
ISBN-13   978 0 7494 4336 8

British Library Cataloguing-in-Publication Data

A CIP record for this book is available from the British Library.

Library of Congress Cataloging-in-Publication Data

Szwarc, Paul.
    Researching customer satisfaction and loyalty/Paul Szwarc.
        p. cm. – (Market research in practice series)
    Includes bibliographical references and index.
    ISBN 0–7494–4336–7
    1. Consumer satisfaction. 2. Customer loyalty. I. Title. II. Series.
HF5415.335.S95 2005
658.8'12 – dc22
                                                                            2005011073

Typeset by Datamatics Technologies Ltd, Mumbai, India
Printed and bound in Great Britain by MPG Books Ltd, Bodmin, Cornwall

Contents

The editorial board

SERIES EDITORS

David Barr has been Director General of The Market Research Society since July 1997. He previously spent over 25 years in business information services and publishing. He has held management positions with Xerox Publishing Group, the British Tourist Authority and Reed International plc. His experience of market research is therefore all on the client side, having commissioned many projects for NPD and M&A purposes. A graduate of Glasgow and Sheffield Universities, David Barr is a Member of the Chartered Management Institute and a Fellow of The Royal Society of Arts.

Robin J Birn has been a marketing and market research practitioner for over 25 years. In 1985 Robin set up Strategy, Research and Action Ltd, a market research company for the map, atlas and travel guide sector, and the book industry. In 2004 he was appointed Head of Consultation and Research at the Institute of Chartered Accountants of England and Wales. He is a Fellow of The Market Research Society and a Fellow of the Chartered Institute of Marketing, and is also the editor of *The International Handbook of Market Research Techniques*.

ADVISORY MEMBERS

Martin Callingham was formerly Group Market Research Director at Whitbread, where he ran the Market Research department for 20 years and was a non-executive director of the company's German restaurant chain for more than 10 years. Martin has also played his part in the market research world. Apart from being on many committees of the MRS, of which he is a Fellow, he was Chairman of the Association of Users of Research (AURA), has been a council member of ESOMAR, and has presented widely, winning the David Winter Award in 2001 at the MRS Conference.

Nigel Culkin is a Fellow of The Market Research Society and member of its Professional Advisory Board. He has been a full member since 1982. He has been in academia since 1991 and is currently Deputy Director, Commercial Development at the University of Hertfordshire, where he is responsible for activities that develop a culture of entrepreneurism and innovation among staff and students. He is Chair of the University's, Film Industry Research Group (FiRG), supervisor to a number of research students and regular contributor to the media on the creative industries.

Professor Merlin Stone is Business Research Leader with IBM's Business Consulting Services, where he works on business research, consulting and marketing with IBM's clients, partners and universities. He runs the IBM Marketing Transformation Group, a network of clients, marketing agencies, consultancies and business partners, focusing on changing marketing. He is a director of QCi Ltd, an Ogilvy One company. Merlin is IBM Professor of Relationship Marketing at Bristol Business School. He has written many articles and 25 books on marketing and customer service, including *Up Close and Personal: CRM @ Work, Customer Relationship Marketing, Successful Customer Relationship Marketing, CRM in Financial Services* and *The Customer Management Scorecard*, all published by Kogan Page, and *The Definitive Guide to Direct and Interactive Marketing*, published by Financial Times-Pitman. He is a Founder Fellow of the Institute of Direct Marketing and a Fellow of the Chartered Institute of Marketing.

Paul Szwarc began his career as a market researcher at the Co-operative Wholesale Society (CWS) Ltd in Manchester in 1975. Since then he has worked at Burke Market Research (Canada), American Express Europe, IPSOS RSL, International Masters Publishers Ltd and PSI Global prior to joining the Network Research board as a director in October 2000. Over the past few years Paul has specialized on the consumer financial sector, directing multi-country projects on customer loyalty and retention, new product/service development, and employee satisfaction in the UK, European and North American markets. Paul is a full member of The Market Research Society. He has presented papers at a number of MRS and ESOMAR seminars and training courses.

Preface

Two themes run through this book. The first is that staff in customer-centric organizations understand the relationship between customer satisfaction, loyalty and profits. They also understand how to use market research to provide a competitive edge. However, they recognize that there is no simple management model or research technique that will provide a clear and unambiguous answer as to what drives customer satisfaction and customer loyalty.

The second theme is that market researchers have the business tools that can enable organizations to fully understand their customers' perceptions, attitudes and behaviours. However, some of these tools reside within client companies and others reside with professional market research agencies. These two groups of professionals must work together to help customer-centric companies realize their full potential. To achieve this, market researchers need to become 'business enablers' and not just 'information providers'. Market researchers therefore must be prepared to broaden their knowledge in the other disciplines of business, from finance to operations, from marketing to strategic planning and from employee relations to customer service.

People who are interested in learning more about the processes and issues involved in researching customer satisfaction and loyalty should find something of interest in this book. It is by design not highly technical. It provides an introduction to market research and theories of customer satisfaction and loyalty for three different audiences: management who work with, or rely upon, market research to provide input to business decisions; market researchers at the start of their careers; and students of marketing and related subjects.

The book is in five sections. Part I sets the scene by looking at how interest in customer satisfaction and loyalty has developed over the past three decades. It also briefly describes some of the more common management theories about customer satisfaction and loyalty. Finally it provides a short introduction to the concepts of qualitative and quantitative research for those readers who are not market researchers.

Part II examines, from the client and supplier perspectives, how market research projects on customer satisfaction and loyalty are commissioned. It looks at the factors that both client and agency researchers need to consider when preparing a research brief and proposal. There are also chapters covering the issues around research methodology, such as sampling, as well as a chapter on questionnaire design.

Part III is relatively short, and covers what is involved in getting a survey into the field.

Part IV covers the important topics of data analysis and reporting of customer satisfaction and loyalty research. It examines this topic from both the research supplier and the client perspectives.

Part V looks at how interest in this area is changing. It briefly recaps the key themes in the book and asks the question: what does the future hold for researching customer satisfaction and loyalty?

Acknowledgements

I have been very fortunate in having worked for three very different client companies: the Co-operative Wholesale Company (a large UK retailer), American Express Europe Ltd and International Masters Publishers (a Scandinavian publishing company). In addition, I have worked in three market research agencies: Burke Market Research (a small Canadian agency), IPSOS RSL (the UK arm of an international full service agency) and Network Research (a mid-sized UK agency). Some of these companies are publicly owned, some privately owned. However, all have one thing in common – a customer-centric approach to business.

In addition, I have also been fortunate in having a number of very inspirational managers who provided encouragement and opportunities for me to learn new skills, experiment with new ideas and look at things through the eyes of others. While they are too many to mention in detail, a few deserve special mention, namely Brenda Graham (Co-operative Wholesale Society), Peter Bartram, Tommaso Zanzotto and Chris Rodrigues (American Express), Dawn Mitchell and Mike Denny (IPSOS RSL), Geoff Fuller (International Masters Publishers) and Eamonn Santry, Virginia Monk, Petra van der Heijden and Derek Mesure (Network Research).

In regard to this, my first book, I must express my appreciation to a few more people in particular. Firstly, my thanks to David Barr, Robin Birn and the other members of the Market Research Society's Book Publishing Committee for accepting my synopsis and providing a novice author with an opportunity to see what he can do, and to Pauline Goodwin and Jon Finch at Kogan Page, and Susan Curran at Curran Publishing Services, for their help in editing and marketing the book. To Derek Mesure, Martin Callingham and Janet Wilkinson I offer sincere thanks for reading the early drafts of this work and providing much needed encouragement and suggestions for improvements, and Stephen Watson of Network Research for his charting skills. All were very much appreciated.

Finally, I must thank my wife Sally. As a sole trader providing organizational development and management consultancy to a diverse range of clients, her ability to continually provide first-class customer service while coping with the constantly changing demands of clients is an inspiration to behold. I am also indebted for the patience she has shown over the last six months while I have been writing this book rather than spending the time with her.

Part I

INTRODUCTION AND THEORY

1 Introduction to customer satisfaction and loyalty

What are customer satisfaction and customer loyalty? Why are companies and other organizations so interested in them? Are there simple solutions to these questions, as some consultants suggest? How do employees contribute to customer satisfaction and loyalty? These are some of the questions this chapter explores in order to provide a context for the chapters that follow.

> What concerns me is not the way things are, but rather the way people think things are.
>
> **Epictetus, Greek philosopher**

This book is about how to research customer satisfaction and loyalty. It looks at what is involved from three different angles. The first is from the view of an organization wishing to understand, and measure, how satisfied its customers are with the products and services they receive from it. The second is from the perspective of a research agency that has been asked to obtain feedback from customers about their experiences when dealing with companies. Finally, it considers the issue from the perspective of consumers who participate in customer satisfaction surveys, including both business customers and members of the general public.

Throughout this book, I use the words 'organization' and 'company' interchangeably. This is simply because if I referred to 'company' throughout some readers who work in organizations might mistakenly believe this book is not referring to them, and vice versa.

WHAT CUSTOMER SATISFACTION IS

I have heard it said that measuring customer satisfaction cannot be very difficult. After all, you are either satisfied with the service you receive or you are not. If you get what you want you are satisfied, if you don't you are not.

If it is that easy, then obtaining people's opinions about how satisfied they are with the products and services they receive from organizations should be a relatively straightforward matter – or is it? Let us look at a typical situation that many people face every day – their journey to work. I consider myself typical of the thousands of commuters who take a train each morning. Leaving my home, I walk to the local station. On arrival, I glance at the indicator board to see if my train is running on time. It is, so I walk to a particular section of the platform where I know the carriage is likely to have some empty seats, and where I expect the train doors to be when the train stops, as this will enable me to get into the carriage quickly. Commuting into London each day, this is a necessity, as more and more people are travelling to work by train but the train company cannot provide any extra trains to cope with the increased number of passengers because the rail infrastructure cannot handle any further increases in traffic volume within current safety regulations. As a result, not everyone who joins the train at my local station this morning will get a seat.

The imminent arrival of the train is announced, but the announcer also tells us that this morning there will be only four carriages instead of the usual eight 'due to a shortage of available rolling stock'. No doubt this announcement is seen as providing a service, as it enables us to know that there is now very little likelihood of getting a seat on the train, and that when the train stops at stations further up the line, the journey will become very uncomfortable as more and more commuters board.

By the time the train arrives at my destination, it is running a few minutes late because of delays at the various stations up the line caused by commuters trying desperately to board it when it is already overcrowded.

How do I evaluate the service I have just received? If I had been asked as I walked to the station, would my opinion have been the same as at the end of my journey? I suspect not. However, would a reasonable person feel the train company has provided a poor service? It is not responsible for the regulations limiting the number of trains that can run on the tracks. It is hampered by the lead times for any expansion of the rail infrastructure (which is measured in years, because of the regulatory need to consult people who could be affected). While it is true that the shortage of rolling stock led to uncomfortable conditions for everyone, the ticket I purchased actually only promised to transport me from my station to my destination; it made no mention about the degree of comfort I could expect. It also did not actually guarantee to get me there at an exact time, merely within five minutes of the published time. Interestingly, in the decade that I have been commuting on this particular line, the train operator has found it necessary to lengthen the projected trip time by over five minutes – and between September and December the trains have a separate timetable, arriving about five minutes earlier at my station than in the rest of the year. (The arrival time at the destination remains the same all year round.) This increased journey time is to allow for anticipated delays caused by trees shedding their leaves on the line and the like. So, one could say that the train operating company has done everything it could to provide a service; and since I am a regular commuter, it has given me a discount on my rail fare in recognition of my loyalty (and my willingness to help its cash flow by paying for the service in advance).

However, let us continue my journey. As I leave the station, I cross the road and walk on towards my office. Along the way, I notice a new Mercedes, and remember my uncle's story of how his local Mercedes dealer upgraded his cassette radio to a CD and radio unit. It took just 20 minutes, and when he drove off he noticed the staff had pre-tuned the radio to the same stations to which his old radio had been tuned – and they had not even mentioned it as part of the service! I recall too how different that was from the service I used to receive from my local car dealer – the mechanics used to leave grease marks on the upholstery to let me know they had serviced the car. (I no longer buy cars from that dealership.)

Then, as I approach my office I call into the local Pret A Manger for a takeaway coffee, and as the smell of the freshly made Danish pastries is so tempting, I buy one of those too. The people behind the counter greet me cheerfully and confirm my order, packing it into a bag together with paper napkins. They wish me a good day and thank me for my purchase. Perhaps they realize that that my small £2.25 daily morning expenditure adds up to over £500 a year for them. Arriving at the office, my phone is ringing. It is a research company wanting to ask a few questions about how satisfied I was with …

What influences our opinions about service

Every day we encounter situations that can affect our views of a particular product or service. Emotional and rational factors (as shown by the train journey experience) shape our opinions. In addition, the opinions and experiences of others who we view as advocates (as in the Mercedes example) shape our opinions, and so too do our sensory experiences and the service we receive from other companies (such as Pret A Manger). In addition, Pret A Manger has earned my loyalty through their cheerful service despite there being three competitors within 100 yards of its outlet, some of which have lower prices. Unfortunately for my train operator my views are conditioned partially by my being a 'captive' customer. I do not have a choice which train company to use – only one runs on my route.

We are also subjected to a barrage of advertising and other 'messages' from companies and the media that can influence our view of organizations and the service we receive from them. So *customer satisfaction* is how customers view an organization's products or services in light of their experiences with that organization (or product), as well as by comparison with what they have heard or seen about other companies or organizations. Therefore, measuring customer satisfaction has to take all these matters into account, as will be explored in more detail in this book.

THE EVOLUTION IN CUSTOMER SATISFACTION MEASUREMENT

The 1950s to the 1970s

In the mid-1970s hardly anyone, except perhaps travellers returning from the United States or Canada, spoke very much about customer service. This was in part the legacy of the Second World War. During the 1950s, reconstruction of consumer economies in the Western world was paramount. By the 1960s, the period of consumer restraint and rationing was long forgotten, as economies expanded and consumers once again had money to spend on new goods and services. It is not surprising therefore that for most companies, gaining new customers was considered fairly easy, as they launched wave upon wave of new and better products and services. Perhaps not surprisingly, organizations did not focus as much time and attention on customer service and the concept of customer satisfaction. During this period senior management and management gurus debated issues such as whether customers 'bought' products or whether they were 'sold' them, and how to segment markets demographically and psychographically to gain market share. However, this was all to change over the following two decades, as two major economic recessions rocked countries in Western Europe, North America and Japan.

The 1980s

During the 1980s, the major European and US business schools, together with major international businesses, developed a number of new management theories to help companies improve their financial performance. These theories usually focused on improving operational efficiencies, based as they were on emerging production line concepts developed in Japan, then one of the world's financial and economic superpowers. New management theories such as 'just-in-time' (JIT) management and 'Total Quality Management' (TQM) transformed the way businesses were operated and how they were structured. These changes emerged in response to an economic downturn in the United States and most Western European countries at the start of the 1980s. Commercial companies starting tightening their purse strings, but they continued investing money in marketing and advertising to entice more customers to buy, or continue buying, their products or services.

However, senior executives also started looking seriously at their operations to see if they could save money. Leading management thinkers of the time, such as William E Rothschild of the US General Electric Corporation, noticed that a strategic advantage could be gained if customer service was treated as a strategic business tool rather than as a support for business. Companies such as RCA (for televisions) and Sears (for home appliances) introduced the concept of selling 'post-sales' service contracts in the United States. For an annual fee consumers could have their televisions, washing machines and other home appliances 'insured' against repair. Companies soon realized that if they had control over their own service network they could deliver a reliable after-sales service, albeit at a cost. However, it quickly became apparent that the size and growth in investment required to correct product defects was huge, in spite of the money customers paid for these after-sales programmes. Not surprisingly, therefore, companies started looking at ways to improve their 'product breakdown' service – and market research was one of the business tools they used.[1]

Market research techniques were developed to examine customer reactions to the way companies 'corrected' the faults that had emerged and how quickly they could be corrected. Mystery shopping was one such tool. 'Mystery shoppers' were trained individuals who would pose as customers while checking out whether certain operational procedures were being adhered to in the establishments they were monitoring. They were 'mystery' shoppers because they did not let themselves be known to the management of the premises they were frequenting. They simply had to act the part of a normal customer, then on leaving the premises they would note down which company policies or procedures were not being adhered to. This concept was not limited to companies that dealt with customers in a face-to-face situation. For example, companies offering services such as the rapid replacement of lost or stolen traveller's cheques or credit cards could check if the promises they were making to their customers were actually being met through the use of mystery shoppers.

Meanwhile, in Japan, the concept of 'zero defects' was emerging as a competitive strategic tool. Rather than building and then maintaining an expensive after-sales service network, Japanese companies believed it would be cheaper to build defect-free products. And because they believed in investing in the quality of their product, they began offering extended warranties and free after-service care. This 'bundling' of service as part of the product a customer was purchasing changed customers' opinions, and 'service' rose in importance as a result (Rothschild, 1984: 125).

The 1990s

By the early 1990s, when the world economy went into another major recession, many millions of employees, mainly but not exclusively middle management, lost their jobs as a result of companies 'down-sizing' in response to the latest business management theory, business process re-engineering (BPR). This perhaps more than anything else changed people's opinions about the concept of 'loyalty' in regard to employers and employment. No longer were employees to view a job with a company as a 'job for life'. In addition, those fortunate enough to remain in employment found the adjustment to the new work environment difficult. Many companies had not considered the effect that downsizing would have on the morale, health and productivity of those employees who had not lost their jobs.

However, two concepts also emerged during this period that changed how companies viewed, and managed, customer service. These concepts were the balanced scorecard and customer relationship management (CRM).

Robert S Kaplan (professor of accounting at Harvard Business School) and David P Norton (president of Nolan, Norton and Company, a Massachusetts-based information technology consulting firm) created the balanced scorecard in 1991. It was designed to provide senior executives with a better performance management system for their organizations than the traditional financial and operational measures most organizations used. These older systems had been developed in an industrial age and were now considered by some to be inadequate, particularly for service companies, which were growing in importance in most Western economies. What Kaplan and Norton provided was a set of measures that gave management a fast and comprehensive view of an organization by complementing the financial and operational measures with two new perspectives, a measure of customer satisfaction and a measure of the way an organization 'learns' – an innovation and improvement perspective (Kaplan and Norton, 1991).

As the balanced scorecard became embedded in many organizations, performance 'reward' programmes based on what customers really thought of the products and services they bought rose in popularity in many boardrooms. Market research was used to gather much of the 'evidence' that provided the customer satisfaction perspective, and so interest and expenditure on customer satisfaction research grew dramatically throughout the 1990s.

Alongside the emergence of the balanced scorecard, technological developments provided companies with an ability rapidly to process and analyse their internal operational data. This contributed to the rise of CRM. Very simply, the advocates of CRM suggested that an organization could equip front-line staff with a better understanding of its individual customers through providing them with a link to its computer systems, and so provide customers with a better experience when contacting the company, or when the company wished to contact them. It aimed to improve the way products were customized to meet individual customer requirements. It helped provide a more targeted focus for marketing and sales campaigns, and it also provided customer-facing staff with more information about the customers they were serving. At a strategic level, it was seen as a way of developing relationships with profitable customers and managing the cost of business with less profitable customers (Foss and Stone, 2002: 14).

CUSTOMER LOYALTY

There were other developments around the start of the 1990s that were to have a profound affect on how companies viewed their customers. For many years Xerox had regularly monitored the satisfaction of its customers through market research. As Dennis McCarthy reports in *The Loyalty Link* (1997), Xerox, like most companies, had always organized its customer response surveys around a satisfaction scale of 1 to 5, and had set a corporate goal of achieving at least 100 per cent at level 4 (that is, 'satisfied'). However, in 1991, after analysing over 500,000 responses collected over the years, management discovered that loyalty rates among 'satisfied' customers were six times less than among 'completely satisfied' customers (McCarthy, 1997: 12).

Within a couple of years, work conducted at Bain and Company (a US management consultancy) revealed that the proportion of customers who claimed to be 'satisfied' or 'completely satisfied' who defected could be as high as 65 to 85 per cent, depending upon the industry (Reichheld, 1993: 71). McCarthy claims that many companies responded to this by cutting prices, as they mistakenly believed that price equated to loyalty. The lower the price, it was argued, the more likely it was that customers would stay with the company.

What many companies had failed to realize in the 1980s was that customer satisfaction was not necessarily a reflection that customers were feeling positive about their organizations; rather it was that they were not feeling negative about them. That is, they had no reason to defect. If the companies had thought about why many of their price promotions were successful in attracting new customers, they might have realized that what they were gaining were not necessarily new customers to the market, but existing customers who were switching their brand allegiance.

During the recession of the early 1990s many companies examined very closely the performance of their marketing and sales expenditure. They discovered that it cost a lot more to acquire new customers than to retain existing ones. They also discovered that new customers cost a lot more to 'manage', in that they were more likely to call the company at peak times, and often did not understand what exactly they had purchased (especially in certain areas such as financial services). The support and servicing costs for these new customers were higher, and so the attraction of retaining existing customers grew.

However, during this period (and up to the present) many organizations noticed that levels of customer satisfaction reported in their surveys remained relatively stable. In fact, it was not necessary to conduct market research to see this (although researchers who conducted customer service tracking surveys during this period could attest to it). It was not very difficult to find news headlines reporting growing customer dissatisfaction with the performance of railways, government services and so on. Why is this? Dennis McCarthy believes it is partly because organizations view customer satisfaction as a cost rather than an investment, and in particular, fail to invest in people at the front line. Satisfied customers are not something you can buy, their loyalty has to be earned, he argues. It builds with every single touch point with an organization. As a result, companies need a stable and highly motivated workforce to be able to deliver a good service.

One unfortunate trend that has emerged during the late 1990s and early 2000s is that some companies have begun to feel that advances in technology will not only improve their service proposition, but also deliver lower costs (and therefore higher profits). So, there has been a proliferation of interactive voice recognition systems to help speed up customer calls for routine services such as checking balances on bank accounts. Instead of being put on hold when you call your bank, you can be offered a menu of services accessible though your telephone keypad or through voice responses. These would all be very sensible initiatives were it not for the fact that most people are social animals and enjoy actually talking to other human beings rather than to a computer.

In addition, some companies have begun off-shoring their customer service to countries in Asia and the Far East where costs can be up to 10 times lower than in Western countries. Again the economic argument for such decisions is very strong, but it is based on the assumption that customers will be loath to change suppliers and will remain loyal to their current one. No doubt these companies do not recall that while in manufacturing, quality management techniques increase productivity by reducing waste and lowering production costs, in the service industries productivity is measured by customer satisfaction and increased sales. The customer is the judge of service quality, and it is nearly always people who deliver service.

Even where a machine provides service, loyalty cannot be taken for granted. A cash machine for example can only deliver the services for which it is programmed. If it is out of cash, and a customer wants to use it to get cash, the customer will seek another machine. It may be a competitor's machine, but if it delivers customers the cash they want, they may be tempted to use it again in the future, especially if there is no extra charge for doing so. In other words, as Jacques Horovitz says, 'Services exist in human experience. For service industries service consists of two dimensions: basic features sought by the customer and the service experience at the time of consumption' (Horovitz, 1990: 6).

The other aspect that these companies may be overlooking is that customers these days have more choice than in the past. While companies may think their customers see the use of automated voice recognition systems as a way of keeping costs down, customers may see it rather differently, as meaning less personalized service than they used to receive. If prices are not reduced as a result of these changes, customers may well believe that service is getting worse. The risk of losing the customer increases as customer frustration grows, and as choice of supplier increases and the ease of switching supplier becomes easier. As Michael Johnson and Anders Gustafsson say in *Improving Customer Satisfaction, Loyalty and Profit* (2000: 7), 'loyalty' is about a customer's intention or predisposition to buy, but 'retention' is the actual act of buying again. 'Retention' is a stronger measure than 'loyalty'. It can also be measured using internal company data, while 'loyalty' usually has to be measured through market research surveys.

There is another subtle distinction between 'satisfied' customers and 'loyal' customers. They contribute to company profitability in different ways. Satisfied customers are more likely to 'promote' the company, because satisfaction is something people will talk about. Loyal customers however are more profitable because they are more likely to buy additional products, often without shopping around for the best price. Of course dissatisfied customers are a real cost to a company, because they criticize the company to others – and research has shown that dissatisfied customers are likely to tell more people about their dissatisfaction than satisfied customers tell about why they are satisfied.

However, not everyone would agree with the concept that loyalty is about repurchasing. Work originating in the late 1980s in South Africa by Dr J Hofmeyr (2004) suggested that there is a difference between loyalty and commitment. A 'loyal' customer might be someone who repurchases products and services but is not necessarily committed to the organization. He or she might be repurchasing out of habit or for some other reason. A committed customer has a stronger emotional bond to the organization, and so is less likely to buy elsewhere, and more likely to be tolerant if things go slightly wrong. Dr Hofmeyr's work is covered in more detail in Chapter 2.

THE LINK: CUSTOMER SATISFACTION PLUS LOYALTY EQUALS INCREASED PROFITS

During the past two decades there has been a growing body of evidence to show there is a link between having committed (loyal) customers and profits. Michael Johnson and Anders Gustafsson make a case in their book that through creating an integrated customer measurement and management system focusing on quality, customer satisfaction and loyalty, organizations will ultimately see an improvement in their bottom-line financial performance. They argue that what the last three decades have basically shown is that the three factors of quality, customer satisfaction and loyalty do not work independently of each other. They are part of a whole that needs to be measured and managed in a holistic way, with a clear understanding of the customer experience at the heart of the system. To achieve this, Johnson and Gustafsson say, you continually need to pursue three activities:

1. Gather customer information about the product and service features that customers value, and understand the more abstract

consequences and benefits these attributes provide and the personal values they serve.
2. Spread that information throughout the organization.
3. Use the information to maintain, improve or innovate in products, services or processes so as to increase satisfaction, loyalty and profitability (Johnson and Gustaffson 2000: 4).

EMPLOYEES AND THEIR CONTRIBUTION TO CUSTOMER SATISFACTION AND LOYALTY

In most companies, with e-commerce-oriented companies possibly being the one exception, service is usually provided through employees interacting with customers. These interactions can be face to face (as in retail outlets and restaurants for example) or via the telephone, e-mail or in writing.

Employees can be customers of their company as well. Therefore it is important to recognize the contribution they make to ensuring the company has satisfied and loyal customers. If employees are not treated well, you can be fairly certain that the message will get through to customers. It can also be very costly to the organization. Dissatisfied employees will take more time off through sickness (thereby raising the burden of work on their colleagues), show less enthusiasm for their company's products and services, and can even do so publicly.

Sometimes this dissatisfaction is brought about by a sense of frustration that the company could and should do more for their customers. At other times it is in revenge for the way the employees perceive they themselves are, or have been, treated. Whatever the cause, imagine the effect this can have on customers. The London *Evening Standard* recently reported some announcements that the city's underground train drivers have allegedly made to their passengers. They included, 'This is the Line Control Room at Baker Street. The Bakerloo line is running normally today, so you may expect delays to all destinations,' and 'May I remind you to take your rubbish with you. Despite the fact that you are in something that is metal, round, filthy and smells, this is a tube train and not a bin on wheels' (Paine, 2004).

Employees play a crucial role in delivering customer service. As a result, their views on the company, its products and services, and their involvement in and contribution to its success are vital. Jack Mitchell perhaps best sums up this point in *Hug Your Customers* (2003). He runs Mitchells/Richards, a large (US $65 million turnover) profitable high-end clothing business in Connecticut. His family firm, founded in 1958, is based on the philosophy that great service comes before great product,

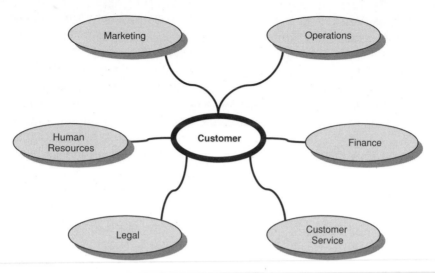

Figure 1.1 A customer-centric organization

and that great people to give that service come above both. Why? Because, in his words, 'you don't give service in a vacuum. People give service. You can have the best service philosophy in the world, but if you don't have great players to execute it, you've lost the game' (Mitchell, 2003: 90).

THE CUSTOMER-CENTRIC ORGANIZATION

Throughout this book there are references to a 'customer-centric' organization, but what does this mean? I use the term to depict a company in which all employees consider the effect of their plans and actions from the perspective of a customer, or potential customer (see Figure 1.1).

However, this is not quite as simple as Figure 1.1 suggests, because it also requires employees to consider their plans or actions not just from the viewpoint of their own department, product or service, but also from the perspective of all the products and services offered by the company. For example, typically what happens in larger organizations is that the Marketing department develops a new product or acquisition campaign with a 'one time only' special offer. In other words, it is 'wooing' the potential customer to the organization (akin to setting out to get a date with someone you would like to meet and get to know better). If this is successful, the target becomes a customer (which is akin to getting married or moving in together). With the honeymoon period now progressing nicely, Marketing sends out more offers, and everyone is feeling good about the relationship. Then Accounts sends out a warning notice that it has not yet received payment for the last transaction, and that unless payment arrives soon, further steps will be taken to recover the debt. The honeymoon is over.

However, what Marketing might have overlooked was that this 'new' customer was in fact an existing customer of another part of the organization, and that the special joining offer actually enticed customers to move their business from the other part of the organization to take advantage of the one-time offer. In other words, it cannibalized its own business. In addition, Accounts might not have realized that while this customer was in arrears on one particular transaction, he or she (or it) also had three other relationships with the organization, which together were worth 50 times more than the transaction in arrears. CRM systems have been developed over the past few years to minimize the occurrence of this type of scenario (see Chapter 2), but systems alone will not stop it happening. It requires all employees to take a much wider perspective when considering their plans and actions.

WHAT THE GROWTH IN MEASURING CUSTOMER SATISFACTION MEANS FOR MARKET RESEARCHERS

For researchers this whole period has meant an evolution in their approach to researching customer satisfaction with products and services. At the start of the period most 'tracking' surveys were done to measure the impact of advertising campaigns. Customer satisfaction research was usually an *ad hoc* project focusing on operational 'breakdown of service' issues. As management became more interested in customer service and loyalty, so new research techniques and models were developed (such as Simalto and SERVQUAL). Today this has expanded even further, with research departments changing their focus (and name in some cases) from 'market research', with its technical connotations, to 'consumer insight'. Their remit has also broadened to include the researching of employee satisfaction and benchmarking (how customers rate the service from their supplier against that of competitors).

It has also meant that market researchers, particularly, but not exclusively in client companies, need to acquire knowledge and skills in regulatory, financial and operational matters, and especially company politics, if they are to be able to deal with the growing requirements of their internal clients. These and other related matters are covered in more detail in the rest of this book.

2 Theories and strategies for measuring and improving customer satisfaction and loyalty

This chapter provides a brief introduction to some of the more common theories and strategies that are used by organizations to improve customer satisfaction and loyalty in their pursuit of improving profits and shareholder value. A basic understanding of these approaches should help market researchers, on both the client and supply sides of the profession, to design appropriate research. The chapter has been spilt into three sections. The first section looks at some of the more common models of customer satisfaction used at a strategic level within organizations. The second section looks at some of the more common operational models, while the third section addresses some issues pertaining to market research.

It isn't that we build such bad cars; it's that they are such lousy customers.
Charles F Kettering, president and chairman of the board,
General Motors, 1925–49[1]

It would be impossible to cover in any detail in an introductory textbook such as this the vast number of different business models and theories that have been developed over the last couple of decades to improve customer satisfaction, loyalty and company profitability. Therefore, this chapter will briefly describe a number of the more common ones being used today. Some, such as Six Sigma, help organizations improve customer satisfaction, loyalty and profitability by concentrating on improving internal processes or operations through rigorous data gathering and analysis of those areas important to the customer. Some organizations use business tools such as the balanced scorecard and the service profit chain. These ensure that the organization's strategic plan is understood and implemented by all employees. The plans are built on the premise that if the organization focuses on delivering the type of quality service desired by loyal customers and providing real management and systems support to front-line employees, profits will follow.

These tools not only include a customer perspective but also provide recognition of the contribution of employees, and can show the value derived from a customer-centric culture. There are also programmes that provide external recognition that a company operates a quality management system, such as ISO 9000, the Malcolm Baldridge National Quality Award and the EFQM European Quality Award. These are valuable to companies through their focus on what is achieved by 'best in class' companies. Finally there are a number of research methodologies that have been developed, and heavily promoted, as being the way to achieve a clear understanding of customer satisfaction. Three of the more frequently mentioned are summarized here: SERVQUAL, Simalto and the conversion model.

All these strategies and methodologies contain recurring themes. They include a desire to understand what drives customer satisfaction and loyalty, clear leadership and commitment to change, a requirement to measure what is being done (as what gets measured gets done) and an obvious focus on bottom-line results. However, for some public sector organizations there may be less of a bottom-line focus and more of an aim to reduce usage: for example, in the employment services one aim is to reduce the number of unemployed people.

STRATEGIC-LEVEL MODELS

Strategic-level models fall into two categories: those that help companies shape their competitiveness through being at the heart of an organization's strategy, and those that provide an external benchmark of how far the organization is meeting its strategic objectives.

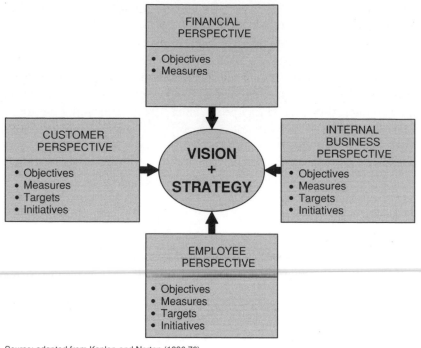

Source: adapted from Kaplan and Norton (1996:76).

Figure 2.1 *High-level view of the balanced scorecard*

The balanced scorecard

As was mentioned in Chapter 1, the balanced scorecard was developed by Robert S Kaplan and David P Norton. It focuses on addressing the needs of various stakeholders in a business in a highly integrated way. It links shorter-term operational requirements with an organization's long-term goals and aspirations. In this way it provides senior management with a series of measures to help them guide their business towards its strategic goals, in much the same way that airline pilots use a series of different gauges on the dashboard to help them guide the aircraft safely to its final destination.

The balanced scorecard has four main components: a financial perspective, a customer perspective, an internal business operational perspective and a learning and growth perspective.

As can be deduced from Figure 2.1, this strategic model focuses on the future, whereas many of the operational models mentioned later in this chapter address 'correcting' and 'learning' based on what has occurred in the past. Basically the balanced scorecard approach asks four 'simple' questions:

- 'To succeed financially, how should we appear to our shareholders?' (financial perspective)
- 'To achieve our vision, how should we appear to our customers?' (customer perspective)
- 'To satisfy our shareholders and customers, what business processes must we excel at?' (internal business perspective)
- 'To achieve our vision, how will we sustain our ability to change and improve?' (learning and growth perspective) (Kaplan and Norton, 1996: 9).

Measurable performance targets can be developed for each perspective, so the financial perspective focuses on matters pertaining to market value, profitability and revenue, while the customer perspective focuses on customer satisfaction and loyalty. The internal perspective can be quite wide-ranging, covering employee satisfaction through to the quality of internal processes. The learning and growth perspective addresses goals for training, the development of new products and services, and so on.

What makes this approach so popular is that the goals can be cascaded through an organization so that each individual employee can have his or her own personal scorecard, thereby ensuring that the whole organization is 'aligned' and addresses the strategy and financial performance requirements set by senior management. For example, the process enables front-line employees to understand the ultimate financial consequences of their actions. Under a balanced scorecard system, management has to take a more considered view of the issues arising from strategic goals and actions, rather than focusing on just the short-term financial impact of those issues.

The service profit chain

The service profit chain is a concept that links profit and growth to employee loyalty, satisfaction and productivity as well as to customer satisfaction and loyalty. But just as importantly, it links all of these to strategy. As the creators of the service profit chain, Professors James Heskett, W Earl Sasser Jr and Leonard Schlesinger, say:

> The service profit chain focuses management thinking on just two very important ideas: (1) do what is necessary to detect the needs and ensure the satisfaction and loyalty of targeted customers and (2) achieve this, in most cases, by giving employees the latitude and support necessary to deliver high value to desired customers.
>
> **(Heskett, Sasser and Schlesinger, 1997: 236)**

This is perhaps best demonstrated using the example reported by the model's creators. Southwest Airlines was founded in 1971 and has been one of the most consistently profitable airlines in the United States. It focuses on building customer loyalty through providing a dependable frequent service delivered by friendly employees at low fares. It does not provide meals on board, onward connections to other flights or a number of other services that many of its competitors offer. Its business strategy and operating model enables it to turn around its aircraft from arrival to departure far more rapidly than most other airlines. How? Southwest Airlines shunned the 'hub and spoke' system used by other airlines in the United States. It meticulously selected routes that used less-congested airports, and because it caters for short-haul flyers who expect little in the way of baggage handling, catering and other amenities, its ground crews can turn the aircraft in less than half the time required by other airlines. Furthermore, it enables its employees to own part of the company through its profit-sharing plan, encourages and provides training and support and flexible working practices, and provides its customer-facing employees with a degree of latitude that enables them to make on-the-spot decisions regarding customer service issues.[2]

The service profit chain evolved from research originally conducted in the 1980s by Professor Heskett. At that time he developed a 'strategic service vision'. This was a four-point blueprint that involved targeting a market segment, conceptualizing how the service would be seen by customers, developing an operating strategy, then designing an efficient and effective service delivery system to turn the strategic vision into reality (Heskett, 1986).

During the early 1990s, Earl Sasser and Thomas O Jones, building on the earlier learning from Xerox that having satisfied customers was not enough to guarantee customer loyalty, developed a set of operational ideas that would enable companies to secure the loyalty of their best customers. These ideas included clearly defining the target market, systematically measuring customer service, employing a variety of measurement methods, translating customer satisfaction information into loyalty measures, and providing customers with first-class support services (and recovery programmes if needed).

Around the same time Leonard Schlesinger was discovering that satisfied employees are loyal and productive, and that what drives them is a desire to deliver results to customers. In order to deliver results to customers these employees not only need the ability to relate to customers, they also need the latitude to use their judgement in doing so (as well as receiving the appropriate reward and recognition) (Heskett, Sasser and Schlesinger, 1997: 8–11).

From these three strands of evidence, the service profit chain emerged. What differentiates this model from other theoretical models is that the creators provide managers with a series of operational ideas that can be adapted to create a relevant chain for any business or operation. The chain focuses management thinking on finding out what drives satisfaction and loyalty among those customers the organization wants to retain, and on providing employees with the freedom and support to deliver the services these customers desire.

STRATEGIC BENCHMARKING

Benchmarking is about comparing performance against a standard or a fixed reference point over a period of time. It can take a number of different forms. For example, internal benchmarks compare how well the organization adheres to internally set standards of performance. Alternatively, the organization can be benchmarked against a set of nationally recognized standards (such as ISO 9000). Another option is to benchmark operational performance against that of other organizations to see if it is 'best in class' (as is done by the Malcolm Baldridge Award). For this reason, benchmarking is very popular with companies that track customer service performance and customer loyalty. There are many benefits arising from a comparison of an organization's performance against a benchmark, including:

- development within the organization of a desire for continuous improvement and innovation;
- creation of a better understanding of the organization's competitive situation;
- heightened sensitivity to changing customer needs;
- establishment of realistic action plans (Murphy, 2001: 205–7).

ISO 9000

ISO 9000 is a series of five standards published in 1987 by the International Organization for Standardization (ISO). It provides guidelines for the selection and use of the ISO standards. ISO 9001 provides guidelines for organizations that research, design, manufacture, ship or install service products. ISO 9002 provides standards for manufacturing companies. ISO 9003 applies to warehousing and distribution businesses, while ISO 9004 is concerned about the application of quality management systems (Robbins and Decenzo, 2001).

As with the Malcolm Baldridge National Quality Award (see below), independent auditors attest that an organization has met the quality management standards. In this way customers can be assured that the company has followed certain processes to test its products and services, and that it maintains records of its formalized activities. In addition, customers know that these companies continuously train their employees to ensure they have the most up-to-date skills and knowledge.

Companies that adopt the standard can have a competitive business advantage, as certain companies will only work with organizations that have achieved the standard.

The ISO has not limited itself to this standard alone. For example, in 1997 it introduced ISO 14000, a standard that demonstrates that a company is environmentally sound.

UK Charter Marks

In 1992 the UK government introduced an award scheme for organizations that receive at least 10 per cent of their funding from government, and that deal directly or indirectly with the public or voluntary sector. The aim of the scheme is to improve the level of customer service these organizations provide. The criteria for the award can be summarized as follows:

- The organization sets clear standards of performance and service by consulting with customers, monitors performance against those standards, and publishes the results.
- The organization actively consults and works with customers, partners and staff to ensure delivery of high-quality services, while providing full information about its costs and how well it performs.
- The organization makes services easily available to everyone who needs them, offering choice where possible and treating everybody fairly in terms of access to these services (paying particular attention to people with special needs).
- The organization continuously improves and develops services and facilities, putting things right quickly and effectively while learning from the results of complaints, compliments and suggestions.
- The organization uses resources effectively and imaginatively to provide best value for taxpayers and customers.
- The organization contributes to improving opportunity and quality of life in the communities served (Cook, 2004: 106–7).

Malcolm Baldrige National Quality Award

Malcolm Baldrige was a US Secretary of Commerce who believed that the management of quality would be a key to the future prosperity of the United States. Shortly after he died in a rodeo accident in July 1987, a quality improvement act passed by the US Congress was named the Malcolm Baldrige National Quality Improvement Act in recognition of the work he had done.

The Malcolm Baldrige National Quality Award is an annual benchmarking award that recognizes companies for their achievements in business excellence and quality. The award is managed by the US National Institute of Standards and Technology (NIST). Companies that wish to apply for the award need to submit an application, providing details of their achievements and improvements on seven criteria:

- leadership;
- strategic planning;
- customer and market focus;
- information and analysis;
- human resource focus;
- process management;
- business results.

Each year these categories are reviewed to ensure they reflect changes in knowledge and application in the field of Total Quality Management. Each applicant's submission is thoroughly reviewed. Organizations receive at least 300 hours of review from a panel of at least eight business and quality experts. Those organizations that pass this initial screening process receive a site visit to verify the information they provided in their submission and to clarify any questions that may emerge during the review. These organizations receive over 1000 hours of in-depth review and analysis. Finally, a detailed report of the applicant organization's strengths and opportunities for improvement is produced by the independent board of examiners.

The NIST claims that for many organizations, the use of the Award's assessment criteria results in better employee relations, higher productivity, greater customer satisfaction, increased market share and improved profitability (NIST, 2003). A maximum of three awards may be given each year in each of the following categories: Education, Health Care, Manufacturing, Service and Small Business. Interestingly, one of the early recipients of the Award was Xerox Corp.

EFQM Excellence Model

While the United States has the Malcolm Baldrige National Quality Award, Europe has the European Quality Award, a programme managed by the European Foundation for Quality Management (EFQM®). The Foundation is a membership-based not-for-profit organization. It was created in 1988 by 14 leading European businesses. Its aim is 'to become the driving force for sustainable excellence in Europe and a vision of a world in which European organizations excel' (EFQM, 1999).

The EFQM Excellence Model is a business tool launched in 1991 to help organizations improve their business performance. It took two years to develop, with many leading European organizations contributing to its development, including AB Electrolux (Sweden), Netas (Turkey), PSA Peugeot Citroën (France), IBM and PriceWaterhouseCoopers (Italy), Renfe (Spain), Lloyds TSB Group, the Council for Business Excellence, Post Office Counters and BT (UK), Neste Belgium and Honeywell Europe (Belgium), the Jellinek Centre (Netherlands), Xerox and Joh. Vaillant (Germany), the University of St Gallen (Switzerland) and Neste Oy (Finland).

What is particularly different about this model is that it provides a framework for organizations to use to improve their own working practices. The model uses nine criteria, five of which are known as 'enablers' (that is, what an organization does) and four 'results' (that is, what an organization achieves). The enablers cover aspects relating to leadership, people, processes, policy and strategy, and partnerships and resources. The results are viewed in terms of key performance indicators, people, customers and society.

The Foundation has developed a variety of tools to help its members achieve their goals, such as the Pathfinder Card (a self-assessment tool for identifying opportunities for improvement) and the ЯADAR Scoring Matrix® (a method for evaluating applications for the European Quality Award among other purposes).

The American Customer Satisfaction Index (ACSI)

The ACSI was launched in 1994. The model links customer expectations (from experiences of the product or service, word of mouth and so on), perceived quality (that is, overall quality, reliability and meeting customers' needs) and perceived value (based on perceptions of overall price given the quality and vice versa) to customer satisfaction. It also includes data on customer complaints and customer loyalty (the latter being measured by likelihood to buy another product or service from the company for different levels of price).

Telephone interviewing is used to gather the data. Information is gathered quarterly and over 65,000 interviews are conducted each year. The survey is operated jointly by the American Society for Quality, the

Stephen M Ross Business School at the University of Michigan and the CFI Group (an international consulting company).[3] As Derek Allen observes (2004: 13), the ASCI is one of the few projects to collect longitudinal data relating to customer satisfaction, retention and financial performance.

One other benefit has emerged from this survey. By using the same questions as those used in the ACSI, smaller US companies can benchmark themselves against the results obtained from the ACSI at industry level.

OPERATIONAL-LEVEL MODELS

In this section, two very different approaches to operational improvements are briefly covered, Six Sigma and customer relationship management (CRM).

Six Sigma

Six Sigma focuses on the measurement of product quality and the improvement of operational processes. Through process improvements, cost savings are made. But Six Sigma is more than just a cost-cutting programme. It aims to cut costs while at the same time improve the value to the customer by focusing improvements on those that really matter to the customer. However, it is not enough to improve processes in the Six Sigma approach. The aim of Six Sigma is to achieve error-free processes – in other words, 'to get it right first time and every time'. Furthermore, it aims to build quality into a product and service rather than just to eliminate it after the product or service is operational.

Six Sigma was first developed in the 1980s at Motorola. It really gained popularity after General Electric reported some very positive business results in the United States following its adoption of this approach. It has been claimed that the estimated benefits General Electric achieved in the first five years following implementation in 1995 were of the order of US $10 billion (Six Sigma, 2004).

Six Sigma is actually a statistic, represented by the Greek letter σ (sigma). It is used to describe the variability, or standard deviation, in a set of figures. The higher the sigma rating, the lower the number of defects. So, a Six Sigma quality rating equates to 99.99966 per cent – or to put it another way, no more than 3.4 defects per million 'opportunities'.

What differentiates Six Sigma from other measurement tools is that it is adapted specifically for each organization. An organization is not benchmarking itself against other organizations. Instead, it focuses entirely on the quality of the output from processes totally under its own control.

Six Sigma is based on a five-step improvement strategy. It starts with determining what is important to customers, then works to identify those vital attributes that have the most impact on quality. The next step is to measure performance on these characteristics. The third step is to analyse the results to identify any gaps between current performance and 'desired' performance. Step four involves finding better ways of handling the critical tasks that have been identified. Finally controls are put in place to ensure that the gains made are retained (Six Sigma, 2004). Companies embarking on a Six Sigma approach will need to make major investments in terms of people and resources. However, one of its benefits is that it can deliver business results quickly.

Customer Relationship Management (CRM)

CRM usually refers to system-based tools that enable an organization to manage the type of relationship it has with its customers. However, it involves more than just gathering data from various marketing and operational computer systems, developing programmes to identify the most profitable customers, then 'managing' the relationship by offering them more suitable products and services. As Merlin Stone and his co-authors point out in *Customer Insight*:

> In markets in which buyers and sellers do experience benefits from developing relationships, these are rarely simple relationships in which a consumer is 100 per cent loyal to one company or to another. Most relationships develop in stages with consumers sampling different products and often remaining 'switchers' or 'multi-sourcers' – buying from several companies.

(Stone *et al*, 2004: 90)

Handled well, CRM can allow for these stages in the relationship to be identified and managed. For example, credit card companies have a huge amount of transactional data in their operating systems. These data can be used for security purposes to identify, for example, a potential lost or stolen card very rapidly through a change in the normal pattern of use, sometimes even before a customer has realized the card has been lost or stolen. However, there are many other customer management applications for these systems. For example, when customers first acquire a new product or use a new service, they usually experiment with it as they explore the various features it offers. However, very shortly afterwards their usage settles down to a more regular pattern. Customer loyalty however is partially dependent on customers maintaining their belief in the value of the product, and this can be seen through how they use it. So companies have two choices: they can watch and wait for a customer's usage to change and then take 'corrective action', or they can try to manage customer behaviour. If they take the former route they will often discover that the customer has already drifted away from them and it is too late to resurrect the relationship. This is particularly noticeable in the banking industry, where customers allow existing accounts to become dormant following a switch to another supplier, often because they feel it is too much hassle to close the account. After all it doesn't cost the customer anything to keep the account open – but it certainly costs the bank money. Some really disgruntled customers do this on purpose to get their own back on the bank for some perceived mistreatment.

However, the organizations that use CRM systems sensibly can often change customers' opinions and behaviour. By segmenting their customers they can identify how they contribute to the organization's profitability, then create a strategy to enhance the customer's loyalty to the organization (or develop programmes to increase the profitability and loyalty of other customers). For example, one credit card organization developed a service programme that enabled its customer service staff in contact centres to identify customers quickly in the first year of the relationship. The agents were trained to check that the customers were happy with their card, and to ask if they had any questions about it. In addition, by looking at their transaction history the agents were able to offer these customers other ideas on how or where they could use the card. The marketing department could target special mailings to them, informing them of outlets in the vicinity of their home or office that had promotions or other special offers for their customers. The whole aim of the programme was to cement the relationships with customers and to 'encourage' the usage of their product in such a way that customers felt they had made the right choice when acquiring the card.

Recently the benefits of CRM have been brought into question. The huge investments that many companies made in the late 1990s in CRM technology failed to deliver the anticipated increase in company profits. Some of this may be because organizations specified hugely ambitious requirements that simply were too costly to build. Other systems failed possibly because of a lack of insight into what customers really wanted from their suppliers – namely core products and services delivered faultlessly each and every time they were used.

RESEARCH MODELS

There are a plethora of research agencies that claim their model or approach for measuring customer satisfaction will provide an organization with a competitive edge or some other business benefit. Many of these models usually contain one or more of the following elements:

- employee perceptions or satisfaction;
- customer satisfaction;
- brand values and image;
- price or value for money;
- advocacy and loyalty;
- competitive benchmarking;
- financial outputs (that is cost savings or gains in terms of new customers or incremental business).

The models (or more accurately, set of hypotheses) can be relatively simple or more complex, as shown in the fictitious examples outlined in Figures 2.2 and 2.3.

Unfortunately, many of the models agencies promote are proprietary, and they are difficult to evaluate either because detailed results

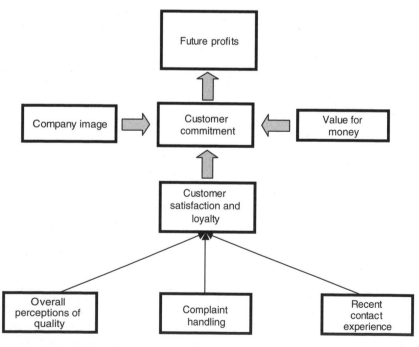

Figure 2.2 *A simple customer satisfaction model*

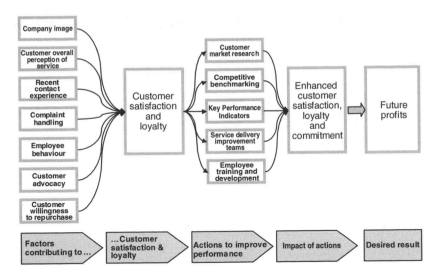

Figure 2.3 A more complex customer satisfaction model

are not published or because they involve the use of proprietary data analyses whose 'black box' sophistication is protected by company copyright. However, there are two well-documented research tools that have been used extensively in customer satisfaction research. These are Simalto and SERVQUAL.

Simalto

Simalto (an acronym for **si**multaneous **m**ulti-attribute **l**evel **t**rade-**o**ff) is a research scale that was developed in 1977 to help more clearly measure the elements of service delivery. It is based on a 'trade-off' approach. Respondents are usually given a grid (this method works best in a face-to-face situation) on which a series of attributes (elements of service, such as availability of service or time to answer the phone) are listed in rows and different levels of service or product service options are presented in columns, as shown in Table 2.1.

Each respondent is asked to indicate for each attribute which of the 'levels' a top-quality company would provide to its customers, which level his or her current supplier provides, and which, if any, of the options offered rates as unacceptable. In addition, respondents are asked to indicate which of the attributes they consider to be 'most important'. Users of the approach claim that up to 35 attributes across nine levels can be measured. However, critics of trade-off methodologies argue that the process quickly becomes tiring for respondents, and that the fewer attributes and levels, the better.

Table 2.1 Example of a Simalto grid

Element of service	Levels			
Availability of customer service	9 am to 5 pm Mondays to Fridays, excluding National holidays	9 am to 9 pm Monday to Saturdays, excluding National holidays	9 am to 9 pm seven days a week, every day of the year	24 hours a day, every day of the year
Time to answer the phone	Phone never answered	Phone answered after 10 or more rings	Phone answered within 4–9 rings	Phone answered immediately (3 rings or less)

One of the benefits of this approach is that the question of price can form part of the exercise. Usually questions to do with price are treated separately, but using Simalto respondents can be asked to either select different levels of service for a particular price, or indicate what level of price they are prepared to pay for the level of service they have indicated.

Another benefit of this approach is that the 'levels' can be constructed using the consumer's language. Often these 'levels' have been developed and pre-tested in qualitative research, so each 'level' will be clear and unambiguous to the respondent.

Supporters of this method also like the ability to determine performance targets. As each attribute can show the 'best in class' rating, an individual organization's rating and the relative degree of importance for that attribute, so the company can decide which of the 'gaps' it should focus on closing first. Furthermore, because the performance level is actually specified, there is no debate about what that level refers to. That is, if the performance of the best in class is to answer the phone within three rings and respondents rate this as critically important (such as might be the case when calling the emergency services, for example), everyone knows the performance target is to answer the phone in three rings. In other methods, where people give ratings on a scale out of 5 or 7 or 10, and the results are shown as averages (such as 7.9), then perceptually employees have a difficulty trying to visualize what closing the gap might actually mean. For example, how motivating is it to be told that you must improve your average rating from a 7.9 to an 8.7 by this time next month, if you cannot visualize what an 8.7 level of service entails?

Besides the drawback already mentioned, there are a number of other pitfalls with this model. For example, each of the attributes should be independent of each other and not overlap, but this is not always possible (see the first line in Table 2.1). Second, it is important that all the attributes that could pertain to a service (from a customer's viewpoint) are included in the list. Third, it is essential that the 'levels' are measurable (otherwise there is no difference from using a 10-point rating scale). Finally, this is not really a measure of customer satisfaction, but more a measure of service delivery performance (albeit driven by what apparently matters most to customers).

SERVQUAL

SERVQUAL is a research methodology designed to identify the gaps between what customers expect from an excellent product or service provider and what they perceive the service to be from their current supplier of that product or service. In particular, it looks at five different dimensions of service quality:

- tangibles (the physical appearance of people and facilities);
- reliability (people or companies doing what they say they will, on time and to specification);
- responsiveness (a willingness to help and meet individual requirements);
- assurance (displaying trust and confidence and having the necessary skills to get the job done);
- empathy (understanding customer needs and providing individualized service).

A battery of 22 service attributes is used to differentiate and classify these five service dimensions. A seven-point Likert scale is used to gather customer feedback about expectations and perceptions of service across the battery of service attributes. The 'gap' between the expected service and the perceived service provides the measure of perceived service quality. The higher the 'perception minus expectation' gap, the higher the level of perceived service quality. Finally respondents are asked to rate the five dimensions in terms of the relative importance of each dimension to them. They do this by distributing 100 points across the five dimensions.

The approach was first developed in the mid to late 1980s by Parasuraman, Zeithaml and Berry (1985). They subsequently refined it in 1991. Their theory is that the key to maintaining satisfied customers is to ensure that their perceptions of service are as close as possible to their expectations.

The approach has been widely adopted and used throughout the world, by companies, other organizations and academics. However, it has also been one of the most discussed research methodologies for measuring customer satisfaction, with many researchers questioning its value and validity.

The strengths of the SERVQUAL approach are:

- It can be used across many different industries, and so is of help not only for measuring how a company performs against others in the same field, but also how the industry fares against others. This can be important for companies in industries where customer perceptions of service are generally low, as the size of the task to improve service quality is all the greater.
- As the battery of service dimensions is large, more data is generated, allowing for a greater depth of analysis (assuming there is a sufficient volume of interviews conducted).
- It can enable users to segment their customers according to expectations and perceptions, and these segments can then be analysed with other data such as demographics.
- The internal consistency of the SERVQUAL scale has been shown to be high in various studies done on it over the years.
- Managers like it because it provides them with data they can understand, and because it has been used by many organizations around the world. In addition, the basic premise sounds very plausible – people's evaluation of the service they receive is based, in part, on their expectations.

Critics of the SERVQUAL approach have a number of concerns:

- The five SERVQUAL dimensions are not generic, with some observers claiming they should be more industry-specific. Some industries may have only one or two dimensions of service, while others may be more complex, having four or five. SERVQUAL makes no allowance for this.
- Some have argued that if customers have a negative experience with service they will tend to overstate their expectations (thereby creating a larger gap), while those customers having a positive experience will tend to understate their expectations (thereby creating a smaller gap).
- In many SERVQUAL studies the 'expectations' scores are quite high, which has led some critics to suggest that it would be better to measure only the 'performance' side of the equation. Some believe that the high levels reported are caused by a 'social desirability' bias (that is, respondents give answers they believe the researcher is expecting to hear, rather than ones that truly accord with their feelings).
- Another concern raised by some critics is that respondents may interpret the 'performance' rating in different ways. So, for example, some

respondents may answer the scale according to their perception of how they think their chosen company would perform, while others may rate it in terms of how well they think the company will perform given the amount of money or business the customer has given them.

- Researchers who have tested and then retested the scale using the same respondents over different periods of time have found that while the 'expectations' results are fairly stable over time, results for 'perceptions' (especially the assurance and empathy aspects) are not. However this has been challenged on the grounds that these aspects of service are more difficult for customers to evaluate.
- SERVQUAL focuses heavily on the process of service delivery and not on the resulting outcome of the service experience. For example, one of the most important aspects of customer service from the customer's point of view is whether the product did what it was supposed to do (for example, the cash machine dispensed the right amount of cash if the purpose of the visit was to get cash from the machine). Some researchers argue that it is important to include both process and outcomes to get a better measure for service quality.
- The process of using the scales (with its two 'rounds' of questioning, one to measure expectation and the other to measure performance) can be time-consuming and possibly boring for respondents.
- The process may work better for some research methods (such as self-completion or face to face) than others (such as telephone). In a self-completion and face-to-face approach respondents can be shown 'show cards' to remind them of the scales being used, so they can literally see the seven points on the Likert scale. Over the telephone, respondents have to visualize the seven-point scale and may not answer in the same way.
- Finally, on a more technical note, some critics have evaluated the impact of the way the attributes are worded. For example, some of the dimensions contain only negatively worded statements, while others contain only positively worded statements. While it is good research practice to have a combination of positively and negatively worded statements (to avoid everyone falling into a pattern of responding), some researchers have noted that there are significant differences between the positively worded and negatively worded statements in terms of perceptions, expectations and gap scores.

For those who are interested in reading more about the strengths and weaknesses of SERVQUAL, the following papers can be recommended: 'SERVQUAL: Review, critique, research agenda' by Francis Buttle of Manchester Business School (1996); Simon S K Lam and Ka Shing Woo, 'Measuring service quality: a test-retest reliability investigation of

SERVQUAL' (1997); and Lisa J Morrison Coulthard, 'Measuring service quality, A review and critique of research using SERVQUAL' (2004). There are many more articles on the subject, and all these papers contain an extensive list of references.

The conversion model

One research model that is often cited is the 'conversion model'. Dr Jannie Hofmeyr and Butch Rice developed this model in South Africa in the late 1980s. Its roots lie in the work done at the University of Cape Town, where Dr Hofmeyr was conducting research into why some people were more committed to their religions than others, and what led people to convert from one religion (or none) to another. From this he developed a psychological model to explain the rationale behind changes in people's religious beliefs.

The model measures the strength of the relationship between customers and products or services. Unlike other models that are based on behaviour, this model is based on psychology: in particular, the recognition that commitment underpins loyalty, but they are not one and the same.[4] Loyalty is based on what people 'do' (such as their likelihood to repurchase based on past behaviour), while commitment is based on how people feel. That is, people might buy a particular brand or use a particular service repeatedly not because they are committed to it but out of habit.

According to this model customers display four levels of commitment:

- entrenched: spend most of their budget for the item with the organization, and have a high likelihood of purchasing again;
- average: spend less with the organization, and have a lower likelihood of repurchase;
- shallow: the likelihood to repurchase from the organization is low as these consumers are already using other brands or suppliers;
- convertible: the group with the lowest likelihood to repurchase.

Non-customers are also catered for in this model as they can be surveyed and classified into one of four categories:

- available: those who prefer the organization's product or service and so are most likely to switch from their current supplier;
- ambivalent: unsure as to whether to switch suppliers or not;
- weakly unavailable: open to switching but with a closer affinity to other suppliers;
- strongly unavailable: very little affinity to the company or brand and least likely to switch.

The claimed strength of this model is its ability to identify why customers (or non-customers) are not committed to the company or organization. It may be that they are dissatisfied. However, it could also be that they prefer a competitor or that they have no strong feelings either way. The other strength of this model is that it can be used in conjunction with other surveys on customer satisfaction. In this regard, it means that the learning from earlier surveys is not necessarily wasted. Finally, the model can be applied to employees as well as to customers, and so it can provide a more holistic view of commitment from both the employee and customer/target customer perspectives.

PUTTING THEORIES INTO ACTION

In *Firing On All Cylinders* (1993), Jim Clemmer provides a blueprint for action for any organization that has identified its service vision. It encapsulates many of the theories mentioned in this chapter. To achieve its vision, an organization needs to ensure that the company's values are understood and acted upon by all staff, that the staff themselves are given the right coaching and skills, and that the organization's processes, its reward and recognition programmes and its marketing programmes are in alignment with the vision. Furthermore, everyone in the organization needs to know what is required of them and that progress towards the vision is measurable and reported upon.

Clemmer identifies 12 actions that organizations need to take if they are to achieve and sustain ever higher levels of service and quality. These are:

- The organization must continually monitor its changing external customers' needs and establish the service/quality objectives and indicators for each customer–supplier group in the entire service/quality chain.
- Senior executives must visibly and actively lead the cultural change process and continuous improvement journey. At the start of the process, they should answer in unison:
  - What business are we in (the *strategic niche*)?
  - What do we believe in (the *values* that will guide everyone's behaviour)?
  - Where are we going (the *vision* of the preferred future)?
- Management and staff support groups at all levels need to serve the front-line producers, deliverers and supporters of the organization's basic products and services.

- Everyone in the organization should be given a thorough introduction to why service and quality are critical. The message needs to be constantly repeated and reinforced.
- Continuous learning must become entrenched at all organizational levels.
- Hiring, orientation and promotion practices must reflect service/quality principles and the organization's values.
- There must be a process of wide-scale continuous skill building for everyone involved in, supporting and leading the improvement process.
- All organizational systems (such as financial and human resource systems) and structures must be aligned to serve the customer and the needs of the front-line team.
- Team and individual reward and recognition processes and practices need to be aligned to reinforce service/quality principles and organizational values.
- Staff at all levels throughout the organization need to be active and contributing members of their teams.
- Measurements and standards must start from the outside and move into the organization along the customer–supplier chain of service and quality.
- Sales, marketing and public relations strategies need to be aligned continually, in order to move the organization closer to its strategic niche and maintain a two-way communication channel with external customers and other stakeholders (Clemmer, 1993: 97–98).

CLOSING COMMENTS

It is not possible to cover in one chapter all the theories and models that have been developed to explain the drivers and links underpinning customer satisfaction, loyalty and profitability. For example, the work that Zeithaml, Berry and Parasuraman (1996) have done on the behavioural consequences of service quality (exploring how the effects of service quality may be more cumulative and gradual and that it is possible to see evidence through customers' behaviours that they are forging bonds with an organization) has not been discussed in detail here.

Another fascinating area is the work being done in the field of psychology and customer satisfaction. For example, at the Manchester School of Management, Robertson, Lewis, Bardzil and Nikolaou (2004) have explored the influence of personality on customers' assessments of service quality. Their work looks at how individuals' reactions to service may be determined, at least in part, by their underlying personality.

3 Qualitative research

This chapter provides a brief introduction to the exploratory and diagnostic research techniques that are commonly referred to as qualitative research. It examines four different ways of conducting qualitative research to gain a better understanding of customer satisfaction and loyalty.

> Know how to listen and you will profit even from those who talk badly.
> **Plutarch, Greek biographer**

WHAT QUALITATIVE RESEARCH IS

Many researchers suggest that the best way to begin an exploration about customer service and loyalty is to conduct some exploratory, small-scale research among customers, lapsed customers and possibly even employees. Many benefits are advocated for support of this approach. The main ones are that the researcher will hear the language customers use to describe the experience of dealing with a company's products or services, and will learn about the range of issues that frustrate customers most, as well as those that delight them. Some agencies also use qualitative survey methods to help identify which issues customers (or ex-customers or employees) consider as important for gaining their commitment to a particular product, brand or organization.

Qualitative research does not have to be conducted solely at the start of a research programme. It can also be used to further investigate findings emerging from a quantitative survey. So, for example, perhaps some quantitative research has been conducted to understand how customers rate the service they receive when contacting a company. However, it is noticed during the analysis of the data that people who have been customers of the company for a number of years are less likely to recommend it than are newer customers. There could be a number of hypotheses why this is so, but rather than rely on instinct, managers might want to get a better understanding of what prevents longer-tenured customers from being advocates. Could it be that all their friends and colleagues are now customers too, so there is no one else in their social circle that they can tell about the wonderful service they have received over the years? Perhaps the company no longer provides the level of service they require, and while they have remained customers, it is more a result of inertia than through active loyalty on their part. Perhaps they no longer plan to buy any more goods or services, so the subject no longer comes up in conversation. On the other hand, perhaps the company has been ignoring them and they feel it no longer cares about them.

QUALITATIVE RESEARCH METHODS

Qualitative research also differs from quantitative research in one other way. It usually provides the researcher with more flexibility. Many of the methods it uses allow the researcher to change direction or try other techniques to elicit data, in ways that could not easily be matched in a quantitative research survey, where the focus has to be on maintaining a degree of consistency of approach.

There is a large array of methods available for the qualitative researcher. Depending on the needs of the project, these can include:

- observational research;
- focus groups;
- in-depth interviews;
- mystery shopping.

OBSERVATIONAL RESEARCH

The history of observational research

Observational research actually began in the 1930s when companies such as AC Neilsen and Attwoods began auditing product sales in retail outlets by counting stock and deliveries on a regular basis. No interviews were involved. Then just before the Second World War, the

British government sponsored a study of the nation (called the Mass Observation Project), which was extended during the war to measure the mood of the nation.

What observational research is

There is a saying, 'a picture is worth a thousand words'. Observational research is all about providing a picture, and until recently, that was done without the words. Now that cameras and optical technology have become more sophisticated, words can be provided along with the pictures. Observational research has become more commonplace in certain situations, such as monitoring how people shop in stores or how they navigate their way around shopping malls. It is also used to help interpret how people are reacting to what others are saying (this is often referred to as 'body language').

Some researchers believe that current research techniques are seriously flawed. Their argument is that current techniques are based on the assumption that people are rational, and select products and services based on their perceived benefits. Scientists in the field of human cognition and communication suggest that this may not be the case. Dan Hill, President of Sensory Logic Inc, points out that linguists estimate that 80 per cent of human communication is non-verbal, and that scientists now reckon that two-thirds of all stimuli reaching the brain are visual (Hill, 2003: 1). Furthermore, they would argue that recent scientific tests on the brain show that the brain's emotional thermometer (the amygdala) plays a major role in how people form assessments and reach decisions. In other words, people are emotional thinkers as well as rational ones, but the emotions kick in quicker – after all, how many of us have not made 'impulse buys' when out shopping? What triggered it? Was it something sensual such as the smell of a new perfume or of freshly brewed coffee? In addition, if our decisions are reached in a split second, then we need research techniques that can capture the information in 'real time'. In some circumstances, observational research can provide 'real time' information.

Simple observational research

Today, observational research can take many forms and can often provide valuable information that customers would not recall if answering questions in a survey. Paul and Nick Hague and Carol-Ann Morgan point out the value in *Market Research in Practice* (2004), when they describe how the security cameras in stores can pick up other behavioural information:

Do we deliberate over our purchase of a can of beans? Do we read the label? What influence and pressure comes from the accompanying kids? Do we pick up other brands and examine them or do we just fly down the aisles throwing cans in the trolley without even checking prices?

This form of observation is known as 'simple observation' as it involves watching and recording activities that are occurring in 'real time' (Hague *et al*, 2004: 74).

Participant observation

The other type of observational research involves the participation of the person being observed. This is usually referred to as 'participant observation'. An accompanied shopping trip is a good example of this. A researcher accompanies the respondent on a shopping trip and at various moments asks why he or she is carrying out a particular action, or asks what he or she is thinking about at a particular point in time (for example if he or she pauses halfway down an aisle). At the same time the interviewer may videotape the expedition. The difficulty with this type of observation is that in a normal situation the respondent would not have been accompanied, or asked to think about why he or she had paused at a particular spot. In fact, where the respondent had stopped might have had nothing to do with the shopping trip (or other action being observed), but be a result of something totally unrelated, like remembering he or she had to call in at the dry cleaners on the way home. In addition, merely the fact that the respondent is being accompanied may well influence the behaviour he or she displays.

Using observational research to provide a deeper understanding of customer satisfaction for managing expectations

A classic use of observational research is to understand the difference between what customers say or think and the more measurable 'fact' of what actually occurs. For example, customers may say they queued for five minutes to reach an open counter at a post office, or to reach the checkout clerk in a supermarket, when an actual recording using a lapsed timer would show that in fact they queued for a considerably shorter period. Armed with this piece of information, management could devise ways of managing customers' expectations. This is most noticeable in popular tourist attractions or theme parks, where there are often signs that tell customers they have reached the point in the queue where they can expect a further wait of five (or 10, or 30) minutes.

CASE STUDY

The problem

A direct marketing company found that whenever it conducted focus groups, respondents would tell the convener that the insertion of scratch cards in a direct mail pack was a waste of time and money. The research participants could not understand why these direct marketing companies continued to insert them in the mailings. After all, every time they opened a mailing containing a scratch card they found they were the 'lucky winner' of the best prize on offer. While this might have fooled them on the first occasion, by the third time they had realized luck had nothing to do with it. However, contrary to this research finding, the direct marketing company had the results of hundreds of test mailings that proved that the inclusion of a scratch card in a mail pack lifted response rates dramatically. So the dilemma was that if respondents were telling the truth in the focus groups, could organizations using scratch cards be damaging their image and reputation, or negatively affecting the satisfaction or loyalty of their customers?

The solution

The direct marketing company decided to film respondents in their own homes, using a small camera built into a pair of glasses worn by the interviewer. The respondents (some of whom were existing customers and others potential customers) were told they were being filmed, and that the survey was to understand how they handled the mail they received at home. On at least four occasions over the following six weeks the participants were visited at their home at the time when they would usually open their mail. During the course of the visit they were observed handling direct marketing materials that had been sent to them through the mail. Not surprisingly a few contained scratch cards. In every case the respondents scratched the cards. When asked why they had scratched the cards, they said they knew it was stupid as they knew they were going to find that they had a winning combination, but they did it because they liked the feeling it gave them. 'Everyone likes to be a winner' was a common response.

Lesson learnt

Select the research method carefully and do not discard out of hand contradictory evidence from other sources. Where findings are in conflict, look for possible causes, and time permitting, conduct further tests to improve learning and knowledge.

One difficulty encountered with observational research is that it can be more expensive and time-consuming than more conventional research approaches. In addition, the observations can be open to different interpretations, even when respondents give their own point of view of what is happening.

FOCUS GROUPS

A focus group is a gathering of typically from eight to ten people, recruited to discuss a topic in which they have some interest. Focus groups can last up to two hours, although some have been known to take longer. (They are referred to as 'extended' groups if they are designed to last longer.) It is a qualitative research technique because the findings arising from the group cannot be assumed (in any statistical sense) to be representative of the population from which they have been drawn.

How focus groups can provide insights into customer service

The purpose of a focus group approach is to allow the participants, through the course of a 'guided' discussion, to interact with each other in such a way that a range of insights on the topic of conversation will be uncovered. For customer satisfaction and loyalty research focus groups can provide a wide range of opinions about customer perceptions of service (and loyalty), about which companies are considered to provide great service, and the reasons this is so. They can also provide insights into underlying assumptions about service. Customers always have stories about excellent and poor service encounters, and unlike some other topics, they are usually more than happy to share these tales with others. Consequently, focus groups are a popular research method for gaining insights into the many different aspects of customer service, satisfaction and loyalty.

While focus groups are widely used for consumer research, they can be more difficult for business research, especially if it is necessary to recruit companies from the same business area. Normally there will be a reluctance to participate in this situation, as the companies do not want their competitors to learn something that could be to their advantage. However, they do work very well when companies from non-competing areas are recruited, as often participants find their businesses have more in common than they think.

Factors contributing to a successful focus group

A number of factors contribute to the success of focus groups. These include recruiting the right participants, having an excellent facilitator (also known as a moderator) to lead the discussion, providing a comfortable environment, and having customer-focused topics to be discussed.

The mix of respondents

Just as with quantitative research, finding the correct mix of individuals is important for a focus group. It is necessary to recruit a representative sample of people from the target audience. As each group is normally drawn from a small geographical area, it may be necessary to hold groups in different parts of the country if it is believed there may be regional variations in customer perceptions. Likewise, it is important to consider the dynamics of the group. Would a mixed group of men and women work? Imagine a situation where the men were more interested in creating an impression with the female participants than in discussing the topic seriously. While flirting can be amusing, some clients may feel that they are not paying for a dating service. In addition, mixing age groups can be difficult for some topics, especially where generational differences in opinions can vary, such as in attitudes to borrowing money. Finally, it is important to be aware of cultural differences. In some countries it can be very difficult to get respondents to be critical of a company's service (or products) because it is not deemed polite to criticize in public. Likewise, people from some cultures think it impolite (not to say difficult) to have a male moderating a group of female respondents.

Moderating focus groups

Facilitation of focus groups is something that is best left to experts. Most focus groups take the form of a discussion structured around a pre-agreed topic guide. The moderator has to 'manage' the discussion to ensure that all participants have an opportunity to express their opinion, and no single participant dominates the group, while also ensuring that enough time is spent on each topic. In addition they have to be actively listening to what each participant is saying, and how he or she is saying it, as well as watching the person's body language for clues about his or her depth of feeling (or lack of it). Moderators may also be required to use stimulus material or other 'aids' to help explore certain topics. This is not a task for the novice or the faint-hearted.

Location

Focus groups can be sited either in specially designed facilities or in someone's home. These days it is more common for groups to be held in facilities that have been specially adapted for recording and viewing purposes. Usually these offices have rooms that can be laid out in different ways to suit the purpose of the group. They can replicate a comfortable living room, with easy chairs and sofa, a coffee table, television set and so on, or they can be transformed into boardroom-style seating if needed for business-to-business research. In all cases the comfort of respondents has to be paramount, so they will feel relaxed and at ease. After all, agreeing to participate in a focus group is a unique experience for most people, and some will approach it with a little apprehension.

A good qualitative research company will have provided the participants in advance with details as to what they can expect when attending the session. It will also provide appropriate refreshments, and some will provide transport home after the group. Participants are generally paid for attending the group as an appreciation of their giving up their time.

Content and subject matter

Another critical element for a successful focus group is the topic guide. This is a list of topics that the moderator uses to lead the discussion. To maintain the respondents' interest it is essential that it focuses on those issues that are important to the customer. Following a brief introduction of each of the participants, most topic guides start with a general discussion about an aspect of the subject in which everyone can participate. This is critical, as the moderator needs to get everyone involved in the discussion as early as possible. After all, it is not like a gathering of friends. These are strangers who have been brought to a venue they have never visited before, to experience something most of them have never faced before – a discussion on a subject they may not even have thought much about before. Following the 'ice-breaking', the topic guide usually follows a pattern of first skimming the surface of the subject area, then diving deeper and deeper into various aspects of it.

How many groups?

One question all researchers grapple with is how many groups to hold. One is not usually enough because it is impossible to determine if the output is representative or not. However if two are held it may turn out that the discussions and conclusions differ, and then it is necessary to hold a third in the hope that the 'best two out of three' will provide enough reliable information to meet the client's requirements.

However, if it is necessary to survey a number of different market segments, the number of focus groups can quickly mount up. To conduct too many groups is not only expensive, the moderator (or more probably moderators) will have a more difficult job trying to summarize all the data that has been generated. I recall one project consisted of 32 focus groups that were geographically spread across the United States. A number of moderators were involved, and the client was keen to attend some of the sessions and to have interim weekly debriefs as the project progressed. While the findings were very revealing, the size and scope of the project was at times very draining on all concerned.

Business-to-business research often does not require as many focus groups as consumer research. This is because many businesses have the same structure and face similar problems, so it is normally possible to get a clear picture from as few as three groups.

Clients and focus groups, a potentially explosive mixture

There is a final point to be made about focus group research that most researchers will have to experience sooner or later – the enthusiasm that some clients can exhibit while observing focus groups, and their enthusiasm for 'instant feedback'.

Observing focus groups

It is not unusual for clients to ask to observe a focus group. This is an opportunity for them to see customers at first hand. They will hear what customers think about the service they receive, or see their reaction to new ideas that the organization has probably been working on for months. However, there are certain safeguards that need to be followed (such as protection of respondents' anonymity). It is therefore essential that any client attending the sessions should be carefully briefed about what to expect, what is required of him or her, and about the risks of 'selective hearing'.

'Selective hearing' is a condition that arises when the observers suddenly latch on to one aspect of the discussion that they had not expected, and start to criticize the whole session. Alternatively, they hear something they like and ignore everything else that is being said. While this can be amusing to an independent observer, it can lead to some very serious client–supplier difficulties. How many agency researchers have been in the situation where their client claimed that the people recruited for a group were obviously not the 'right' people because they criticized the client's products while praising their competitors' products?

Clients and the desire for instant feedback on findings

'Instant feedback' must be the greatest concern of all moderators. Having just spent a couple of hours running a group, the moderator is then asked to produce an instant summary of the 'key findings' that emerged from the session. This does not allow any time for the moderator to reflect on all that has happened. Neither does it allow him or her to determine how different this group was from others he or she (or his/her colleagues) has conducted on the subject. Meanwhile, there is a risk that the client has drawn his or her own conclusions, and is keen to see if the moderator has similar 'findings'. In some cases this situation arises because of the different personalities involved. The researchers are 'judging' types, weighing up all the evidence and reaching considered conclusions. The client is often a business person who is used to making decisions based on the information to hand. Therefore, in such situations, the client can get quite agitated if the researcher is reluctant to draw conclusions based on the focus group that has just ended.

CASE STUDY

The problem

A major retail chain was concerned with the amount of profit it lost through breakages when customers bought eggs in store. It had noticed that customers always opened the egg cartons before putting them in their shopping trolleys, presumably to check that the eggs were not cracked or broken. Some customers dropped the eggs or the cartons while checking the contents. Therefore in response to this problem a packaging manufacturer developed a new range of transparent egg cartons for the retail chain. The retailer decided to conduct focus groups among customers before committing to an in-store test of the new cartons. (They were more expensive to produce than the traditional containers, so it would be very costly to go directly to an in-store test.)

During the initial focus group the participants praised the sense and practicality of the new packaging. However, at the end of the session they were invited to help themselves to the eggs (as they would not keep), and in every case they picked the traditional cartons for taking the eggs away in, rather than the new cartons they had said were so much better. The question the client immediately wanted answered was how much notice it should take of the participants' actions.

The solution

After a discussion with the client it was agreed that it was too early to judge if the actions of this group of participants would be typical of all egg purchasers. Therefore the client agreed to await the outcome from the remaining three groups that were to be held over the next couple of days. It was also agreed that the respondents should be invited to help themselves to the eggs earlier in the session, to see if they had a concern over the strength of the carton (being transparent it looked less substantial than traditional packaging) or whether some other factor was involved.

Lessons learnt

Drawing conclusions based on a single focus group can be difficult, especially when it involves new products or services. Often it is necessary to conduct a few groups to get a better understanding of customers' motivations. In addition, researchers may need to change the content or focus of the qualitative research if early indications are unclear or raise important questions that need to be added to the study.

Videotaping or recording focus groups

It is usual to videotape or audio record focus groups. This can be very helpful to moderators, as it means they can concentrate on their task of moderating the discussion in the knowledge that they can listen to and/or view the tapes before preparing their report. However two factors need to be considered when taping group discussions. First, permission must be sought from the participants at the start of the session to ensure that they do not have any objections to the taping. Second, safeguards must be in place if the tapes are to be played or supplied to people outside the research organization conducting the research. Video recordings present the biggest difficulty concerning the second point, as a respondent could be recognized from videotape. Here the researchers have to tread very carefully to avoid breaching the data protection legislation that exists in many countries.

IN-DEPTH INTERVIEWS

Depth interviewing is a different form of qualitative research. In *Market Research in Practice* (2004), Paul and Nick Hague and Carol-Ann Morgan identify six situations where depth interviews would be a more appropriate choice as a qualitative research technique than focus groups. These situations are:

- when respondents are geographically scattered;
- if it is important to avoid other people influencing the responses given by an individual (as may occur in a focus group);
- where the aim is to collect individual case stories from an individual;
- where significant comment is needed from an individual (in a focus group each person usually only talks for around 10 minutes during a group lasting one and a half hours);
- where individuals' responses and behaviour need to be tracked;
- where the topic area is sensitive (such as talking about personal wealth, personal hygiene, drugs or alcohol) (Hague *et al*, 2004: 62).

Face-to-face and telephone interviews

Depth interviews can be conducted either face to face or by the telephone. These are not usually complementary methods, except where a telephone has been used to recruit a respondent or to make an appointment for an interview. Each of these approaches has different strengths, and the method to choose will depend on the specific circumstances.

In a face-to-face interview, the interviewer can observe the respondent's body language and facial expression. It is also easier to 'pace' the interview. The telephone, on the other hand, is becoming a method of choice for many respondents, especially those that lead busy lives and have little spare time. However, it is more difficult with a telephone interview to gauge a respondent's demeanour and whether or not he or she is getting bored with the interview (although experience has shown there are obvious clues that respondents give out when they are reaching this point). In business-to-business research, a telephone interview can be easier to arrange than a personal interview, especially among senior management in large companies.

The depth interview questionnaire

Depth interview questionnaires can take two forms, semi-structured or structured. In a structured approach, the interviewer has a strict set of questions to be followed. In a semi-structured interview there is more latitude for the interviewer to explore matters that are raised in the interview itself. Both approaches use open-ended questions (these are questions that do not have a pre-set list of potential answers, but a space for recording responses 'word for word'). If the purpose of the research is to elicit the words and phrases that people use to help with the development of a questionnaire for the next stage of the research, or to aid the shaping of communications about products and services, a semi-structured approach is best.

Alternative approaches for conducting depth interviews for insights into customer satisfaction or loyalty

Researchers can use a number of different approaches when conducting depth interviewing. They do not all have to be 'one-on-one' face-to-face interviews. For example if the aim is to find out how different people view customer service, one option is to have two people to discuss the topic, with the moderator guiding the conversation. (Here the main purpose is for the two people to have a conversation on the subject, not a question and answer session between the moderator and each of the respondents.) This method works especially well in the United States. Respondents are particularly open to sharing their experiences of good and poor service. At times during the discussion, the moderator leaves the room, leaving the tape recording running, and the two respondents continue their discussion without him or her. These types of interview are referred to as 'paired depths' in the UK and 'dyadic interviews' in the United States. Triadic interviews are a variant of this, where three respondents are interviewed at the same time.

Clients and depth interviews

Unlike focus groups, it is not common for the client to accompany the interviewer for a depth interview. One reason is that the client is more likely to know the potential respondent. This is particularly so in business-to-business research, or in research into a select segment of the market (such as people who have a private banking relationship in the financial sector). Obviously this affects respondent confidentiality, as well as increasing the risk that respondents will not be as open and honest about their feelings when face-to-face with the client.

Depth interviewing skills

As with focus groups, it is very advisable to use a properly briefed and trained interviewer for depth interviewing. For successful in-depth interviews, the interviewer has to be able to quickly put the individual at ease. In addition he or she needs to build a rapport and sound genuinely interested in what the respondent has to say. In the business-to-business market the interviewer may also need to establish credibility by being either knowledgeable about the client's field of business or sounding experienced and authoritative. Naturally interviewers need to be skilled in using probing questioning techniques, and have first-class active listening skills. This is especially important with telephone depth interviews.

How many depth interviews to conduct

Normally with depth interviews the focus of interest is the quality of the responses rather than the quantity of them. As a result, most practitioners suggest that between 10 and 30 interviews are sufficient for most surveys. As you can imagine, with a typical depth interview lasting about 45 minutes, a huge amount of information can be gathered.

Factors influencing the cost of depth interviews

Depth interviews are not cheap. A face-to-face depth interview costs about 10 times more than a similar survey conducted over the telephone. The difference is of course, that it is only possible to keep someone's attention on the telephone for around 20 minutes whereas in a face-to-face situation interviews can last for up to 45 minutes. In addition, it is very common to incentivize respondents to participate in a face-to-face depth interview. This incentive can take the form of a cash payment or a donation to a charity of their choice.

Depth interviews take a lot of organizing. They also have other challenges, such as getting potential respondents to agree to participate. Various techniques can be used to obtain cooperation. If the research is a customer satisfaction study and the client is providing a list of customers (or lapsed customers) for the survey, the client may be willing to let its sponsorship be revealed near the start of the survey. Often this can make a difference between respondents agreeing to participate and declining. Certainly in the business-to-business arena, customers are more likely to participate if the client is a well-known company. If the client agrees to pre-notify the potential respondents about a possible survey, the proportion of people refusing to participate is lower.

INTERNET-ADAPTED QUALITATIVE RESEARCH

The internet has provided researchers with an additional business tool. It has obvious uses in the area of desk research, and provides an updated version of traditional self-completion surveys. Small companies, and other clients without a lot of money to spend on market research, may well find that the Internet is a useful medium for gathering customer feedback, provided their customers have access to it.

While it has drawbacks, many of the limitations are the same as those of other self-completion survey methods: low response rates, an uncertainty as to who answered the survey (and whether or not it is his or her sole opinion or that of others who were with them at the time), and how representative the respondents are of the customer base. Some feel that respondents cannot express their emotions as well through this medium, but others claim it is not a problem, as people can use capital letters or 'smileys' to convey their attitude.

Strengths of internet research

The strengths of internet questionnaires are also similar to those of the self-completion survey: respondents can read each question and see the range of answer codes on offer. There is no risk of interviewer bias. In addition, it is possible to show video clips (useful for advertising research) as well as pictures, and ask respondents for their immediate impressions.

Employee research is one area where internet surveys are potentially very useful. Most employees have access to e-mail and so it is possible to send out an internet (or intranet)-based survey via e-mail that they can respond to quickly and easily. There are many inexpensive software packages that can be bought to set up a survey of this type, that even novices can use.

Another area that has been attracting attention is internet focus groups. There is technology available to enable discussions to be held by telephone via the internet. Alternatively, moderated online focus groups can be held, where participants discuss issues in real time using chat room technology. The online groups do not tend to last as long as traditional focus groups (around 45 minutes compared with 90 minutes for a traditional focus group in the UK, but in the United States they can last up to an hour and a half). Clients can 'attend' these types of groups through the chat room facility.

Internet focus groups can provide a broader geographical coverage than is possible with traditional focus groups. They also reduce the travel costs that are normally incurred with traditional face-to-face methodologies. David Van Nuys (1999) has identified other potential savings, especially where a client can provide potential respondents' e-mail addresses and telephone numbers. In his estimate, the savings can be up to 20 per cent of what would be charged for a face-to-face group, in addition to travel cost savings. Another saving is the efficiency cost associated with management time. Instead of management having to spend time travelling, waiting in airport lounges, spending evenings away from their families, they can be at work right up until the moment they need to dial in to their virtual focus group. In the United States, Van Nuys claims that online groups work best with six to seven respondents.

Another variant of this is the bulletin board approach. Here participants respond to questions posted on bulletin boards by a moderator. A bulletin board discussion can last a week or more. As a result, respondents tend to give more 'considered' replies as they have more time to respond.

Limitations of internet research

There are limitations to web-based or internet research. Besides those mentioned above, MORI, a UK research agency, has found that the cost savings are not as great as originally anticipated. It claims that participants' comments are far briefer, that people are more reflective when using the bulletin board approach, and that chat room-based discussions can be trickier because of the time lag in comments appearing on the screen. It has also found that older participants feel less comfortable with this medium than younger customers (who feel very at home with it) (MORI, 2004).

MYSTERY SHOPPING AND CUSTOMER SATISFACTION MEASUREMENT

'Mystery shopping' involves the use of evaluators who are trained to observe and note the quality of services being offered by organizations to their customers. Companies employ this approach to measure whether their service levels are meeting internal policies or procedures. They may also use it to test the service levels of their competitors. However there are some restrictions in the UK and Europe about how these methods can be employed. For example market researchers must not undertake mystery shopping surveys to be used for non-research purposes such as checking the performance of certain identifiable employees for possible disciplinary purposes. Neither must they use the technique to artificially boost sales of a particular product or service to create the impression of an apparent consumer demand. Finally they must not be used where they would waste an organization's time or money.

While mystery shopping can be considered a quantitative research technique, I have included it in this chapter because in most cases the observations are often based on a small number of cases. For example, a bank or a shop may want to see if its policies and procedures are being followed in each of its outlets. This may involve many hundreds of 'readings' (hence the research is quantitative), but each individual outlet may only have one visit a month. Therefore for the individual outlet it is really a piece of qualitative research.

Mystery shoppers are not the same as satisfied customers

Usually these mystery shoppers behave like normal customers, and make enquiries or purchase products without revealing their presence to the outlet or organization concerned. It must be remembered, though, that in many cases these mystery shoppers are *not* customers in the true sense of the word. They may not actually be acting as they would if they were making a purchase on their own. As they have been carefully trained, they have a heightened awareness of what is happening around them, so while they can be useful for providing factual feedback on the event they are observing, their own thoughts and opinions about the service should be treated with caution.

Lisa Morrison, Andrew Colman and Carolyn Preston (1997) point out other problems that should be borne in mind when interpreting the evidence from mystery shopping surveys. For example, many people prefer to give favourable reports rather than unfavourable ones (especially if the people in the target organization seem pleasant or easy to empathise with). They also note that women are likely to provide more accurate mystery customer reports than men, but that as customers, women are also likely to be better treated than men. In addition, they have found that the age of the assessor is also likely to affect the results (with younger adults being more accurate). Finally, they point out that a mystery shop is a two-way encounter between individuals. As such, the behaviour and appearance of both individuals can influence the outcome.

The need to involve and inform employees

When mystery shopping calls are conducted within the client's own organization, it is advisable to inform staff and any staff associations that the organization plans to undertake the study. In some European countries this is a legal requirement. While staff do not need to know exactly when these visits or calls will be made, they should be told the reasons for the study, and that no disciplinary actions will be taken against any individual as a result of what is observed during the visit. In addition, if staff are incentivized on sales or volume of calls handled, any potential losses in their bonuses as a result of spending time with this 'false' customer should be taken into account.

ESOMAR (the European Society for Opinion and Marketing Research) (1999) points out that if mystery-shopping calls are being made on non-client organizations, researchers should follow certain guidelines. For example, the interviewing of staff should last only two to three minutes, and where a purchase is made, the call should be commensurate with the value of the product or service being purchased. In other cases they suggest that, unless there are strong technical reasons for doing so, calls should be limited to 10 minutes' duration in manufacturing and retail businesses and 15 to 20 minutes in other service industries and businesses. Where calls are made to self-employed or professional people, and the time spent on the call may literally cost them (lost) business, consideration should be given for reimbursing them at an appropriate professional rate.

What mystery shopping should focus on

As mentioned earlier, many organizations commission mystery shopping surveys to measure the adherence to company policies and procedures designed to enhance the customer service experience. As such, they can be seen as a hurdle to watch out for by employees rather than as a business tool to recognize and reward examples of outstanding service and desired employee behaviours. The case study shows how mystery shopping can be used in a positive way for the benefit of employees and customers alike.

CASE STUDY

Pret A Manger is a chain of about 150 shops in the UK that make and sell sandwiches using natural, preservative-free ingredients. Its management is fanatical about the quality of the food and service provided in the shops. Sandwiches are freshly made throughout the day in the organization's own kitchens. Charities for the homeless are offered any unsold sandwiches at the end of each day (and these are transported to them in vans bought by the company). The company recognizes the critical role that its staff play in delivering its service vision. It has commissioned Bond Street jewellers Tiffany & Co to make solid silver stars, which are sent to staff members whenever a member of the public calls or writes to congratulate a specific person for being helpful or professional. In addition, a member of the management team will reply to the person giving feedback, and thank him or her for taking the time to pass on the comments. As Pret A Manger says in its promotional literature, 'Do call or e-mail, we have a brilliant team standing by. Our founder, Julian, will answer your queries and questions if you like. Alternatively, our MD Clive Schlee hasn't got much to do; hassle him! If you are a Pret customer, you have a right to be heard and listened to.'[1]

This innovative company also has turned the traditional approach to mystery shopping on its head. Each week mystery shoppers visit every one of its outlets. If the service received by the mystery shopper meets all the necessary criteria, the mystery shopper gives the service provider a £50 reward. As a result, the programme is well accepted by employees (Cook, 2004: 63).

CLOSING COMMENT

The intention of this chapter was to provide a short introduction to qualitative research. For those wishing to read more about qualitative research, a good starting point is the seven books in the series *Qualitative Market Research: Principles and Practice* edited by Gill Ereault, Mike Imms and Martin Callingham (2002).

4 Quantitative research

Just as the previous chapter addressed the basics of qualitative research, this chapter looks at similar issues with respect to quantitative research, again with references to researching customer satisfaction and loyalty.

> Not everything that can be counted counts, and not everything that counts can be counted.
>
> **Albert Einstein**

Quantitative research is concerned with measurement. It is used, for example, to measure the size of a market or segment, to validate a finding arising from another source, or to test hypotheses. It usually involves obtaining data from relatively large numbers of respondents who have been sampled in a rigorous manner. The wording of questions in a quantitative survey is fixed, and they are usually asked in a fixed order (except where rotation or randomization is required to minimize bias – a topic covered in a later chapter). There are many different methods researchers can use to conduct a quantitative survey. In this chapter we look at the main approaches used for customer satisfaction and loyalty research. These are mail (postal), face-to-face, telephone, internet, and customer comment cards. The chapter closes with a brief overview of some other quantitative methods that are less commonly used for customer satisfaction surveys, including consumer panels, syndicated surveys and omnibus surveys.

MAIL

The benefits of mail surveys

Mail surveys (referred to as postal surveys in the UK) have a number of benefits for the researcher on a tight budget. They are relatively cheap compared with most other traditional research methods (although the cost of printing, packing and distribution should not be underestimated). Provided the addresses are accurate, they need not be restricted in terms of geographic coverage. In addition, all questions are 'asked' in an identical fashion and so there is no risk of interviewer bias. As a research method it can appear the least intrusive to people, and if they do not like the subject matter they can decide not to respond. If they do decide to respond, they can complete the survey at a time convenient to them. They can read all the questions and be assured that there is nothing to fear from what is being asked. In addition, visual 'prompts' can be provided.

Limitations of mail surveys

Mail surveys have a number of limitations. One potential problem is that respondents are able to see all the questions being asked, and this makes collecting 'initial thoughts' impossible: when they see the whole questionnaire, ideas that may not have occurred to respondents spontaneously will be put in their minds. So, for example, in interpreting responses to an initial 'overall satisfaction' question it is important to bear in mind that the opinions expressed are more considered than when a similar question is asked at the start of a telephone survey.

While mail surveys are cheaper than most other forms of market research, they can take longer to conduct, as sufficient time must be allowed for respondents to send back their completed questionnaires. Many research practitioners advise sending a reminder about 10 days after the initial mailing to boost response levels, but depending on the size of the mailing, this may not always be a cost-effective option. Three weeks after the initial mailing, probably about 90 per cent of all likely responses will have been received. Some practitioners always send mail surveys out on a Wednesday or Thursday so that they arrive in time for the weekend, when consumers are more likely to have time to complete them.

Besides the use of a reminder, some agencies recommend that an incentive is offered to boost response rates. Again, opinion about the use of incentives is divided. Response rates can vary enormously depending upon the incentive used. For many years the inclusion of a

US dollar bill would outpull any other incentive in Europe, even though some banks charged a fee greater than the local value of a dollar if anyone tried to convert it into local currency! Another popular incentive is a pen – the theory being that respondents will drop everything they are doing there and then to complete the survey. The promise of a donation to charity or of a summary report of the survey is often used in business-to-business mail surveys.

Other factors that can affect response rates are the layout of the questionnaire and the topic of the survey. Questionnaires can appear difficult or time-consuming to complete if they use small typefaces and have lots of 'tick boxes'. The topic can have a dramatic effect on response rates. Response rates to surveys about personal vacations or travel are usually higher than response rates to surveys about banking or finance.

CASE STUDY

Background

A US financial company launched a new product in the UK, targeting the affluent sector of the market. The product offered a highly personalized and discreet service. A few months after the launch, the company decided to research its customers to see how satisfied they were with the level of service they were receiving, and to find out if any aspects of the service were falling short of expectations. However, it felt it could not conduct the research using face-to-face or telephone research as these methods might appear intrusive, so it decided to conduct a mail survey. However, it was concerned about the low response rates that mail surveys traditionally got, so working with its direct marketing agency, it devised a mail survey that would, it hoped, achieve an acceptable level of response. It succeeded. The response rate exceeded 70 per cent.

Secrets of success

The following factors were considered instrumental in achieving this level of response. First, the questionnaire was accompanied by a letter personally signed by the company's managing director inviting feedback from the 'charter members' of this new service. This was the first time the term 'charter member' had been used in any mailing to these customers, and it was felt that it added an element of exclusivity. Second, it invited these charter members to provide feedback on the things the company had done well and aspects that it had not done so well during their first half-year of product ownership. It also invited them to add suggestions for how the service could be improved. The questionnaire was printed on very high-quality paper and a first-class stamped return envelope was provided. Obviously, the mailing list was very accurate and up to date. Finally, the subject matter was highly appropriate to the audience.

CASE STUDY

Background

A publishing company wanted to create a new recipe magazine for the cookery market. However, it recognized that there were hundreds of recipe books and magazines already in print, and that every week many magazines and newspapers carry articles on cookery or offer new recipe ideas, so to stand any chance of success it had to really understand what people liked and disliked about cooking and recipes. However, as with all new product development, any money spent on the product was speculative, and there was a risk that the financial backers would not see a return on their investment. Therefore, the publisher decided to conduct a mail survey targeted at people with an interest in cookery.

It bought lists of such people for the mailing. Recognizing it would have only one shot for getting the information required, it devised a 28-page self-completion questionnaire. The researchers were highly concerned about the likely response rate, but the publisher insisted the questionnaire be mailed. It achieved a response rate in excess of 50 per cent.

Reasons for success

It was concluded that the length of the questionnaire actually contributed to its success among the target audience. People who are passionate about a subject cannot get enough information about it, and are also more than willing to share their views with others on the subject – provided they feel their level of interest will be reciprocated by the other party. In this case the publisher had already produced several successful cookery publications and the audience would have recognized that fact. In addition, the publisher offered to send all respondents some new recipes it had developed as an incentive.

While the two case studies show what can be achieved from mail surveys, it must be noted that generally response levels to mail self-completion surveys are quite low (typically around 20 to 25 per cent). Response rates of this level raise the question about how representative the results of the surveys can be when such a low proportion of the target universe responds.

Another limitation of mail surveys is the inability to clarify or probe responses to open-ended questions. Some people find it very difficult to express why they have taken a particular action or have a particular opinion. In other forms of research the interviewer can probe for further information, but in self-completion surveys it is necessary to rely on respondents being able to articulate their thoughts in writing. It is also difficult to gauge how much space to leave on the page for responses to open-ended questions. People with large handwriting need a large amount of space, or else they may truncate their response to fit the available space. However, if plenty of space is left, people with small handwriting may feel pressured into writing more than they intended because they feel that a lot is required.

Another concern with mail surveys is that the researcher cannot be certain who has completed the questionnaire. It may have been completed by the intended respondent, but there is no way of knowing if he or she has reported his/her own opinions or those of others he or she may have canvassed. This situation may occur more in business-to-business surveys, where the 'targeted' respondent passes the survey on to a subordinate with the instruction to 'complete as much as you can and then return it to me for a final sign-off and review'.

Finally, there is little likelihood of determining whether the respondent has misunderstood any of the questions, so questions have to be kept relatively easy to understand and complete. This, of course, should be the case for all surveys, but in other approaches it is possible for interviewers to ask clarifying questions if they feel respondents have misunderstood. This option is not available in a self-completion mail survey.

FACE TO FACE

Advantages of face-to-face interviewing

Face-to-face interviewing has a number of advantages over other forms of data collection. For example, many different types of sensory aids such as videos or pictures, music or sounds, tactile materials and scents can be used.

In a face-to-face situation interviewers can also employ observational research techniques to help put the interview or the respondent's comments into context. For example they can watch, or record, people's reactions to a particular question or stimulus material. How did they handle it? What did they look at first? Did they find it difficult to open? This is not a very common practice, but the case study shows the value of this approach.

CASE STUDY

The situation

A US company developed an advertising campaign to support the launch of a proposed new service for its main business customers

---

(and hopefully to attract new customers in the process). The new service aimed to reduce the amount of administrative paperwork its clients had to complete each month. The campaign employed humour to show harassed managers' lives becoming more bearable through the use of this new service. The agency proposed face-to-face research. While not the main focus of the research, the client asked if the agency's interviewers could also make a note of the working environment of the companies they visited.

The complication

Most respondents, while answering the questions asked, agreed that the new service would be a very useful service for business people. However, many of the interviewers noticed that most of the managers they visited had very clean and orderly offices. Furthermore, they noticed that when the respondent had to get some information in order to answer a particular question, they simply entered a few commands into their computers and the answer was provided. In other words, in spite of what the respondents were saying, there wasn't a need for the proposed service because respondents had computer systems that dispensed with the need for paper records. In so doing they had reduced the amount of time spent on administrative matters.

Lesson learnt

While customers will answer questions asked, it is important to consider other factors that may have a bearing on the business issue. In this case the choice of research approach had an important bearing on the issue. The type of information noted by the interviewers simply would not have been available from a telephone or a self-completion survey. As a result of the interviewers' observations, the client decided to change the focus of the proposed campaign and to target it at a different customer segment.

Other advantages of face-to-face interviewing are that interviewers can be certain they are talking to the correct individual, they can also see if the respondent is having difficulties understanding a particular question, and complex questions can be more easily explained through the use of 'show cards' and other stimulus materials. In addition, verbatim responses can be probed for clarity of understanding.

The development of laptop computers has provided face-to-face interviewing with even more facilities than in the past. The advent of CAPI (computer assisted personal interviewing) has meant that video clips can be shown to respondents during an interview. In addition, sensitive questions that interviewers or interviewees may have been embarrassed to ask about or answer can now be asked, and the interviewer can simply pass the laptop to respondents to type in their answers. CAPI software is now so sophisticated that it is possible to design the questionnaire so that the responses a customer gives to earlier questions can appear as part of the text in later questions.

Disadvantages of face-to-face interviewing

So what are the disadvantages of face-to-face interviewing? First, there is cost. It calls for highly skilled and presentable interviewers, especially if the interviews are with senior executives in business or government. These interviewers need to have been properly briefed, and this can necessitate personal briefings. If customers are widely dispersed across the country, there are travel and other related costs to consider.

Geographic location is another potential problem. In some countries there are 'no go' areas where it is unsafe for interviewers to enter after dark or on their own. In the United States and Canada it is uncommon for 'door to door' (also known as 'in-home') research to be conducted because of the vast distances involved. However, there is a large and thriving research market for face-to-face surveys conducted in shopping malls. In the United Kingdom there are far fewer malls, so on-street interviewing is conducted, as well as in-hall tests (which usually involve the recruitment of respondents on nearby streets). Sampling issues relating to face-to-face surveys are covered in a later chapter.

As with qualitative research, face-to-face research can also be affected by social bias. (This occurs when respondents feel they need to provide a particular answer to a question in order to be seen in a good light by the interviewer.) This matter is covered in more detail in the chapter on questionnaires.

TELEPHONE

Over the past 30 years telephone research has grown in popularity along with the growth in telephone ownership. However, it now faces a new challenge with the increasing popularity of the mobile phone.

The benefits of telephone interviewing

Telephone research offers many benefits over other methods of market research. First, as most telephone research is conducted from specialist telephone centres, there is more supervision and control over the quality of the interviewing than for face-to-face surveys conducted in malls or in the home. Most agencies have a supervisor for every five to ten interviewers, who can check the quality of the interviewing as it happens. Because most telephone interviewing is conducted from telephone centres, it is possible to provide personal briefing for the interviewers. Therefore there is less chance they will misunderstand the instructions for the project, and they can raise questions for clarification that may not have occurred to the other interviewers until later. So in this sense it is more efficient. A related benefit is that clients can attend the initial briefings and provide additional background, or an immediate answer to an unforeseen matter, which helps to avoid delaying the start of the interviewing.

Sensitive questions can be asked over the telephone because the interviewee and interviewer are not facing each other, and so neither can display any embarrassment about asking or answering the question. Of course the question has to be relevant to the survey, and follow the guidelines laid out by local laws (such as the UK Data Protection Act) and the local market research association's code of conduct.

Telephone interviewers, like face-to-face interviewers, can ask open-ended questions and probe for clarification of any ambiguous answers. In addition, a qualitative aspect can be added to the survey. For example, if a respondent states that he or she believes the service he or she receives from company 'x' is poor, the interviewer can then be instructed to ask why the respondent thought the service was poor, and to record the response in the customer's own words.

The development of CATI (computer assisted telephone interviewing) has, like CAPI, provided a number of additional benefits. There is flexibility in that the questionnaire can be routed according to the answers provided by the respondent. In this way only relevant questions are asked, which should make the interview more interesting to the respondent. Second, there is speed. Through this technology, answers to all the interviews conducted by a certain point in time can be reviewed almost immediately, which means that interim results can be provided if required by the client. Certain quality aspects have already been covered in so far as the questionnaire can be pre-tested before it goes into the field, and any incorrect routeing of questions can be corrected. Interviewers are therefore unlikely to ask questions in the wrong order (or ask inappropriate questions) as the software will guide them through the interview. Another quality aspect is that incorrect answers cannot be entered. So, for example, if the question asks the respondent to pick one item out of a list of five as being the most important, the software will not allow the interviewer to code two items as being the most important.

The final benefit of telephone interviewing is cost. It is cheaper than face-to-face interviewing, as there are no travel or distribution costs. It is also possible to conduct multi-country telephone surveys from a central location in one country (provided there are interviewers available to conduct the survey in the respondents' native languages). This is likely to reduce survey costs, as it is not necessary for one agency to brief agencies in other countries to conduct and monitor the survey, although of course the agency (and in turn the client) will have to pay the cost of the international telephone calls and a premium for multilingual interviewers. In addition, response rates for some international surveys can be higher than for telephone surveys conducted in the home country, especially for business-to-business research, as respondents are more likely to participate in an international survey provided they feel the topic is relevant and important.

Disadvantages of telephone interviewing

So what are the disadvantages of telephone research? The first has to be the inability to show respondents stimulus materials (although the development of video phones may change this situation). Another limitation is questionnaire content. If the questionnaire contains dozens of attributes for respondents to rate, the process can become very tedious for the respondent and the interviewer. If the respondent loses interest in the survey, the risk of him or her terminating the interview increases dramatically.

The advent of answerphones and call screening technology has impacted this research approach, as many people now use answerphones as a way of avoiding unsolicited calls. As a result research agencies need to constantly monitor the proportion of customers who are screened out of the survey, as there is a risk that the final sample of people surveyed will no longer be representative of the target population. This is similar to the problem of non-response faced by mail surveys.

Telephone interviewing also presents interviewers with a particular challenge. They have to try to build an immediate rapport with a stranger, and hold his or her interest during the interview. This aspect of telephone interviewing is covered in more detail in the chapter on fieldwork.

Finally, I mentioned earlier the challenge facing the profession caused by the spread of mobile phones. Often people are less willing to conduct a survey over a mobile phone, because they may have called at an inappropriate time, or could feel embarrassed about answering a series of questions in a public location. Time will tell if this situation changes. Certainly commuters overhear many different types of conversation, and some of these calls contain highly personal information!

INTERNET/E-MAIL

Strictly speaking there is a difference between internet and e-mail surveys. An e-mail survey involves sending a questionnaire to a potential respondent to complete offline and then e-mail back to the sender. As such it is more akin to the mail approach mentioned earlier. An internet survey is one that is completed online, usually from logging on to a specific website. Internet surveys can be accessed by a 'pop up': the respondent visits a particular website and is invited to provide his or her opinions about the site or the service he or she has received from it. Alternatively, respondents can be accessed via an e-mail inviting them to participate in a survey, and providing a hyperlink to connect them directly to the questionnaire on the hosting website.

Strengths of internet/e-mail surveys

Internet/e-mail surveys have a number of advantages over other types of research. For example, unlike mail surveys, responses to internet surveys are usually quite quick. Furthermore, with the technology available today questionnaires can be made to look very inviting and easy to respond to. Instead of ticking 'check boxes' that appear on mail surveys, it is possible to use radio buttons that change to ticks or other graphics to make the experience more interesting and lively for the participant.

It is also possible to purchase internet questionnaire software and to create, conduct and analyse the results in-house. Apart from the amount of time that staff will be involved in the project and the purchase of the software, there are very few additional costs to consider.

Weaknesses of internet/e-mail surveys

Unfortunately, internet/e-mail surveys have a number of disadvantages. They share many of the disadvantages mentioned earlier about mail surveys (such as non-response bias, not being certain who responded to the survey, and the quality of open-ended responses). In addition, many consumers are suspicious about opening documents that have file attachments because of the risk of inadvertently downloading viruses. Some anti-virus or internet security software may block access to unrecognized sites, and this again may limit the usefulness of this approach. In addition, some potential respondents may not have the appropriate software to open the questionnaire even though they can access the hosting website, or are suspicious of downloading new software to enable them to open the questionnaire. In business, so many e-mails are now received that many managers suffer from having mailboxes brimming to overflowing, and so are less likely to respond to any but the most urgent and relevant to their business.

Using the internet to measure customer satisfaction

One aspect that needs to be considered with internet surveys in particular is when to conduct them. Very often they take the form of pop-up surveys that appear during a potential respondent's visit to a website. The benefit of this approach is that it is known the person has visited the site, but the disadvantage is the difficulty of gauging how relevant the survey will be to the visitor. For example, if this method is being used to obtain reactions to the service people have received in the past from the company, the survey will have no relevance to first-time visitors to the site. In addition, if it is to gather opinions about how easy the site is to use and whether or not the visit met the visitor's needs, the timing of the pop-up is important. If it appears too early into the visit, respondents may not be able to answer all the questions and it will increase their annoyance level. Leave it too late, however, and you run the risk that respondent will leave the site before the questionnaire pop-up appears, or that they will not complete it because they want to move on to other matters.

Internet usage has grown enormously in the United States and the UK in the past decade, so internet/e-mail surveys are no doubt here to stay, but there is still much to learn about how to get the most benefit from them.

CUSTOMER COMMENT CARDS AS A DEVICE TO MEASURE CUSTOMER SATISFACTION

If you have ever stayed in a hotel or dined out in a restaurant then chances are you will have come across customer comment cards. They are usually located in hotel bedrooms or by the checkouts in restaurants. The idea behind these cards is very simple – to invite guests to leave their comments about their recent visit to the establishment so the management can evaluate how satisfied their customers were with the service they received or the quality of the location's facilities.

The cards often consist of a few questions with simple 'tick boxes' for respondents to use for their answers. The questions are usually very short and to the point (for example, 'How would you rate the politeness of our staff?' The answer options could be a simple scale such as 'excellent, very good, good, fair or poor'). The questions are usually limited in number in order to encourage the customer to respond, as the form only takes a couple of minutes to complete. The establishment usually provides a special postbox where the cards can be deposited before the guest leaves the premises. However, for those guests who do not have time to complete the survey there and then, these questionnaires usually also include a reply-paid mailing address so they can be posted back.

While these cards are relatively cheap to produce and distribute, they are limited by the number of questions they can contain and the fact that the respondents are self-selecting. Typically, less than 1 per cent of customers reply to this type of survey, and these tend to be those that are either very happy or very unhappy with the service provided.

CONSUMER PANELS

Consumer panels are not used frequently for customer satisfaction and loyalty surveys, which is a shame as they potentially have a lot to offer. They typically consist of individuals who have agreed to be contacted on a number of future occasions for their views on a particular subject or subjects. They are often paid a fee for their participation, and they can be recruited for a short period of time (say, three to six months) or indefinitely. Agencies are keen to sign up people to panels because, with falling response rates, it is getting harder and more expensive to find certain categories of respondents (such as people who drive luxury cars , who use bespoke services, or who have three or more homes). If agreement is obtained from these types of people to be contacted again, the recruitment costs can be kept to a reasonable level. Of course, the challenge for agencies is to not abuse their panel of respondents by calling on them too often, or the respondents will find the constant requests for interviews becoming intrusive and will withdraw from the panel.

A variation on this type of panel is one where respondents are specifically recruited to provide regular information about, for example, their purchases or television viewing habits.

The use of customer advocate panels for gaining feedback on customer satisfaction

Consumer advocate panels are a particular type of panel used for monitoring customer satisfaction and marketing programmes. This type of panel is actually a hybrid of the two types of panels mentioned above. Respondents are recruited from customers of the sponsoring company. They are then surveyed on a regular basis about one or more aspects of their experience of its service or products. For example, a financial services company might ask them to record all the details about each piece of correspondence they receive from the company in a particular time period. Then they send back all the material to the sponsoring company. So, for example, the company can determine how long the postal system takes to handle its mail shots. In addition it can evaluate the quality of the mailing pack and its contents, the accuracy of the mailing addresses on its databases, and so on. Some larger companies might even discover that their subsidiaries are mailing their customers with multiple offers in a relatively short time period, and that some of the offers are actually in competition with others from the same company.

One large US financial service provider used to invite its panel members to come and meet its senior executives three or four times a year to discuss how the company could improve its services. Not surprisingly, these 'customers' became very knowledgeable about the organization, and some executives began to question the validity of the exercise. However, others rather enjoyed the opportunity to talk directly with customers, no matter how 'expert' they had become.

All these different types of panels face certain common problems. The first is the recruitment and then maintenance of a large enough representative sample of respondents. Usually these panels need to be over-recruited initially in order to cope with any drop-outs during their lifetime. In addition, it can be questioned how representative their panel members' behaviour and views are. Most panels are used to measure behaviour (for instance, purchases made or television programmes watched), and it is well known that in the first few weeks of panel membership, new panel members' behaviour is not typical of their usual behaviour. Therefore their data records are usually ignored for the first few weeks they are panel members. It is also difficult to determine at what point respondents' views and opinions become conditioned by their being members of a panel. However, used wisely, panel data has one major benefit: it can provide longitudinal data. Thus it has the potential, for example, to show whether very satisfied customers purchase more products (from a supplier) than those who are less satisfied.

SYNDICATED SURVEYS

The idea behind syndicated surveys is to save money by pooling resources. These surveys can take one of two forms. In the first, an agency identifies a gap in the market for information that most client companies would find too expensive to commission as a proprietary survey. It then carries out this survey and sells the results to several companies, for a lower cost than an exclusively commissioned survey. For example, the agency might conduct a survey among students about their banking habits and their opinions about how well the banks they have contacted have treated them. Individual banks can then buy data about the market as a whole (that is, how students generally view the banking market) and specific feedback about their own services. In this way they can monitor if they are perceived by students as being better than their competitors, about the same or worse. These surveys are typically conducted every two or three years, so the syndicate members also have the opportunity to see how the market is changing, and how their own performance is changing over time.

The benefit of this approach is that it is in the agency's interest to ensure that the survey is technically sound, so clients can be confident the survey data they are purchasing is as valid as it can be. However the downside to this approach is that no syndicate member gains a competitive advantage over the other members, since all have access to the same information. This therefore places an emphasis on the quality of data interpretation by in-house researchers and others who make use of it.

In the second form of survey, a group of client companies get together and jointly decide to commission a single survey, the results of which they share. These surveys can be quite similar in form to agency-led surveys. Sometimes the syndicate participants are not in the same industry. For example, a group of companies interested in international business travellers might form a syndicate and commission a survey. The syndicate might include a car hire company, a financial services company that sells traveller's cheques, a credit card organization, a major international hotel chain and an airline. Each respondent is asked questions about various aspects of his or her travel experience, and the results are openly shared (if this is agreed beforehand) among the client syndicate members. The idea behind this concept is that each member gains important information from relatively hard-to-reach groups of respondents that is not available to its competitors. The challenge is to get the members to agree to the questions, research methodology and so on. This type of syndicated survey requires a lot of time and effort to set up, and a lot of stamina and diplomacy to design a project that all members will be happy to invest in.

OMNIBUS SURVEYS

Omnibus surveys are a cost-effective way of gathering data if a client has only a few questions that need to be answered. They work like this. Each week a research agency conducts a survey among a representative sample of 1,000 or 2,000 adults (or 'households in some cases). Some agencies conduct these surveys face-to-face while others conduct them over the telephone. A client buys 'space' on the questionnaire, based on the number and type of questions it wishes to ask. Most agencies charge on a 'per question' basis.

What makes these surveys cost-effective is that the clients are in effect sharing the administration, interviewing and analysis costs. In addition, because the surveys are conducted weekly, they can provide results within a short space of time. Further, because omnibus surveys exist in most European countries (although the sampling methods vary), this provides a very quick and cost-effective way of gathering data across a range of countries if needed.

However, omnibus surveys do have some limitations:

- Deadlines must be strictly adhered to. If an organization's questions are not finalized in time it will 'miss the bus' and have to wait for the next survey.
- The agency may not provide a questionnaire design service (although it will tell clients if it thinks their questions are unworkable!).
- The agency typically provides a limited set of data analyses but no data interpretation.
- Finally, organizations are unlikely to know what other companies are using the service or where on the questionnaire their questions will appear. This can present a problem if they are asking the same question over several different surveys, as the context in which a question is asked may differ from week to week. This could influence the results, as too could the effect of 'drop-outs' (that is, those people who do not complete the survey). Some agencies are reluctant to ask questions about some industries near the start of their omnibus surveys, as they feel customers would be discouraged from completing the survey. Banking and financial services is one industry that has in the past been burdened in this way. Therefore it is important for clients to ask the agencies to supply them with the demographic details of the sample that replied, and not to rely on the demographic details of the sample that started the survey.

CLOSING COMMENT

The intention of this chapter was to provide a short introduction to quantitative research. I am not aware of a definitive textbook that only covers quantitative market research, so if the reader wishes to read more about this aspect of market research, a good starting point is Didy Ward's chapter 'Quantitative research' in the *ESOMAR Handbook of Market and Opinion Research* (Ward, 1998).

Part II

GETTING STARTED

5 The project briefing

This chapter looks at the working environment of client researchers and the underlying factors that can influence the way they do their work. Following this, it outlines the issues they face in putting together a brief for customer satisfaction research. It provides some ideas for how to get their sponsors to clearly articulate requirements, to consider the ramifications of the possible outcomes from the research and to identify who else needs to be consulted about it. Funding and resource issues are discussed, as well as other internal constraints arising from company policies and procedures and data protection legislation. Other matters covered include an exploration of what form the research may need to take from the client perspective: for example, should it have an operational or strategic focus, is it to contribute to an internal performance measurement programme, is there a requirement for an external competitive benchmarking of performance? The chapter ends with suggestions on how to determine which research agencies should be invited to tender for the project and how to brief them.

> Never criticize your neighbour until you have walked a mile in his moccasins.
>
> **Native American saying**

This chapter and the next cover issues that client-based and supplier-based researchers face when setting up a research project for measuring customer satisfaction. Many of the points covered are applicable to any type of market research project. Experienced researchers working on the client side of the business might wish to skip this chapter, but I hope even the experienced will find something new or interesting to stimulate them. For new client-based researchers and those who have never worked in a client environment, it should provide insights into the life of colleagues on the client side of the business.

THE CLIENT RESEARCHER'S OPERATING ENVIRONMENT

What is life really like for a client-based researcher? Is it true that they spend most of their time on the telephone talking with agencies and the other half out wining and dining them? In my experience there is a great misconception about what is involved in being a client-based researcher among many agency researchers who have never worked in a client organization. If an agency person does not understand the role or the operating environment in which his or her client works, how can they work together as business partners?

There are many different types of organization in which a client researcher can work. For those working in a small company, in all probability market research will be just one of their many responsibilities. They might also, for example, be responsible for marketing and sales. In addition, they will usually not have a lot of money to spend on market research, so will rely on the internet and other sources of information to provide their information needs. They may not be very highly trained in market research, and could need to depend on the support and advice of agency staff when the time comes to commission it.

At the other end of the spectrum are large research departments with many highly skilled researchers. These departments can usually be found in multinational corporations or in the public sector. Researchers working in these organizations often know exactly what they require from a research agency, and often have spent part of their career learning the trade in a research agency.

However, most researchers work as lone individuals within small to medium-sized organizations. They need to provide management with expert advice as well as handle most aspects of a research project. Usually they have a small budget for research, or have access to funds set aside for research purposes.

THE ROLE OF A CLIENT RESEARCHER

The role of the client researcher can vary. For example, a company might expect its researchers to be 'information providers' rather than 'business partners'. An information provider tends to focus more on 'facts' rather than hypotheses or theories when specifying the output from projects. Those with a business partner orientation, in contrast, will probably look to research agencies to discuss the business ramifications of any research findings. These discussions can cover many different aspects of a business including organizational restructuring, financial impact and marketing.

Factors that impact a client researcher's contribution

There are three key factors that impact the role and contribution a client researcher can make. These are the business environment in which the company operates, the situation within the organization itself, and finally, the researcher's personal aspirations.

The business environment

In regard to the business environment, client researchers are expected to understand how changes in the economy, legislation, the political arena and technology can impact their organization (and their customers). In addition they need to keep abreast of longer-term changes in society. Finally, they need to be aware of what competing companies are doing in their market.

The company environment

There are many factors within the organization itself that can influence the contribution that client researchers can make to the business. For example, the larger the organization, the greater the bureaucratic structure and the longer the decision-making chain can be. All companies have strategic plans and business goals. In some organizations these plans are treated as if they were a national secret. To achieve the respect of senior management and so be taken into their confidence, researchers need to demonstrate their business acumen and foresight. This is achieved by the type of analysis and business understanding they display through their questions, their interest in the organization, and their presentations and reports. It is also reflected by the types of research companies and research personnel they employ on their projects.

Client researchers also need to be aware of the financial health of the organization, as this can influence the level of resources available at their disposal, the types of issues to be researched, and for suppliers, how quickly their invoices are paid! However, it is the culture within the organization that is probably the most difficult aspect of company life for the client researcher to understand and apply. This is crucial if they are to get things accomplished, especially in large organizations. The main aspects a researcher needs to identify are:

- Which departments 'drive' the company (for example finance, marketing, production). Usually this can be determined by looking at the career backgrounds of the senior staff and those who are rising rapidly up the corporate ladder. In my experience, the best organizations are those where there is a balanced senior management team, each member of which has a different set of background skills and experience.
- How other people in the organization get things accomplished. A company may have all sorts of rules and regulations, manuals and procedures, but if the people who get things done usually show a healthy disrespect for these rules and regulations or show an entrepreneurial flair to get things accomplished, this could be the path to follow.
- What the management considers the company's key success factors to be. Is it customer retention and satisfaction, is it financial prudence, is it marketing flair or product innovation?

The personal environment

Finally, there are the personal aspects that client researchers face in their organizations. Client researchers' effectiveness can be influenced by their career aspirations and management seniority. During the early part of their career, client researchers often have to concentrate on learning about the organization, its products and services while at the same time honing their market research skills. As they progress, they will be given more responsibility, and with this comes project management, departmental management, and possibly moves into other areas of the business (which can take them away from their research role). In addition, client researchers will have a set of goals on which their performance will be assessed. These goals can include their record of financial management (such as keeping within budget), their project management skills (including timeliness, planning, resource allocation and decision making) and their people management (that is, team and thought leadership, career counselling, appraisal skills and so on). Finally their direct line manager's influence must not be overlooked. If a manager is seen as a potential 'superstar', the likelihood is that he or she will not be in that position very long. A very ambitious manager may put inordinate pressure on the client researcher to produce results that make the manager look good. Client researchers who know how to manage their managers are usually the most effective. This usually means ensuring the manager has no surprises, that both researcher and manager are focusing on the same goals, and that the researcher is sensitive to the pressures the manager is facing.

There is a more detailed, in-depth examination of the client based research environment in Martin Callingham's excellent *Market Intelligence* (2004).

PREPARING THE BRIEF

The starting point of any project has to be an understanding of what is required from the market research that is to be carried out. This is normally produced in a briefing document (although it is not always in writing). Basically, a brief is a statement from the research initiator, or sponsor, setting out the objectives for the research and providing any necessary background information that the researcher will find useful in understanding the scope and nature of the issue.

First, a brief should tell the reader why the research is being carried out, and provide a summary of the background to the research. Obviously it should contain a set of objectives (that is, an indication of what the sponsor wants to know from the research and what business decisions it will be contributing to). It should contain details of the target audience – that is, the people whose opinions the organization is interested in receiving, or from whom it wishes to gather information. In addition, it should provide an indication of the budget and when the results are required (and in what format).

A more detailed briefing document might also contain information about previous learning or surveys conducted on the subject, and whether or not previous research might need to be replicated.

If it is an international survey the researcher will need to know which countries are to be covered and if there are any specific language requirements (for example, reports to be produced in three languages, one for each of three countries covered).

If the sponsor is planning to make a business decision that will be heavily dependent upon the results from the survey, the researcher will need to know the degree of accuracy the sponsor requires from the survey in order to feel confident about using it to make the decision.

Of course, it is wise for a commissioning client to ask for an outline of the agency's experience of the type of work it wants it to conduct, and some details about the staff who will be working on the project. In addition there is often a section relating to terms and conditions of business. This might, for example, include a requirement to consult the client over the choice of any sub-contractors, and specification of the procedures if the research or the report does not meet an acceptable standard, or if essential deadlines are not met. The very best briefs ask the research agency to identify in its proposal what they will expect from the client if the project is to be completed as specified. These requirements apply to all research projects, not just surveys about customer satisfaction.

BRIEFING ISSUES FACED BY CLIENT RESEARCHERS

The main problem with the scenario described above is that it all too rarely happens. Client researchers are often not given a complete briefing. Sometimes they receive a request for information at second or third hand. If the requirement is initiated at the top of a large organization, it can be filtered through a range of people who add their own interpretation to the request, especially if the original brief is of a broadly conceptual nature. The case study gives an example.

CASE STUDY

The chairman of a large multinational organization received a call from his wife (who was abroad on vacation) to tell him she was disappointed to find that the service from the company in her holiday resort was not as widely available or as prompt as it was in their home country. The chairman immediately fired off a note to his executive assistant to find out more about the situation in country 'x'.

The executive assistant called the head of the region concerned. The regional head wrongly assumed she was being told there was a major problem in her region, and that the chairman wanted facts and figures to determine the extent of it (as well as plans for solving it). So she decided she needed market research to tell her how widespread the problem was, and gathered her strategic planners, customer service and marketing people together to determine what actions they would take if (and when) the research proved that there was a problem in their area. After all, if the chairman said there was a problem, there obviously had to be one somewhere.

In due course, the researcher received a brief to measure the size and scale of the problem. Because no one had checked with head office when the results were needed, it was assumed that as the work was for the chairman's office they were needed as soon as possible, so should take priority over other work. The local management team also decided on the size of the project (large: they did not want to be accused of not having surveyed enough people) and the questions to be asked (plenty: they did not want to

---

refer back to head office and give the impression it was being bothered with mere 'details'). Finally it was decided that the report had better be produced in colour and translated into the language of the country where head office was located, even though no one in the local office was really fluent in that language.

How can a client researcher overcome these (and other similar) problems? One way is to seek answers or clarification on the following matters:

- Who is the internal client and what is the business issue he or she is addressing?
- What are the questions that the research sponsor actually wants answering?
- By when is the information required?
- In what format is the information to be provided?
- Who else in the organization will need to be involved in the process?
- Who will be funding the project and what resources and budget are available for it?
- Can the issues be addressed from existing internal company data, external published data, or will it require proprietary market research to be conducted with customers or the general public?

UNDERSTANDING WHO THE INTERNAL CLIENTS ARE FOR CUSTOMER SATISFACTION AND LOYALTY RESEARCH

Right from the start of any project, it is important to know who the sponsor (or initiator) is and what his or her goals and aspirations are. There are many different types of request for customer satisfaction and loyalty research. Here are just a few examples:

- The company has received some bad publicity about its slow responses to customer complaints. The client researcher is asked to prove that most customers who contact the company receive a prompt and courteous response, and their issues are resolved at the first time of contact. Assuming this hypothesis is proven correct, the findings from the survey will be used in a response to the media.
- Senior management has decided to implement a 'balanced scorecard' as part of a strategy to improve financial performance. Customer satisfaction is one of the elements to be measured. It will

form part of the management incentive programme, and so will need to be measured on a continuous basis.

- Marketing has noticed that sales are falling, as customers are cancelling or not repeating their orders, and moving their business to competitors. Yet the company's pricing is very competitive and its sales force report no problems when they call on clients. The marketing department suspects the problem lies in a slow or poor response to customer requests, or another service matter such as poor administration. The research is intended to determine the cause of customer defections.
- Following an intensive training programme, the customer service department has introduced some new 'behaviours' that it wants agents to display when dealing with customers. Research is needed to measure what differences, if any, customers have noticed over the past few months when contacting the company.
- The company has been conducting a customer satisfaction survey for several years, and customer satisfaction ratings have hardly changed over the period in spite of the company acting on the results. Research is needed to find out why this is so.
- Senior management has outsourced the customer service function, and wants monitoring to be carried out to ensure call standards are being maintained by the subcontractor. If customer perceptions have changed, it wants to know to what extent this is a result of the outsourcing.
- The company has recently appointed a new chief executive who is placing satisfying customers at the heart of his strategy. He believes the programme currently in place is outdated, too all-encompassing and out of line with emerging theories about how to really measure customer satisfaction. He therefore insists that it be replaced as soon as possible.
- A new business wants to learn more about its customers' requirements and their satisfaction with the service they have received from it so far.

HOW TO GET INTERNAL CLIENTS TO ARTICULATE THEIR CUSTOMER SATISFACTION RESEARCH NEEDS

As these examples show, requests for customer satisfaction and loyalty research can emerge from any part of an organization, and can provide a range of interesting and diverse challenges for the market researcher. The best research briefs usually come from companies where the research sponsor and other relevant end users within the client company have been involved in developing a detailed list of requirements. Through their involvement, they take ownership of the project. Not only have they usually thought through quite clearly what their requirements are, they are often also receptive to ideas from others. The client researcher can contribute to shaping the research project requirements, and also provide guidance to the sponsors on critical areas of a research project such as sampling, questionnaire design and content.

Unfortunately, there are still many companies where the researcher can encounter difficulties getting management to clearly articulate their requirements. Here are a few techniques that I have found useful when faced with this situation:

Three useful techniques

First, ask internal clients to write out the list of questions to which they would like answers. These will not necessarily be the exact questions used in the questionnaire (as they normally have to be converted into questions that address the matter from a customer's perspective). This might sound very easy, but many managers find it exceedingly difficult. This is because it forces them to think through their requirements quite carefully in order to make them clear and easy to understand. This technique can often lead to a change in requirements or emphasis for the research survey.

Another technique is to gather together the managers whose departments or work could be affected by the subject under discussion, to thrash out the details of the request. The researcher needs to emphasize that the need for the research is not being questioned; the aim is to ensure that all the interested parties' requirements are met as fully as possible by it. While this sounds like a recipe for disaster, in fact it usually works extremely well, since it brings new issues to the surface. It can lead to refinements in the brief; sometimes it becomes apparent that the company is not yet clear about its needs, and the detailed research needs to be postponed until they have been clarified.

However, not everyone is willing to participate in meetings or to put things in writing. In such situations a good option is to produce the brief and then circulate back to the research sponsors, asking for confirmation that it shows full understanding of their needs and that nothing has been omitted. The researcher can of course say that until 'sign off' is received he or she will not take the matter forward. Again this approach has the benefit of getting the initiators to give approval, but it runs the risk that an initiator might not read the document thoroughly, and just give approval because it seems to cover the main points.

IDENTIFYING WHO ELSE IN THE ORGANIZATION NEEDS TO BE CONSULTED FOR A CUSTOMER SATISFACTION SURVEY

One of the biggest challenges a client researcher faces when setting up a project is determining who else in the organization needs to be consulted. The case study shows why this is necessary.

CASE STUDY

When credit and charge cards were launched, customers had to sign a three-part receipt to confirm the transaction. The store or hotel or restaurant gave one sheet to the customer, retained one part for its own records, and sent the final part to the credit or charge card company for payment. As two copies were required, each receipt consisted of three sheets of paper interleaved with two sheets of carbon paper. The sales assistant removed the carbon sheets and destroyed them, as they contained sensitive data (details of the transaction, the card number, the card holder's name and a copy of his or her signature). This method of payment was therefore dirty (as anyone who has ever handled carbon paper can tell you, the ink comes off on your hands and is very difficult to wash off), and open to fraud by unscrupulous employees.

Therefore, when a company came up with a way of impregnating the lower two sheets so that information written on the top sheet was transferred to them without the need for carbon paper, it was felt that both customers and outlets would warmly welcome the development. Customers would like it because it would lessen their concern that unscrupulous employees could get hold of their card details and make bogus purchases (or pass on their details to other fraudsters). Establishments would also welcome it because it would make life cleaner for their employees. But these new carbonless receipts cost more to produce and had to be kept in controlled environmental conditions to ensure they did not get 'bruised'. If they became bruised, it caused difficulties for the optical scanners the card companies used to capture the details from them. So the company that had developed this new technology decided that research was needed to determine if the establishments would see the benefits of accepting the new receipts, and if they would be willing to absorb any increase in the fees they paid the card companies to help offset the development and other costs. In addition, management was keen to see if it would increase the loyalty of card holders because of the obvious security benefits.

The sales team were consulted as they were looking for additional material to support their sales arguments when trying to sign

---

up new establishments, and when handling calls from existing establishments about the introduction of the new receipts. The marketing department was involved as it needed customer feedback from both establishments and card holders about the benefits of the new service. Operations personnel were spoken to as they needed to know how establishments stored receipts and what difficulties, if any, they could see arising from the change. The audit department requested that the proposal include the internal company requirement that three competitive quotes would be obtained for the research, while the finance department wanted assurance that any requisite purchase orders had been completed for the project with the appropriate level of management sign-off. The legal department needed to approve the text that would appear on the receipts, and wanted to ensure there would be no unforeseen difficulties as a result of scanners failing to read the carbonless receipts correctly. Not surprisingly, this consultative process took the client researcher a couple of weeks to complete.

The situation described in the case study is not unique to the corporate business sector. For example, in the public sector there is normally a requirement to consult a wide variety of stakeholders. In the UK health care field these include patients, doctors and other health workers, the local Trust authority, the local medical practice and social services. Equal opportunities and ethnic monitoring requirements may also need to be taken into account. Therefore client researchers must make sure that they have consulted widely before putting the proposal out to tender.

KEEPING A CUSTOMER PERSPECTIVE

One of the most critical tasks client researchers need to undertake while preparing the brief and consulting with their colleagues is to ensure that the customer's perspective is not forgotten in the process. Merlin Stone has a very clear perspective on this matter. He feels that market researchers have often let their organizations down. In support of his case he points out that many financial services companies have embraced customer satisfaction measures based on internal measures such as their speed of answering letters, while it is the poor performance of their investments that has really dissatisfied their customers. In his words 'If their [market researchers'] halo is to do with thought and understanding, this is what they need to contribute, not just reports and presentations. If market research were managed in this way, then market research clients would be more successful!' (Stone, Bond and Foss, 2004: 128).

Sometimes the survey sponsor may also need reminding to consider the issues from the customer's viewpoint. For example, if the sponsor refers to a need to measure customer perceptions of distribution channels, a client researcher might need to rephrase this in the brief as 'seeking customer opinions about how they go about purchasing the company's goods or about contacting the company for their services'. Customers do not refer to distribution channels; they buy products at outlets, or contact companies in person or in writing, via the internet or over the telephone.

Other ways to get the sponsor to consider the customer perspective include asking sponsors to describe the customer experience or the customer benefits arising from the product or service they wish to measure. Researchers can ask them to articulate in what way this product or service would be important to the customer. Another good way to obtain a customer perspective on an existing service is to read letters that come in from complaining customers. These are often a rich source of material, and while they are usually from a minority of customers, it is the language these customers use to describe the product or service that will help provide the customer perspective for the briefing document.

FUNDING AND RESOURCES

The funding of any research will depend upon how an organization has decided to allocate its budgets. Needless to say, in many organizations a business case needs to be made to justify the investment in the research project. This can necessitate the client researcher obtaining 'ballpark' estimates in order to support the business case for the project. Once made, these 'estimates' often are seen as the full and final costs for the research (which can cause difficulties for all concerned if any of the underlying assumptions prove incorrect). If the funding for the project is coming from a budget other than a central research one, the researcher has to understand what the trade-off will be for the internal client. For example, progressing with a research project may reduce funds allocated for a marketing campaign. This can require delicate handling, especially if the project has been designated as a requirement by senior management who will not be funding it out of their budget.

In addition, the potential research sponsors often do not have any idea how much a research project will cost. This can lead to amusing conversations about the proposed cost for the project. For example, I once met with the senior management of a company that had decided a major piece of international research was required. It would cover 17 countries and would consist of at least 1,000 interviews per country. On receiving the initial ballpark estimate one manager commented, 'Do you realize that with that sort of money I could take all my customers out for a meal? Which do you think would enhance their perceptions of the service they get from our company, a meal or an opportunity to participate in this survey?' (I remember thinking at the time that it would have been a very cheap meal, and therefore the study probably would have the greater lasting benefit.)

A challenge many client-based researchers face when commissioning a 'tracking' survey (which many customer satisfaction surveys end up being) is how best to position the funding requirement. Should it cover the first year's investment only, or is it better in the long run to say it will cost 'x' over the next three years? This is an important issue for any research agency that will need to invest in its infrastructure in order to take on a project. The agency will look for some guarantee that the project has a chance of lasting long enough for it to recoup its investment.

UNDERSTANDING INTERNAL CONSTRAINTS

Many agency researchers who have never worked on the client side have only a partial understanding of the constraints under which client researchers can be expected to work. For example, client researchers may have to obtain cost quotations from three separate agencies to meet internal audit requirements. This is in spite of the fact that they have an existing relationship with a preferred agency. If the preferred agency's proposed fees are much higher than the competitors', it can be more difficult for the client researcher to justify its selection for the project. Usually the client researcher needs other arguments to support the recommendation. These can include:

- The agency has unique expertise for handling this type of project.
- The agency has sufficient resources to handle the project to time and budget.
- The agency is a recognized leader in its field for this type of work.
- The agency is not working for a major competitor (while the other competing agencies are).

Another challenge client-based researchers face is the expectation from their management that they will have a clear view of how they will tackle the issue to be researched. In other words, they are seen as the research specialists, and management does not want to get bogged down in discussions about who should or should not be sampled, which sampling technique is the best to use, which research methodology should be adopted, and so on. However, it very quickly becomes apparent that managers do have views on certain matters that really belong in the researchers' domain, such as the exact wording of the questions they would like answers to and opinions about the placing of questions within a survey. These matters are discussed in more depth in the chapter on questionnaires.

Finally, timing can be an important issue for client researchers. If the results from a satisfaction survey are to be used as part of a staff bonus programme, the timing of the delivery of the data becomes crucial, as it will have an impact on people's pay cheques. In any case, it is always a good practice to have clearly defined delivery dates for any research project.

DECIDING WHAT FORM THE RESEARCH SHOULD TAKE (OPERATIONAL OR STRATEGIC)

Researching customer satisfaction and loyalty can be undertaken at many different levels. For example, a small organization might require an operational survey to determine how customers view its break-down recovery service. In this scenario, it will in all probability be most interested in how quickly things are put right, whether or not customers found the service met their needs, and whether as a result of the experience they plan to continue as customers. It might well also want to find out if customers would recommend the organization to their friends and colleagues based on the service they received.

Alternatively, a researcher might decide it is necessary to take a more strategic approach to answer the needs of management. For example, perhaps the breakdown recovery service has been being measured for some time, but now senior managers want to know whether it is better or worse than competitors' services. The research might well address operational matters in this situation, but it could also explore why customers selected the service provider in the first place, and what, if anything, would cause them to change suppliers.

In larger organizations it is probably necessary to have, or to build, a programme of research that will help the company take a more strategic view of the customer experience. For instance, it could include a measure of employee satisfaction as well as customer satisfaction. When employees in an organization feel less valued, they are less likely to deliver truly outstanding service to their customers. Likewise, even the way employees interact with each other can influence employee satisfaction, which in turn can affect external customer perceptions. This is illustrated by another alleged public service announcement from a London Underground driver: 'We are sorry for the delay. This is due to the incompetence of the signal operators in the Aldgate area' (Paine, 2004). Sarah Cook gives the example of AT&T, which found that a 3 per cent increase in employee satisfaction related to a 1 per cent increase in customer satisfaction (Cook, 2004: 6).

DECIDING WHETHER WORK SHOULD BE DONE IN-HOUSE OR BY A MARKET RESEARCH AGENCY

One question all client researchers face at some time is whether or not the research should be handled by in-house staff. This is not surprising given that it logically appears to most internal managers that this is a more cost-effective (which normally means, cheaper) option. For example, if the organization has a call centre that deals with customer queries, in all probability it is busier at certain times of the day or week than others. During the quieter times call centre staff could be honing their skills, catching up with administrative matters or conducting outbound calls. However, it is not unknown for some companies to expect these staff to make calls to customers who have recently contacted the centre to find out how satisfied they were with the experience. Naturally, these call centre staff have a script to follow and need to record the results of their interviews, either on paper or via a suitable software programme. Managers these days are very attracted by this practice, because they feel they are capturing customers' immediate reactions to their contact experience. In addition, it enables staff to recognize that not all customers are happy with the outcome of their calls or with the way they were treated. The cost benefits of such an approach are obvious. There is no extra cost for the calls or the staff because 'quieter' moments are being used. There is no need to spend management time liaising with external agencies or in gathering and processing samples for use by an external agency. Feedback is almost instantaneous. What sensible organization would not follow such a practice?

Advocates for using external companies to conduct market research usually value the independence and expertise they bring to the situation. The staff that agencies use to conduct interviews have normally been trained in how to actively listen and capture what the respondents are telling them. They are skilled in not 'leading' respondents, either in the way they ask the question or in the way they record their answers. Furthermore, research agencies are specialists in such areas as sampling, questionnaire formulation and data interpretation. In addition, agencies usually work to a set of guidelines or a code of practice in their country, and this ensures that clients receive a professional approach to the project.

HOW TO DRAW UP A SHORT LIST OF AGENCIES FOR A CUSTOMER SATISFACTION SURVEY

If an organization does not conduct much market research, or is planning to conduct some in a foreign country where it does not have contacts in any research agencies, how should it go about finding a suitable agency? Fortunately, there are a number of steps that can be taken to draw up a list of possible agencies.

The first port of call these days will probably be the internet. A quick search on 'market research agencies in {a specific country}' normally brings up dozens of links. The problem with this approach is that it is possible to spend hours trawling through company websites and at the end of the day be none the wiser about which to approach. Refining the search to 'market research customer satisfaction and loyalty' will most likely still generate a large list of companies, but at least all of them should be offering some degree of specialization in customer satisfaction research. However, be aware that some agencies claim to conduct every possible type of research in order to get as many leads as possible. Better agencies should have testimonials on their site, or a list of recent clients who are willing to provide trade references.

The internet is not the sole source of information. In many countries there is a recognized trade or professional association such as the Market Research Society in the UK, ESOMAR (the European Society for Opinion and Marketing Research) based in the Netherlands (and covering most European countries), the Association of Market Research Organizations in Glebe, Australia, and the Council of American Survey Research Organizations based in Port Jefferson, New York, to name just a few. A fuller list is provided in Appendix 1. These industry bodies usually will not recommend a particular agency, but they do provide details of organizations providing market research services who employ at least one full member of their association and of their code of conduct, which is binding on their members.

Another good source of information is industry trade fairs. Market research organizations often take display stands at the bigger fairs, and like all participants are delighted to spend time telling potential clients about their products and services, or discussing their requirements. The difficulty here is that these fairs only happen at certain times of the year, so the timing may not fit client needs.

Many research companies advertise in the specialist trade press, and some practitioners write articles about developments in their field. In addition, many send delegates to conferences, give papers at conferences, and run training programmes on behalf of their national trade associations. These, too, can be a valuable source of leads.

HOW TO BRIEF AN AGENCY FOR THE PROJECT

Once the client researcher has reached consensus within the organization on what needs to be measured, when the results are needed, what budget is available for the customer satisfaction project, and that a market research agency should carry out the survey, the next step is to select a short list of up to three agencies and invite them to pitch for the work.

The most usual way of doing this is to provide a written brief. This has many advantages. It makes it certain, for example, that all the agencies start at the same point. How they interpret the requirements may differ, and this can play an important role in the decision about which agency to select for the work (see also Chapter 6).

An alternative (or additional option) is to brief each agency verbally, either over the telephone or face to face. The great advantage of a face-to-face briefing is that the client gets an early indication how seriously the agency takes the project. However, there is a cost for the agency, and many agencies are reluctant to attend personal briefings as part of a short list of, say, three agencies, unless the potential size of the project warrants it.

A telephone approach to an agency, or a visit to its premises, can reveal a lot about the company, and may help shape the decision whether to include it on the short list – especially for a survey on customer satisfaction. For example, how do its staff answer the telephone? Are callers put on hold, or put through to an answerphone or voicemail, and are they greeted in a warm, friendly and professional manner? When a caller is transferred to another department, does the next contact use his or her name? How are personal visitors greeted? Are parking spaces set aside for them? Are they met promptly, or left waiting in a lobby for five or ten minutes? Are they offered a tour of the facilities and introduced to others who could have an interest in the company or business? Are they offered tea, coffee and biscuits?

My personal approach is to send out a written brief, and tell the agencies in the covering letter when I am available to handle any queries. After selecting an agency for the job, I then invite them for a further briefing and discussion, to ensure they have a clear understanding of the project, and to enable them to submit a new costing should they feel any matters have materially changed from the written proposal. The practice in the UK is to work to fixed-cost proposals, therefore providing this second opportunity is usually warmly welcomed. In addition, I am a great believer in inviting the sponsor for the research to meet the agency staff at this meeting. It helps cement buy-in, as well as providing the agency with an early opportunity to meet one or more of the managers they may well see again when they come to present the results.

So the brief is complete, and the researcher has all the necessary sign-offs or approvals to proceed. What happens next? In the next chapter I explore what occurs at an agency when the invitation to respond to a research brief arrives on its doorstep (or desk, more likely these days, with the use of e-mail and the internet).

6 The proposal

This chapter looks at the issues research suppliers have to consider upon receipt of the customer satisfaction research brief. These include an evaluation of the internal resources and skills they will need to employ on the project, and whether any additional resources will be required from other companies. A number of project management issues such as timing and budget constraints are also discussed, as are contractual issues relating to other bidders, any history or relationship with the client, demands for exclusivity and terms and conditions of business. Often the agency is asked to recommend an appropriate method or methods (such as qualitative, quantitative, panels, diaries, internet, telephone, postal survey or mystery shopping). These aspects are only briefly covered in this chapter, as are related factors such as sample provision, sample size and what approach should be proposed (such as an in-house model versus a bespoke approach).

The chapter also contains suggestions on how to handle difficult situations such as the client proposing a different approach from the agency's, whether the agency should be the single provider or outsource elements of the work to others, what the proposal should contain and how it should be presented and delivered. Finally it addresses factors that influence the cost of the project, how an agency decides on the research team that will work on the project (its size and composition), and what factors the client should consider when selecting the agency it will appoint.

> Never criticize your neighbour until you have walked a mile in his moccasins.
>
> **Native American saying**

In some ways this chapter covers similar issues to Chapter 5, but from a different perspective (hence the use of the same quote to open the chapter!). As was mentioned at the start of Chapter 5, it addresses issues that supplier-based researchers face when setting up a research project for measuring customer satisfaction and loyalty. Many of the points discussed are also applicable to other types of market research, but I focus on how they apply to customer satisfaction research. Experienced researchers working on the supply side of the business may wish to skip this chapter, but I hope even the experienced will find something new or interesting to stimulate them. Relatively new agency researchers and those who have never worked in an agency environment should find it provides insights into the life of colleagues on this side of the business.

Research agencies submit research proposals in response to a research brief. There are many issues a research agency needs to consider when deciding whether or not to respond to a research brief. These issues are shaped by a number of factors, which are outlined in this chapter. The chapter closes with a look at how a client researcher can evaluate which proposal to select from those submitted.

EVALUATION OF INTERNAL RESOURCES AND SKILLS

While most clients realize that they are not the only client (or potential client) for an agency, they need to believe that they are going to receive all the resources and attention their customer satisfaction project deserves. After all, a client researcher may have already spent several days or weeks shaping and discussing the project with internal sponsors, and now there is an eagerness to get it off the ground. Consequently, clients normally expect agencies to be able to respond quickly and with a similar degree of enthusiasm to the brief that they have generated over the previous weeks. It is interesting therefore to note that agencies first hear of many projects via e-mail, or particularly if it is from a government organization, an invitation to tender on a website.

However, receipt of the brief at the agency will require an agency to reappraise immediately current workloads and resources. After all, at any one time a research agency will have a number of projects at different stages of completion, all with clients eager to hear how their project is progressing, or contributing to the questionnaire development, or awaiting results. Furthermore, agencies know that for most projects put out to tender, they stand a one in three chance of winning the work. So a key decision that is made very early in the process is whether to commit resources to submitting a proposal, or to decline the tender. Naturally declining to respond raises concerns. Will this client (or potential client) invite the agency to tender for projects again? What if the project has the potential of leading to more projects in the future that would not be put out to competitive tender, because it would be logical for the same agency to work on the follow-up projects?

Most agencies do not like to turn down an opportunity to submit a proposal, especially from an existing client, but responding positively is not always the wisest course of action. 'Winning' a project that is subsequently not completed to the client's satisfaction can damage not only their own reputation, but also that of the contact within the client's organization. It is also not unknown for projects to change direction once they have been commissioned, and this can sometimes cause difficulties for an agency that has only limited experience or limited resources.

One of the first tasks an agency undertakes upon receipt of a brief is to determine if it has the resources needed for the project. Issues to consider include the following:

- Whether the agency has staff with the right customer satisfaction research skills and sector knowledge for the project. If not, it may be possible (and acceptable to the client) to hire them from elsewhere.
- Whether the agency has enough fieldwork capacity to complete the project in the time required. If not, it may be possible to obtain additional resources from another agency.
- Whether the timing of the project will conflict with any other major projects, creating bottlenecks or excessive workloads at critical moments.
- Whether the agency has enough technical resources to handle the project, and if not, how quickly it could add more.
- Whether the agency has the financial resources to handle the project. This can be very important for a large-scale customer satisfaction project that could put pressure on the company's cash flow, or where it may require hedging for foreign currency if the project is to be billed or payments made in foreign currencies.

These matters are very important for projects that will cover a number of countries, and for customer satisfaction 'tracking' surveys (those that will be repeated on a regular basis). These projects are usually more demanding on an agency's resources, so making a mistake here can prove very costly.

OTHER BIDDERS

Most agencies like to know who their competitors are for the project. This is not because of a macho desire to beat them, but because it can provide the agency with some useful knowledge and may help shape its thinking about how to respond.

In customer satisfaction research, many agencies have developed proprietary methods or theories for researching the subject, while others take a more bespoke approach. This can be an important factor in the decision about which approach the agency should take when responding to the brief. In addition, certain agencies have built their reputation on their specialization in a particular field of research (such as customer satisfaction, loyalty and commitment) or a particular industry (such as telecoms or financial services) or a particular type of respondent (such as captains of industry). This enables them over the years to build a competitive advantage, and knowing this may lead an agency to decline to respond to a brief because it knows it cannot match a competitor's expertise.

Finally, an agency may need to subcontract part of the project to another company or individual, and obviously cannot select one of the other agencies bidding for the project in such a situation (unless, of course, the two agencies agree to submit a joint proposal and the client finds this acceptable).

THE HISTORY OR RELATIONSHIP WITH THE CLIENT

One of the benefits of working with a client for a number of years is that staff get to know not only the client researchers, but also the environment in which they have to work. This can be crucial in determining whether or not an agency wishes to continue working with this client, and the resources it will need to allocate for the project. Some clients are more demanding than others. In one case, a US-based client used a European agency to coordinate a project across 14 European countries, and phoned the agency every day at 1 pm European time for an update on the project. The call usually lasted an hour, because the client wanted a detailed progress update for each of the 14 countries. In addition, because the internal sponsor was a member of the executive committee that ran the company globally, the company contact felt obliged to be as up-to-date as possible at all times. Perhaps not surprisingly, the client could get very annoyed if the main agency researcher was not available to take the call, and let other staff know this in no uncertain terms. When the agency had been briefed for the project originally, it had been told there would be a need for regular updates, but not how regular or how long they would last. Needless to say, the agency underestimated the cost for this element of the project. However, when subsequently it was asked to submit a proposal for a 17-country survey for the same client, it had a better idea of what to expect.

TIMING AND FREQUENCY FOR MEASURING CUSTOMER SATISFACTION AND LOYALTY

The timing for a customer satisfaction survey can vary depending upon its size and complexity. When a brief is received, the agency needs to ascertain if it will be able to complete all the stages of the project in the time outlined by the client. If it feels it cannot, as a result of conflicting pressures, it will need to discuss with the client how far the requirements are cast in stone. Often, clients have a 'target' date rather than one upon which other actions are dependent. However, it is also worth discussing with the client whether there is any likelihood that the *client* will not be able to deliver information on schedule. For example, if the client is supplying the sample for the survey, has it agreed a deadline for provision of the sample internally, or is there a risk this date could move?

If the brief is for a tracking survey, then how often the customer satisfaction and loyalty survey will need to be repeated will depend upon a number of factors. First, there should be enough time between measures for the client to be able to take corrective actions. However, if the business environment in which the client company operates is highly competitive, it may be necessary to monitor the market more frequently than would otherwise be the case.

Pros and cons of continuous interviewing for customer satisfaction research

One of the other aspects the agency needs to consider, particularly if a tracking survey is required, is whether or not to spread the interviews across a particular period (such as Monday to Saturdays each week) or to conduct it in bursts (for example, all the interviewing conducted in one particular week each quarter). The choice of interviewing period will be influenced by the purpose of the research. For example, if the aim is to measure customer satisfaction with a particular event (such as taking out a loan or servicing a car) it may well make sense to conduct the survey as close to the event as possible, in order to capture customers' opinions about the experience while they are still fresh in their minds. However if the aim is to find out customer opinions about service by day of week or time of day (for example, measuring the queuing experience in city centre stores), the right choice could be to interview each day, to see not only if customers' behaviour is affected by the time of day, but also how the time of day affects their opinions about service.

If the aim is to interview a representative sample of customers (or lapsed customers for that matter) to find out their opinions about service from a particular company, it will probably be necessary to widen the interviewing hours and interview between 9 am and 9 pm each day. In this way the sample will not be unintentionally skewed towards one particular demographic group. If researchers telephone people for an interview only between the hours of 9 am and 5 pm, Mondays to Fridays, they tend to find that the majority of people answering the telephone are retired, unemployed, students, homemakers with young pre-school age children, or people who are self-employed and who work from home.

CONTRACTUAL DEMANDS (FOR EXAMPLE FOR EXCLUSIVITY)

Reasons for requesting exclusivity on customer satisfaction projects

Many customer satisfaction surveys, and especially those where staff incentive programmes are involved, can lead to the client asking for an exclusivity agreement with the agency. Their request is based on the premise that the client will be sharing quite sensitive details about its policies and procedures with the supplier, and therefore requires guarantees of confidentiality. One way of achieving this is to ask the agency to sign an exclusivity contract: for example, committing it not to work for a direct competitor for the duration of the contract (and often for a period of up to a year following the end of the contract).

Another reason for requesting exclusivity is that the client does not want any competitor to benefit from any 'learning' gained from the project, either intentionally or unintentionally.

Drawbacks to exclusivity contracts

While the request for an exclusivity contract is usually well intentioned, the benefits often do not outweigh the drawbacks. For example, any such request will result in the agency increasing its fees for the project, as it will not be able to accept any work from direct competitors, even if the work has nothing to do with measuring customer satisfaction. If the agency is considered a market leader in the field, a request for exclusivity will be very expensive indeed. Many agencies are also reluctant to take on such a commitment, as they build their reputation partially through the learning gained from working with a range of clients, including many who operate in the same field. Furthermore, if the agency is a brand leader, its executives will often be asked to give papers or be consulted by industry bodies, which will almost certainly mean they will encounter the management of competing client companies.

Safeguards that agencies can take to ensure client confidentiality

Research companies that operate according to a national code of conduct usually strive to ensure that when carrying out work for different clients that they do not have any clashes of interest. One method favoured by many of the larger agencies is to create separate teams to safeguard client confidentiality. Further steps can be taken, such as running project data through separate computer databases, having all staff sign confidentiality agreements that last for the duration of the contract, and even housing staff on different floors or in different buildings. It is impractical for smaller agencies to take many of these steps, and the client then needs to rely upon the professionalism of the researchers to safeguard confidentiality.

Sometimes clients who want exclusivity also demand that the agency has sufficient experience in the product category concerned – without stopping to think that the best way to obtain experience is to work for competitors.

OPERATIONAL FACTORS

One of the critical elements that can affect the cost and timing for a customer satisfaction and loyalty research project is how easy or difficult it is to locate potential participants. If the survey is being conducted among a client's own customers, the provision of a sample of customers for the survey can be a great benefit. However, there may be a hidden cost for the client, in terms of the time and resources that need to be employed within the client company to gather the sample.

Sample provision

For the agency other matters affect sample provision. These include how it will be sent – will it be provided on a disc, possibly encrypted with security software the agency will have to purchase? Will it be sent in one electronic file or in many files that will have to be merged upon receipt? Will it be sent on paper and thus need data to be entered by the agency? Will the agency have to de-dupe it against other files, such as customers previously contacted within a set period of time? Will the agency have to de-dupe it against other lists that have to be purchased, such as the list for the telephone preference scheme in the UK (or the US 'Do Not Call' Register)?

The UK telephone preference scheme is a list of people who have asked that they not be contacted by telephone for marketing purposes. While market research is exempt from this scheme, many companies ask market researchers not to contact customers who have registered this preference, for fear of upsetting them. Ironically, it has been shown that these customers can react quite positively to a market research survey, and some have been heard to comment along the lines of 'I'm glad you called as you hear about these surveys but I am never asked to give my opinion.'

Sample management

Another factor that agencies have to bear in mind when putting together a cost for the project is how frequently they will have to manage sample files sent from the client. If for example the project is a monthly tracking survey, they will have to run de-duping and cleaning of sample files 12 times a year. However, if this monthly tracking survey is among customers who contacted the organization within the previous 48 hours, a fresh sample will need to be provided every other day, or about 12 times a month.

DECIDING ON SAMPLE SIZE

Another factor that has a direct bearing on costs is the number of interviews to be conducted. If the client has not suggested any figures, the agency will have to decide on an appropriate number of interviews. If the requirement is for an exploratory survey, a few in-depth interviews or focus groups may suffice. However, these are not inexpensive options. If face-to-face interviews are to be conducted that are geographically dispersed across the country, the agency may explore the idea of conducting them by telephone or via the internet if the client's funds are limited.

If the requirement is for a substantive survey that will enable the client to measure quite small shifts in customer attitudes, a quantitative survey will be required. Selecting the optimum sample size is important, as finding the right people in the required volumes is one of the more costly aspects of a research project. How can the best sample size be determined? This depends on the degree of precision that the client is prepared to accept for the project. It also depends on the amount of analysis the client wishes to undertake among subsectors of the population, such as companies in different market sectors or industries, or people who are new customers compared with those who have been customers for two or more years. If the research requires multivariate statistical techniques or other complex analyses, large sample sizes may be necessary.

Let us imagine that the client wants to know from the research how many of its 10,000 customers would consider purchasing from it again (that is, what proportion are 'loyal' customers), and is willing to accept a 95 per cent level of confidence in the results, and a 5 per cent margin of error. In other words, there is a 95 per cent chance that the true population figure lies within 5 per cent of the resulting figure from the survey. Statistical formulae can be used to determine that to achieve this, it is necessary to interview 370 of the customers.

One other factor needs to be borne in mind by the research agency when determining sample size: the shape of the response curve. If say 55 per cent prove to be loyal customers but 45 per cent do not, the degree of accuracy in the result will be less than if say 95 per cent are loyal and just 5 per cent are not.

If the survey is being conducted among a relatively small customer segment (for example, wholesale banking customers), only a few interviews may be required, as they will represent quite a sizable proportion of all such customers.

DECIDING ON THE METHOD OF SAMPLING

Depending on the client's requirements, an appropriate method of sampling will need to be selected. For example, customer satisfaction can be measured at many different levels. One option is to look at an overall relationship level: that is, how customers feel overall about the products or service they have received from the organization. The best way to obtain this perspective is from a random sample of all customers.

However, the client might ask for satisfaction to be measured at a process level. Here its interest would be in issues such as how orders are handled, or how customers view the technical support provided by the organization. In this situation a random sample may not be the most cost-effective method for finding potential respondents. A sample of customers who have had an order processed recently, or who have made a technical enquiry, will fit the project better.

Some clients may want to learn more about how a particular transaction has been handled. If the goal is to uncover perceptions about what actually happened during the transaction, it is imperative that the survey occurs as soon after it as possible. However, if the purpose is to see how the handling affected customers' perceptions about the organization, more time needs to elapse. If the requirement is to get the survey into the field as soon as possible after receipt of the sample, this has implications for the agency in terms of sampling and field preparation.

Finally, the client might ask for a survey to be undertaken at a micro-transaction level. This is almost akin to a mystery shopping exercise, as in these situations the client often wants to understand in minute detail what happened and how customers felt about it. For example, perhaps the topic is how well customers' last transactions using an automated telephone ordering system were handled. The key is again for the client to provide a sample that is as 'fresh' as possible. With the technology available today, it should be possible for a client to provide such samples within minutes of the transactions taking place, and for the agency to get researchers into the field within a couple of hours.

IN-HOUSE MODELS VERSUS BESPOKE APPROACHES

A number of market research agencies have developed from experience different approaches towards measuring or interpreting customer satisfaction. These include Simalto and SERVQUAL (see Chapter 2), and many others. These models provide these agencies with a competitive advantage: the fact that they are tried and tested can be perceived to lower the risk of the research for future clients. One drawback is that agencies may experience a pressure to use their proprietary model to address all customer service research, adapting it if necessary to fit particular research requirements. An executive in such an agency could find it quite difficult (although not impossible) to offer a solution other than the one promoted by the agency, as this could be seen as suggesting that the proprietary model or solution has flaws or is not all-encompassing. Promoting the agency on the back of such models also carries a wider strategic risk: as new learning emerges about customer satisfaction, the model might need to be changed or run the risk of being seen as outdated.

Countering this trend to develop branded models, some other agencies promote the fact that they do not use a particular model, but instead address each research enquiry on its own merits. In other words, they offer a bespoke approach.

WHEN THE CLIENT PROPOSES A DIFFERENT APPROACH FROM THE AGENCY

Sometimes clients decide on the approach they want to see used for their customer satisfaction survey before they have spoken to an agency. This can be for a number of reasons. First, an in-house researcher might have convinced managers that this is the approach that will address their needs. Alternatively management may have heard of an approach and decided that as sponsors for the research, they want it to be adopted. This is not as uncommon as it sounds, and can lead to difficulties for the research agency if it feels the proposed approach is not the most appropriate one. How best can an agency avoid such a situation?

Possible reasons for considering alternative research methodologies

An agency that plans to suggest an alternative methodology from that suggested in the client brief can take any of four basic lines of argument:

- The proposed methodology is not the best for meeting the objectives of the survey.
- There is a more cost-effective approach that would meet the aims of the survey while saving the client money.
- The proposed approach is technically flawed.
- The proposed approach is out of date.

Before suggesting an alternative approach, it is best to ask the client how wedded it is to the approach suggested in the brief. With this approach the client has an opportunity to discuss any ideas the agency puts forward. If the client is convinced by them, the agency may well be in a position to help the client researcher shape the arguments for an alternative approach.

The approach is technically flawed

Which of the four options is the best to use will vary, depending upon the situation the client is facing. For example, to suggest the approach is technically flawed would probably be acceptable if the client does not have a research professional on its staff. However, if it does have a researcher, this could be a double-edged sword. Such an approach would undermine the authority and credibility of the researcher within the organization, even if he or she is relatively new to it. In addition, if the client researcher already has the confidence and support of management, this approach is likely to lessen the chances of the agency being considered for the work.

Furthermore, suggesting that the proposed methodology is flawed is also difficult because all methodologies have strengths and weaknesses. Mail surveys are cheap and easy to manage, but can suffer from low response rates, and allow respondents to read all the questions before answering any of them (which could influence the way they respond to them). Personal interviewing enables respondents to be shown stimulus materials (such as advertisements or correspondence), but respondents faced with interviewers can answer questions more positively, as they want to 'please' the interviewer (or not offend him or her by saying what they really think). Telephone interviews can be quick and are relatively inexpensive, but response rates are falling, and as more people use mobile phones as their telephony of choice, it is an approach that may become more expensive. In addition it is not possible to show people advertising or other stimulus material over the telephone. Internet surveys are growing in popularity with some clients as they can design and monitor the results themselves. However, there are questions over how representative the respondents are, and limitations on how long respondents are willing to take in answering questions on the internet.

The approach is not cost-effective

Suggesting that an approach is not the most cost-effective will gain the support of research departments where cost savings are seen as paramount or where budgets are tight. However, sometimes clients are in a situation where they need to ensure that all the money allocated to their budget is spent, and if it is approaching the end of their financial year and they have not used their entire budget, a cost-saving approach will not be the most effective for changing their mind.

The approach is dated

The suggestion that an approach is out of date also has its weaknesses. For example, an agency may try to convince a client that its proposed mail survey approach (one of the oldest methods of research) is not the best because response rates are so much lower than those achieved by other survey methods. This may be true for many surveys, but it may not apply if the client is a mail order company. It may also not apply if the client has conducted mail surveys before and has built up a bank of normative data that can be used to calibrate results from the proposed survey.

The approach is not suitable

The final suggestion (that the proposed methodology may not be the most suitable) has similar strengths and weaknesses to the suggestion that the methodology is flawed. However, in this scenario, the agency is not questioning the methodology itself so much as the choice of method. Here the agency needs to tread carefully, as the client researcher may well agree that there are better methodologies, but claim that his or her hands are tied in the choice of method. For example, a few years ago an agency suggested to its client that while its suggested approach had its merits, it was really designed to address a different research issue. The client researcher responded that the agency might well be right, but her manager had been to a conference and seen how a respective company in a related field of business had used this methodology to 'solve the problem'. Faced with this scenario, the client researcher had no choice but to follow the instructions of the line manager and specify how this survey was to be done.

THE AGENCY AS SINGLE PROVIDER OR OUTSOURCER

Obviously, if an agency does not have all the skills in house to handle a project it will have to either hire them in, or outsource part of the work to another company. This situation can arise if the agency consists predominantly of consultants whose role is to help a client design, project manage and interpret the findings from the survey. It might not have interviewers, coders, editors or sometimes even data processors on its staff: it buys in these services as necessary. This can also apply when a network of independent consultants gets together to put forward a proposal in response to a brief. Here every member of the network is in effect outsourcing his or her particular set of skills to the project.

Benefits of outsourcing

The great strength of outsourcing some (or most) of the elements of the project to others is that it means the project is not hindered by the weakest element within a single organization. For example, an agency may well advertise itself as a 'full service' agency, meaning that all aspects of the project can be handled in house. However, as these organizations are usually very large, they tend to have a formalized organizational structure (usually along functional lines) and sets of procedures for getting things done. If, for example, the IT function is understaffed or handling large volumes of data, it might not have invested in the latest market research data analysis software, or have the most powerful available hardware (for cost reasons). In contrast, an agency that only processes data for other companies will have the most up-to-date software and hardware, as its livelihood depends on it. Therefore a smaller agency that outsources its data processing to a specialist data processing company will gain the benefit of having the most modern equipment and skilled workers working on that element of the project.

The drawbacks to outsourcing

The weakness of outsourcing an element of the project is that the outsourcing agency needs to ensure that it has excellent communication skills as well as project management skills, so that no delays or mistakes occur as a result of the outsourcing. In addition it needs to be very certain that the company employed has the requisite skills and resources to complete its part of the project to time and budget. Outsourcing can therefore increase the costs of the project as it requires additional administrative time by the subcontracting agency.

Some clients prefer agencies to handle all the work in-house (normally for reasons of confidentiality). It is important therefore for the research agency to check with the client whether it can outsource some of the work or not.

UNDERSTANDING THE TECHNICAL REQUIREMENTS FOR DATA ANALYSIS AND REPORTING

If a project is likely to have a heavy reporting requirement, such as reporting customer satisfaction by retail branch for a nationwide store chain, or by distribution depot for a national transport company, the agency will need to be briefed on the extent of the reporting required. For example, will it need to be done monthly or quarterly, if it is to be a regular monitor of customer satisfaction? Will the client want the reports distributed electronically or to be printed? How quickly does it want the results reported?

Besides the actual reporting of the results, the agency will need to know if the client needs data files sent to it to enable its staff to further interrogate the data, or whether it is expecting the agency to provide additional *ad hoc* data analysis (and reporting). If the latter, the agency will have to make an assumption in the proposal about how much additional *ad hoc* analysis to allow for in the quotation.

If the client wants a data file sent to it, it is a good idea to check how it wants this data to be provided. It might have special software requirements, and if the agency cannot support this requirement it will have to buy in the appropriate software (and learn how to use it), or outsource this part of the project.

LEGAL AND OTHER CONSTRAINTS

There are a host of legal requirements that market research agencies have to abide by these days compared with 20 years ago. In the UK and Europe there has been a raft of data privacy and data protection laws, which enshrine the rights of individuals over what data can be kept about them, how and for how long. This can also extend to data about sole traders and partnerships, and so impact business-to-business research as well. In addition, the various trade associations have data protection requirements built into their codes of conduct. This is very important because without the public's trust and cooperation, there would be no market research profession. So it is very important for an agency to know what plans or requirements a client has in regard to its own use of the data, and to ensure that these plans do not breach the codes and regulations.

In addition, if the survey is to be conducted in one country but the data is to be processed in another, the agency must make certain it does not breach any legislation about cross-border data transference.

Agencies do not just have to be careful about data on respondents. If the survey has a requirement for customers' comments about why they thought a particular service was excellent (or poor) to be explored further through the use of open-ended questions (referred to as verbatim comments in the UK), the agency must also take care not to fall foul of the laws of slander, through passing on comments about named (or recognizable) individuals. To avoid this will require the agency to ensure that every verbatim comment is reviewed, and where necessary any potentially offending comments are edited out before the rest are passed on to the client.

CONTENTS, PRESENTATION AND DELIVERY OF A CUSTOMER SATISFACTION RESEARCH PROPOSAL

A good proposal will contain all the information a client needs to help it decide whether to hire the agency for the project. In this respect it should contain:

- a synopsis of the background to the project and its objectives;
- some further information about the project or the market, to show that the agency understands the scope of the project and will be bringing some relevant information and experience to it;
- details of the methodology that will be used, together with a rationale for why the proposed approach is the best for meeting the client's needs;
- an outline of the interview sample, in terms of any relevant criteria set by the client (for example, existing customers and recent lapsed customers, or customers who have recently contacted the organization);
- a broad outline of what will be covered in the questionnaire (but not the actual questions that will be asked) and, if relevant, what will not be covered in the survey;
- details of any particular reporting outputs such as written reports, PowerPoint charts or data tables (including in what media they will be provided);
- details of what the client will have to provide (such as a random sample of customers with a recent contact) and by when;
- a list of any assumptions upon which the cost estimate has been based (such as average interview length, number of open-ended questions that will require editing, anticipated length of report);
- a broad outline of the time it will take to complete the project, and the key milestone dates for questionnaire design, fieldwork, analysis and reporting;
- a short biography of the key personnel who will be working on the project and their relevant skills and experience;
- the fee for the work as specified;
- the agency's terms and conditions of business.

FACTORS THAT INFLUENCE THE COST OF THE PROJECT

There are a number of elements within a research project that can affect the cost. These elements fall into one of two categories: fixed costs (which are those the company will incur regardless of how well or poorly the project is progressing, such as salaries of full-time staff working on the project, and company overheads such as electricity, rent, rates and so on), and variable costs. These are those costs that are directly influenced by particular aspects of the project. The main variable costs are finding respondents, average length of the interview, the number of open-ended questions that require coding and editing, and the volume and complexity of the analysis and reporting requirements. In addition, most projects will incur 'one-off' set-up costs. These are the costs that are necessary to get the project started but which, in the case of a tracking survey, will be unlikely to occur again. Examples of set-up costs are programming a questionnaire for use in CAPI or CATI, preparing a de-dupe database (for a tracking survey), setting up a reporting program (for example if the client wants to receive a data file in a different computer program from that being used for the fieldwork or normal reporting), preparing any reporting templates (for a tracking survey), preparing the interviewer briefing instructions, and finally, if it is a tracking survey, preparing some 'how to' manuals detailing the procedures that are to be followed on the project.

Recruiting respondents

The ease with which appropriate respondents can be found is a paramount factor in determining the variable costs of a project. Even when the client can provide lists of customers, there can be difficulties. Customers may have no recall of a recent 'event' that the client claims has taken place. In this situation the agency will have incurred the costs of contacting that customer, which could have included a number of contact attempts, to no effect. Most agencies estimate the 'contact rate' and include it in their costs. However, if the customers are harder to contact than had been anticipated, an additional fee may be levied.

Interview length

The average length of an interview is critical from two aspects. The first is that respondents will be prepared to give up only a certain amount of their time to discuss their opinions with an interviewer. Even if interviewers begin by giving an indication how long the interview will last, customers' perceptions of the amount of time they have spent with the interviewer will seriously affect their willingness to continue with the interview. The second aspect is that an agency estimates how many interviews an interviewer can complete in a set period of time, and uses this to estimate how many interviewers it will have to use on the project. This has a direct bearing on the variable costs the agency pays. It also affects its cash flow. If the interviews take longer than was projected, the agency will have to employ more interviewers and so its variable costs will rise. If the estimate was too pessimistic, the final costs of the project should be lower than originally estimated.

Number and types of questions being asked

The number of open-ended answers that require editing and coding is also a variable cost, as it is not always possible to determine exactly how many respondents will answer these questions, or how many of the questions they may qualify for answering. In addition, open-ended questions increase the length of a survey, which will affect the number of interviews an interviewer can complete in a given time period. Finally, if a respondent has a lot to say on a subject, the length of the verbatim response may impact on costs – both in terms of interview length, and in terms of the time it takes to edit the response.

One area that often generates long verbatim responses is asking respondents about any recent problems or complaints. It is often possible to predict how a respondent will answer a question about how well they perceive their complaint was handled, by how long he or she spends telling the interviewer what the complaint was about. It seems that if it has been handled poorly, respondents provide a long explanation of the problem or complaint – probably because they feel they are talking to someone who is interested in hearing what they have to say.

There is also a cost implication when questions are asked as if they are open-ended, but the client insists on a long list of pre-coded potential answers rather than recording the respondents' comments. It can take interviewers quite a bit of time to code these types of responses, as they have to listen to what the respondent is saying, then look at a long list of possible answers to determine which is the most appropriate.

Volume and complexity of reporting

The volume and complexity of reporting can also be a variable cost if the client requires a lot of *ad hoc* analysis to be conducted on the project.

Other factors influencing costs

If the project is a tracking survey there are other matters that can impact costs. For example, if the layout of sample files is not consistent (and to an agreed specification), there will be a cost for 'fixing' the layout, or a risk to the start of interviewing if the file has to be returned to the client because the layout cannot be corrected at the agency. Related to this is the issue of inconsistency in file naming conventions. Here again, both cost and time are impacted as staff have to investigate exactly what file it is they have received.

THE SIZE AND COMPOSITION OF THE RESEARCH TEAM

Once an agency has decided to submit a proposal it will need to decide who will work on the project. This is sometimes an easy decision to reach, particularly for a smaller agency where the whole company may be involved. However, for a larger agency there may be more difficult issues to be addressed. For example, how experienced a team needs to work on the project? (The more senior the team, the more expensive a project will be.) How many staff will need to be involved? The more staff, the more costs will rise, as well as the more difficult it becomes to manage available resources across the other work the company is currently handling. Some projects will require a more senior team to set the project up and steer it through the pilot stages, at which point less experienced researchers may be used to handle its later stages.

If the agency has considerable experience in a particular field, it would not be surprising to discover that a number of competing clients wish to work with it. The challenge for the agency is how to ring-fence the work it is doing for one client from the gaze of its competitors. There are a number of steps that can be taken, as mentioned earlier in the chapter. Their data can be protected either by using separate computers to store and process their information, or by assigning a set of unique passwords to each client, which are only known to the agency personnel working on that client's projects. Separate client teams can be set up if the agency is large enough to ensure that confidentiality is maintained. These teams can be housed on different floors or in different buildings if the agency is large enough.

FACTORS FOR THE CLIENT TO CONSIDER WHEN SELECTING AN AGENCY

The final phase of the project initiation stage involves the client evaluating the proposals and selecting an agency to handle the work. So what are the factors that a client will take into account when selecting an agency?

In my experience a client looks at a number of elements when selecting an agency for a project. The questions clients ask include:

- Does the proposal address all the issues expressed in the brief?
- Has the agency demonstrated any thinking behind its proposal that goes beyond simply responding to the technical aspects of the project?

- Does the agency demonstrate commercial and marketing awareness about the client's business and its industry?
- How well structured is the proposal, and is it clearly written and presented?
- Has the proposal brought the subject to life?
- If required, how much imagination and creativity has been shown by the agency for the project?
- Is the agency keen and hungry for the work?
- Are the proposed agency team people you want to do business with, and that the commissioning client can put in front of his or her internal sponsor?
- What is the agency's track record for completing its projects on time and to budget?

CLOSING COMMENTS

If you have read both this and the previous chapter, then it will be obvious that client researchers approach projects with a different perspective from agency researchers. However, the view that client researchers are business-focused problem solvers who are flexible and proactive, while agency researchers are technocratic, project-focused individuals is no longer applicable. Some agencies are now larger in size than many of the client companies that employ them. Agency researchers can no longer afford to be merely project managers – they have to, and do, understand the commercial realities of business. In fact, they are often closer to the commercial realities of running a business than many client researchers, as the decisions they take can mean the difference between profit and loss for their organization.

It is to be hoped that a clearer understanding of their respective roles and responsibilities, and a recognition that each brings different skills and perspectives to the table, will enable agency researchers to provide a better service to their clients, and for both parties to cement and have an enjoyable longer-term relationship.

7 Sampling

This chapter addresses issues concerning sampling, and in particular deciding who to interview and whether or not they should be pre-notified about the survey. If the customer satisfaction and loyalty survey will involve repeat waves of interviewing, there are issues about the need for building and maintaining contact history databases, and the potential impact of future reorganizations or changes in company strategy on the programme are also covered. Finally, issues arising from constantly changing client customer profiles, and factors influencing any decision about the use of 'random' samples versus 'event-driven' booster samples are discussed.

> He has the deed half done who has made a beginning.
>
> **Horace, Latin poet**

With both the agency and the client now in full agreement about what needs to be done, by when and at what cost, the task of measuring customer satisfaction gets underway. Once it has been decided what is the target population, it is necessary to decide whether to interview everyone in it or to select a sample. In practice, the only time surveys attempt to interview everyone is when a very small group (such as a company's major customers) is being researched. Usually it is necessary to select a sample. However, sampling must be done very carefully, otherwise there is the risk of introducing bias or error that will affect the results from the survey.

SAMPLE RELIABILITY

The first concern is the reliability of the sample. Reliability is about repeatability. For example, if a researcher asked lots of respondents the same question and got exactly the same answer from each of them, it could be said there was high respondent reliability. Similarly, if a researcher asked the same person the same question over a series of months and got exactly the same answer each and every month, there would be high reliability over time. If the survey used a different sample of respondents each month, but produced the same results every time it was repeated, it would have high sample reliability.

When measuring customer satisfaction over a number of different time periods, it is clearly important that the sampling is conducted the same way each time from the same target population, so the data from the survey is relatively free of sampling error and therefore reliable. When researchers talk about a survey having a low sampling error, they are really saying the survey has a highly reliable sample.

BIAS

Bias is a different matter. When something is measured, it is important to be sure that what is being measured is not being influenced by an external factor of any kind. If an external factor does affect the results, then bias has been introduced. For example, let us consider a sample of all the shoppers who use a particular shopping mall, for a survey of how satisfied shoppers are with the mall and its facilities. Because no list of shoppers exists, the researcher decides to visit the mall and sample every fifth person who enters it on a particular day. Would this give a representative sample? The answer is not necessarily. If the researcher chooses a weekday to do the sampling, he or she will not encounter anyone who only visits the mall at weekends. Likewise, if he or she does the sampling on just one day of the week, there could be other factors that influence the reliability of the sampling, such as if certain shops in the mall offer senior citizens discounts for shopping mid-week rather than at weekends. Selecting a midweek day would give a sample containing more senior citizens than would be expected from a sample that had been taken every hour that the mall was open over a period of a week or a month.

There are many other types of bias, and some can affect customer satisfaction surveys in particular. Let us suppose the shopping mall interviewers decide that instead of approaching every fifth person who enters the mall, they will approach all those who are smartly dressed, about their own age and look like they may be willing to participate in the survey. This would also be introducing a bias.

There are lots of ways bias can creep into a survey at the sampling stage. For example, a middle-aged male recruiter might feel uncomfortable approaching younger females out shopping on their own in case they misinterpret his approach. He might also feel uncomfortable approaching a group of young lads who are being boisterous and having a bit of a laugh.

PROBABILITY SAMPLING

There are basically two types of sample: probability and non-probability samples. A probability sample is one where each member of the universe has a known chance of being selected for inclusion in the survey. This type of sample is also often referred to as a random sample.

In order to measure the satisfaction among all of a company's customers, the researcher might obtain a list of them all (not listed in any particular order) then select one at random, then select another from those remaining in the list, and so on until he or she had reached the number he or she felt was required for sampling purposes. It is necessary to bear in mind that not everyone who is contacted will agree to participate in the survey, and some people might not be available at the time of the survey, so it is always necessary to select more people than are actually required for the survey.

Naturally, selecting a sample in this way is a very time-consuming process, so researchers have two other options they can adopt for obtaining a random sample. These are systematic random sampling and stratified random sampling. To produce a systematic random sample, the first step again is a list of all the customers. Let us say there are 15,000 of them, and a sample of 100 is needed. Therefore, in effect, the aim is to sample one person in every 150 of the universe. The researcher selects a number at random between 1 and 150, and this is the starting point. Let us say the number is 20. The first target is therefore the 20th name on the list. The next target is the 170th name on the list (that is 20 + 150), followed by the 320th name (170 + 150), and so on. This method eventually generates a sample of 100 people. But this approach could result in a situation where none of the most important customers are selected for the survey. For example, if the organization has a small number of high-value customers and a large volume of small-value customers, a random sample might exclude most, if not all, of the most important high-value customers. This can be avoided by using a stratified random sampling approach.

This method first splits the customers into separate segments according to a set of criteria that it has been decided are critical to the business (such as contribution to profits, or geographic coverage). The list is then sampled randomly within each segment.

Often there is a case for using a different sampling ratio for each segment. Suppose the customers are split into four segments in terms of contribution to profits, with 50 per cent of the business profits being generated from segment 1, 25 per cent from segment 2, 15 per cent from segment 3 and 10 per cent from segment 4. It could be decided to take 50 per cent of the sample from segment 1, 25 per cent from segment 2, and so on. Probably the segments will vary in size. Many organizations find that as much as 80 per cent of their profits can come from 20 per cent of their customers. If segment 1 has 150 customers, the sampling ratio will be one in every three customers (50 customers to be interviewed from a universe of 150). If the size of segment 2 is 2,500 customers and 25 per cent of the sample is to be from this segment, the sampling ratio for this segment is one in 10 (25 customers from a universe of 2,500), and so on. Note that in this case the final sample would be representative of the profitability structure rather than the numbers of customers.

There are other variations within random sampling techniques, but I cannot go into them here. An excellent, and not too technical, source for further reading is Chapter 8 in Yvonne McGivern's *The Practice of Market and Social Research* (2003).

NON-PROBABILITY SAMPLING

Interviewing random samples can be quite expensive if a survey is to be conducted face to face. Another problem is that sometimes it is not possible to obtain a full list of the population to be surveyed. For these reasons a non-probability sampling approach is used instead. In this case either the person drawing the sample, or an interviewer involved in recruiting it (or both) has some control over the selection of who is to be surveyed.

Using quota sampling for customer satisfaction research

The most common non-probability approach is quota sampling. Imagine the aim is to interview a representative sample of customers who have recently contacted a company, to determine if customers perceive a difference in the quality of service depending upon their method of contact. The company has invested heavily in developing call centres and customer relationship management systems, and hopes the survey will show that telephoning is the preferred contact method.

As well as contacting the company by telephone, customers also contact it by e-mail, via the internet, by letter or by calling in to one of its outlets. It is obviously necessary to analyse the data by each of the channels, to see if it can be demonstrated (and promoted) that telephone is by far the best method for customers to use. However, while the company can provide details on the volume of calls, e-mails, internet contacts and letters it receives, it cannot provide any statistics for the number of customers who call in at its outlets. In addition, some customers use more than one channel to contact the company. For example, a customer might make a telephone complaint and confirm it in writing. Again, the company has no statistics on the proportion of customers who do this. Faced with this situation, the researcher could decide to draw a random sample of customers and then 'find' customers who have used each of these channels through questioning. However, if one or more of the channels is used by fewer people, this could be an expensive way of finding them. It is possible to set quotas to limit the number of customers interviewed for the other contact channels, to keep the costs of the project down, but it is still an inefficient way to find the sample.

One solution is to use non-probability quota sampling. As the company cannot provide any population statistics but can provide lists of customers who have contacted it in an agreed period for each of the methods of contact, the researcher takes a large enough sample from each list to complete a minimum of 100 interviews for each channel. In other words the researcher sets a 'quota' of 100 interviews and ignores the fact that each of the contact channels in reality has a different volume of customers using it. This approach enables the researchers to examine differences by channel, in the knowledge that a minimum number of customers have been surveyed for each channel.

How can it be ensured that the users of each of the channels are representative? After all, if a particular time period is selected, it may well be that seasonality or some other factor will skew the profile of the sample (such as contacting people shortly after a bout of poor publicity about the industry's lack of concern for the damage its products do to the health of the nation). To control for this, quotas can be set for each channel so that the sample represents something approaching the normal pattern of issues that people contact the company about (for example, 30 per cent about billing and other administrative issues, 15 per cent about complaints, and so on).

DECIDING WHO TO INTERVIEW

One of the challenges all customer satisfaction surveys face is deciding who exactly to interview. For example, does the client want to know how customers view the organization at a point in time? If so, then a representative sample of customers should be surveyed. But maybe some of the customers are in litigation with the company, so would it make sense including them in the sample? Perhaps another group of customers are being chased for non-payment. Should they be included in the sample? For some businesses the answer will be 'yes', perhaps because they represent a very small section of the customer base. Other businesses might well decide it would be inappropriate to include them.

Sampling customers with a recent contact with the organization

The research requirement may entail talking with customers who have had a specific recent contact with the organization, so it can be seen how well it is handling these matters. Here the ideal is a representative sample of these customers. However, it is important to bear in mind that these customers may not be representative of the entire customer base. For example, the aim might be to survey customers who have corresponded with the company in writing, and see if staff have handled them in a satisfactory manner, so the correspondence department could be asked to supply a random sample of customers to whom they have written in the last week. But the company might have numerous reasons for writing to customers, including some that are required for regulatory reasons (for example, in the UK, financial institutions are obliged to inform customers every time there is a change in the interest rate being paid on a savings product). These letters are usually 'form' letters rather than personal letters responding to a matter raised by a customer. Should these customers be included in the survey? Customers may have very pertinent views on the style of the letter, but the organization might not be able to do much with the information gathered if the wording used has to conform with certain legal requirements.

Sampling customers about a service that is outsourced

Another complication that can arise is when a company outsources part of its operations. Its customers are also customers of the outsourced organization. In this situation, it is important to understand which organization customers feel they are dealing with, and also how the outsourcing makes them feel about the host organization. For example, in the financial services industry it is not uncommon for a credit card company to offer insurance covering purchases made on the card. If customers make a claim on the insurance, they may well have to deal directly with the insurance company rather than the credit card company. However, their opinions about the service they receive from the insurance company may also reflect on their opinions about the credit card company. Therefore it would be important to sample these customers, but to design the questions in such a way as to identify where any service praise or criticism is to be properly attributed.

Sampling in the business and corporate markets

Business-to-business and corporate customer satisfaction surveys have additional complications that need to be borne in mind when deciding who to include in the sampling process. In the business and corporate markets the client might well want to survey more than one person in the customer organization. Decision making in businesses (and in other large organizations such as government departments) often includes a number of different people and departments. If the objective is to measure the degree of customer satisfaction, is it enough to survey just sales department contacts? It might be more appropriate to also gather the opinions of others such as directors (who usually have the ultimate say regarding strategic business contracts and relationships), or members of the administrative departments who deal with the day-to-day aspects of the contract.

Another interesting aspect to bear in mind when deciding who to survey in the business and corporate market is the structure of the client base. For example, most companies that operate in this area have a few very large 'key accounts'. This group is often treated with kid gloves, and marketing and servicing people can be very hesitant having market researchers march into their most important customers to ask them what they think about existing service, or their thoughts about new ideas to enhance the service they are offered, as the case study demonstrates.

CASE STUDY

The problem

A major US organization had developed a new service for its customers that would not only save its clients money but also make administration simpler and quicker. All the pre-testing conducted among the target market and existing customers was very positive. The project gathered momentum, then the senior management

---

asked, 'What do our top 10 accounts think of this idea?' The results were rather surprising. Virtually all of them hated the new service concept. So what should the management do with these results?

The solution

The immediate response was to review the survey to find fault with the questionnaire. (None could be found.) Managers next wanted to know who had been spoken to (obviously believing the wrong individuals had been sampled) – but the correct target audience had been interviewed.

What the survey demonstrated was the importance of talking with key accounts before launching new service initiatives. What the client had done was to go to an existing group of very satisfied customers that had adapted their internal company processes to work with its own processes. Then after a few years when things had gone smoothly, the client had suddenly appeared to say, in effect, 'all change for the better'. Once this was realized, the solution was obvious. The client went back to these customers and explained that it had developed a new service concept. Realizing how its best customers had built their policies and procedures around the existing service, it offered to put a team of people into each of the companies, at its own cost, to work with them during the change period. It did not lose a single one of these customers, and successfully introduced the new service, which gave it a competitive edge over the other players in the market.

Lessons learnt

Do not accept results on their face value. Look for other possible explanations. And on no account should a researcher allow his or her work to be 'buried' for political reasons. The fact that the results may be unsettling should be welcomed, for it may save the company from making a poor business decision.

Including lapsed customers

Another group of people many companies do not consider worth contacting is 'lapsed' customers – those who used to be customers but are now no longer (or customers who have been 'inactive' for a long period of time, such as mail order customers who have not bought from the company in the past 12 months or more). One reason for excluding them is that the internal company records may be out of date, so it is costly to sample them. Another reason is that as they have 'gone away', what is the point of finding out what they think? Of course the answer is, if the organization does not know why they left, it is important to find out, because the reasons for leaving could be under its control, and could still be affecting other customer relationships.

THE BENEFITS AND DRAWBACKS OF PRE-NOTIFYING RESPONDENTS

It is not uncommon for senior management in many organizations to feel that their customers are different from those of other organizations. This is especially the case with organizations that offer a highly personal service to rich or famous people. They usually request that before any contact or sampling of their customer base is undertaken, they contact their customers directly and ask them if they would mind participating in a survey. Usually these companies provide the customers with an option to opt out of any research. While one can understand their concerns with privacy and not wanting to disturb their customers with calls from an agency, it is often overlooked that these same individuals are customers of many different organizations, and often are more than willing to participate in surveys provided their anonymity is guaranteed.

CASE STUDY

Background

A UK agency was contacted one Thursday to see if it could conduct a telephone survey of 100 of its client's customers in the UK, France and Germany, with results to be presented in the United States the following Tuesday. The client supplied a list of 1,000 customers in each country for the purpose of the survey. After approving the questionnaire, it left the agency to get on with the research.

What happened next

The interviewers were both surprised and delighted to discover that many of the names on the list were of the rich and famous. The required quotas of interviews were achieved, and the interviewers had, by all accounts, a great time trying to get through (and succeeding in many cases) to some of the most well-known names in the world of entertainment. It was subsequently discovered that the agency should not have been sent these names as the company had them listed on its 'special treatment' register, but this fact was overlooked when the instructions for drawing the sample were sent to the company's computer programmer, so these people were included in the sample file sent to the agency.

Results

It is impossible to determine if the survey would have been as successful if these customers had been pre-notified and given an opt-out from participating in the research. Subsequent surveys with a random sample of the company's customers produced very similar

---

results. However, the 'buzz' and interest that this particular survey generated among the interviewers working on the project meant that the survey received more than the usual degree of interest and attention in the field, and the agency reported that later surveys done for the client were always welcomed by the interviewers (no doubt hoping that they would once again be interviewing the rich and famous).

THE NEED FOR CONTACT HISTORY DATABASES

There are a number of reasons for an agency to build and maintain a contact history database. One reason is that it plans to recontact customers to conduct a follow-up survey, either to obtain a deeper understanding of what they have to say, or to gain their opinions about things that have happened since the last contact, or are about to happen (such as introducing a new service or moving call centre operations from one country to another).

Another situation is when a customer tracking survey is planned and the aim is to avoid recontacting customers for a given period. They might, for example, recall the gist, if not the detail, of the survey from the first time they were interviewed, so their responses in the second survey could be conditioned by the experience and recall. In either case the agency needs to build and then maintain a contact database, so that each time a new sample is provided from the client it can be de-duped against the existing database.

Of course, some people whom researchers contact ask that the organization never contact them again. Maintaining a database ensures this request is complied with while the individual continues to reside at the same address (or to use the same telephone number).

A more delicate situation is when a researcher attempts a contact with a named individual only to be told he or she has recently died. In this situation, in the UK there is an obligation for the research agency to alert its client so its own database can be updated.

If the organization does maintain a contact history database, it must ensure that it complies with all relevant data privacy legislation. This may be quite an onerous undertaking.

There are also legal issues to consider if any data about individuals is transferred across international boundaries, perhaps for interviewing or data analysis. Various international agreements affect cross-border transfer of data, and agencies are advised to ensure they comply with them.

THE POTENTIAL IMPACT OF FUTURE REORGANIZATIONS OR CHANGES IN COMPANY STRATEGY

One factor that can seriously affect the sampling of any tracking survey is a company restructuring. For example, an agency might be conducting a customer satisfaction survey for an organization that has outlets spread across the country. The data from the survey is used to report customer feedback at the individual outlet level, as well as at area and national levels. To ensure that sufficient customers have been surveyed to provide reliable data at the individual outlet level, the researcher will in all probability have set outlet-level or area-level quotas on the number of interviews. Then an announcement is made that the company is restructuring its outlets into fewer, larger areas or more smaller areas. This can affect the survey in a number of different ways. If the survey provides tracking data, will it be possible to reanalyse the historic data according to the new structure? If customer service targets have been set at area level, will it be possible to determine how these are affected by the change?

If the sample selection was done at area level, new sampling fractions will need to be determined, and this can be a tricky, time-consuming process as there will be no historical data available to check that the sampling has been done correctly.

In addition, in larger organizations, structural changes are often cascaded through the company, and so do not all take place at once. So one area may be selected to introduce the changes and the rest of the organization will follow in separate 'rollout' waves. This can mean that selecting the sample is different for different areas, depending on where they are in the rollout programme. It can also have implications on reporting, but that is a topic for a later chapter.

ISSUES ARISING FROM CONSTANTLY CHANGING CLIENT CUSTOMER PROFILES

One of the challenges researchers face when conducting customer satisfaction tracking surveys is what to do when the profile of the market they are measuring changes. This can come about because the client company has bought out another company, and so the profile of its customer base changes. Or it might have an ageing customer base and lose more customers than it is gaining, so management initiates various marketing programmes to attract new, younger customers.

The question is whether it is necessary to set quotas on the survey to ensure that the profile of customers being tracked remains constant, so that any changes in the data are not a result of changes in the profile, or whether it is better to accept that the profile is changing and then try to determine whether any changes in the data are caused by profile differences at the analysis stage. My preference is for the latter, if the goal of the survey is to monitor how customers view a company's service. If new customers are left out then the results will not reflect the current customer base, so management will be reliant on data that is increasingly unrepresentative. Alternatively, the researcher could conduct a separate survey among the newer customers, then merge their data into the main tracking survey to provide an overview of the customer base.

RANDOM SAMPLES VERSUS 'EVENT-DRIVEN' SAMPLES

Customers can have many different points of contact with an organization, and the frequency with which they contact it can also vary depending upon circumstance and behaviour. Therefore any customer satisfaction research programme needs to take into account whether it is to measure satisfaction at a strategic level, at an access channel level and at specific moments in time. These factors can influence how a sample is selected (as has been mentioned earlier). So for example, a customer contacting an organization about a change in his or her loan repayments will have a point of view about the organization as a whole, thoughts about the product (the loan), the way the change was communicated, and the way the most recent contact was handled.

Is it necessary to measure all 'events' continuously?

I would suggest that it is not necessary to measure all 'events' continuously. In some situations it is more cost-effective to measure an event and then allow three or six months to elapse before taking another measure. Adopting this approach allows time for the organization to take corrective actions such as re-training, changing policies or procedures, and for these to be 'bedded in' before the next reading. It also allows time for customers to notice whether or not there has been a change, as the researcher can ask them if they consider service today to be better or worse than six months or a year ago.

However, it is useful to measure customers' overall opinions about the company, its products and services on a more continuous basis, as these measures are normally slow to change, so it is important for management to receive as early a warning as possible that things are improving or deteriorating.

How soon after a service contact should customers be surveyed?

Some organizations believe that it is best to interview respondents immediately after a service event so that they can capture respondents' opinions and emotional feedback while it is still very fresh in their minds. Often these surveys are conducted in-house by client service staff, as this enables the client to get the details of the contact followed up very quickly. There is also a belief that by conducting these calls staff will see at first hand how their service encounters are perceived, and that they will, if necessary, be open to changing their behaviour as a result.

One difficulty with this approach is that the sample will not be very representative, as people who contact the organization most frequently will have a greater chance of being surveyed than those who do not. As only a minority of customers usually contact a company frequently, this approach will skew the sample. It will also affect the results, as often the customers who contact a company most frequently are new to the company (and so need more contact to understand how things work), or have a problem that is still unresolved, or have discovered that by complaining frequently they can often get things done or receive certain benefits.

There are two other risks with this approach. First, the staff interviewers may not be trained in the techniques necessary for listening and noting customer opinions in an unbiased way. Second, there is a risk of a 'halo' effect. That is, customers think the matter they called about has been dealt with as a result of this new contact, when in reality it has not, or they have not yet encountered problems but will do so in future. For example, a customer calls up to order a new widget. She is told the widget has been ordered and should be with her in three days, and the money is debited from her credit card or account. She then receives a survey call about this transaction, and it would be reasonable to expect her to be pleased with it and the way it has been handled. However, a week later she still has not received her widget, but has received her credit card bill with the transaction debited. Her opinions at this point are not likely to be the same.

CLOSING COMMENTS

Sampling is one of the most important aspects of a project. It does not matter how good a questionnaire is, how professionally the interviewing has been conducted or how sophisticated the analysis and reporting has been, if an unrepresentative or biased sample has been interviewed. As this chapter has demonstrated, a host of issues need to be discussed and agreed between the client researcher and the internal sponsor, and there is also a need for the agency researcher to monitor regularly that the respondents who are interviewed are representative of the target population that had been originally sampled for the survey.

8 What to ask

This chapter examines three aspects of developing a questionnaire for a customer satisfaction and loyalty survey. First it looks at the issues concerning the construction of the questionnaire: its focus and content, how to 'position' the survey in its introduction or preamble, its length and 'balance', and revealing who is sponsoring the survey. The second area covered in this chapter concerns the design of the questions themselves: for example, how to ensure clarity, how to build attribute scales, and what types of scale to use. The third part of the chapter addresses other critical issues such as derived versus stated importance and issues surrounding changes being made to tracking surveys.

> It is a curious thing that people only ask if you are enjoying yourself when you aren't.
>
> **Edith Nesbit,** *Five of Us, and Madeline,* **1925**

QUESTIONNAIRE CONSTRUCTION

Who is affected by the way a questionnaire is designed?

When designing a customer satisfaction and loyalty questionnaire it is necessary to bear in mind that different people will be affected by it. There is the client, whose concern is that the questions will provide answers that address the research objectives and contribute to the business objectives of the project. Interviewers will want a questionnaire that is clear and easy to administer. Data analysts will want a questionnaire that is relatively easy to programme and to analyse. The agency researcher will be concerned about the specified questionnaire length and with certain other parameters (such as how many open-ended questions it will contain) as he or she will have made certain assumptions on these matters when determining the costs for the project. Finally, respondents will want to be asked questions that are relevant and that enable them to provide their feelings about the subject, in a quick and easy way.

The priority should be to build the questionnaire from the customer's point of view, as the underlying objective of all customer satisfaction surveys is to gauge the customer's feelings and perceptions about an organization's products or services. There is no benefit in asking lots of questions about matters to which respondents have never given much thought. It will only depress response rates if the survey is done by post, or create annoyance if the survey is being conducted on the telephone or face to face. Therefore the golden rule is 'ignore the customer at your peril' when designing the questionnaire.

Where to start when designing a questionnaire

How do researchers go about finding out the things that matter to customers? As has already been mentioned, one option is to read the correspondence they send in to the company. Another is to accompany salespeople on their visits to customers and observe what happens and the issues that are raised. In addition, it is possible to spend time listening to what customers are calling the company about, and noting the tone of voice and other emotional signals they display to help gauge their depth of feeling on the matter.

The critical incident technique

Conducting qualitative research to probe which issues are important can be a worthwhile investment. In this regard, Michael Johnson and Anders Gustafsson (2000: 52–53) recommend using the critical incident technique (CIT) to identify satisfaction drivers. Basically this technique involves getting respondents to identify a specific example of a positive or negative service experience. Then, for the positive experiences, researchers probe what specific characteristic of the product or service customers would like to see every time they encounter that situation. In the case of a negative experience, they probe for the characteristic that would make the customer question the quality of the company. In addition, for each specific incident, it is worthwhile establishing the significance and consequences of the incident as far as the customer was concerned.

Mapping a questionnaire

Assuming there is at least a broad idea of what could be important to the customer, the next step is to map out a draft of how the questionnaire should flow. Normally, researchers start with more general questions and then lead the respondents on to the more specific matters they wish to discuss with them. Finally they close with some demographic questions and any sensitive questions that some respondents may refuse to answer (about personal income, investments, ethnicity and similar topics). This broad guide works well for both qualitative and quantitative research in most situations.

Usually the survey objectives will already have been decided by the time an agency is commissioned to carry out the project. However, as the detailed content of the questionnaire is being developed, researchers often find that there is a need to re-evaluate the purpose of the survey and determine whether more work is required before the main survey can commence. This can arise because within the client company, there is a tendency to look at things from an internal perspective rather than a customer one. So, for example, within companies people talk of 'best practice'. Very rarely have I heard a customer refer to 'best practices'. Customers are more likely to talk about which companies provide the best service, or which companies they like dealing with the most.

The content of the questionnaire

Having decided the structure and shape of the questionnaire, the researcher then needs to consider the content. Anyone who has sat down with a blank sheet of paper to create a questionnaire knows how hard it is to do this.

The introduction

The first, and in many ways the most critical, thing is to determine how to introduce the survey. The introduction has to be short, sharp, to the point and yet engaging enough to make the potential participant want to take part in the survey. Often the client is keen for the introduction to explain why it is interested in hearing what customers have to say, and how it plans to use the results to (further) improve the service it will be providing to their customers. This is yet another example of an inward-facing organization. Most people who agree to participate in a survey do so because they want the organization to hear their views. Therefore, there is probably not a lot to be gained by telling them the organization is going to listen to their views. If people feel that participating in the survey is not going to benefit them in any way, they will usually refuse to take part.

Eligibility questions

Following the introduction it is usually necessary to include some 'eligibility' questions to confirm that the person being interviewed meets the criteria for the survey. Failure to do this can result in wasted effort as, no doubt, during the survey it will become obvious that the respondent cannot answer some of the questions being asked. Even where the client has provided lists of customers who, it claims, meet the criteria for the project, it is worth confirming that the customer is still eligible to take part. For example, the client may have provided an agency with a list of customers who contacted it in the last month. A simple eligibility question can confirm that customers recall the contact about which the aim is to gain their opinion. The researcher (or questionnaire administered remotely) starts by asking, 'Can I confirm that you recently made contact with company {x} about {product}?'

If it becomes apparent that many people are 'failing' the eligibility question, and so not being asked the rest of the questionnaire, it is usually worth asking interviewers if they have any idea why this is so. Often respondents provide further information to an interviewer that is not recorded on the questionnaire. It could be along the lines of 'No, I didn't contact them, but I did receive an annual statement from them about four or five weeks ago.' In fact, many interviewers alert their supervisor as soon as problems such as this start occurring. If this situation arises the researcher can go back to the client to confirm that the sample that has been drawn is as specified. If not, the survey may need to be put on hold until such time as a more representative sample can be provided.

Once the introduction and eligibility questions have been designed, it is now worth mapping out the broad outline of the rest of the interview. This is because it is important to make sure that the content and flow will hold the interest of the respondent. If there is a requirement to go into great detail, it is probably better to design the survey to just cover the one topic, and to alert potential respondents that the questions will be focusing on this particular matter. Interviewers can always offer respondents an opportunity to add their thoughts on any other topic that they may wish to raise at the end of the survey.

The order and sequence of questions

Care has to be taken when designing the order and sequence in which the questions will appear, as this can introduce a range of biases and/or errors. When participating in a customer satisfaction survey, respondents first have to determine exactly what is expected of them. Therefore the early questions should be aimed at ensuring the respondent will not find the process too arduous. That is why in most surveys, whether qualitative or quantitative, the first few questions are fairly easy for the respondent to answer. For this reason, they are usually factual questions.

As the interview proceeds, the answers respondents provide can be influenced by the answers they have already given to earlier questions. For example, the organization might want to ask whether the respondent would recommend or criticize it to others. If this question is asked too early in the interview, respondents' opinions about other matters could be influenced by their response to this advocacy question. However, if the question is put near the end of the survey, the interviewer runs the risk that respondents will provide an answer that appears logical in light of their earlier answers, rather than what they would have said if they had been asked at the start of the questionnaire.

Questionnaire length

There are broad guidelines on how long respondents are willing to spend being interviewed. However, it is not uncommon for respondents to be willing to spend far longer than researchers expect, if they are interested in the subject. Customer satisfaction is one area where most people have a point of view and are willing to spend time telling researchers what their opinions are.

Most industry practitioners claim a postal survey should be no longer than eight sides of A4 paper. However, I have seen response rates in excess of 50 per cent on a 28-page questionnaire. It all depends on how engaging the subject is (as well as the layout and, if offered, the incentive). Business customers will also be willing to spend more time than might be expected if the subject matter is relevant and they feel that the client will take notice of what they have to say. It is not uncommon for business customers to spend 15–30 minutes on a relevant telephone survey. In fact, the people who are most likely to spend the least time are those recruited on the street for an immediate interview. This is because most often they are in a rush to get somewhere else.

Finally, while in-home face-to-face interviews can last half an hour or longer, telephone interviews often last only 10 to 15 minutes on average. As mentioned in an earlier chapter, a qualitative research 'questionnaire' will last much longer on average than most quantitative questionnaires.

Business to business customer satisfaction questionnaires

Customer satisfaction surveys in the business and commercial market can require a lot of planning to ensure the most relevant information is collected. As already discussed in the chapter on sampling, different people in an organization may have different requirements in terms of customer service. For example personnel in a purchasing department may consider the service they receive from a company in terms of its staff's negotiation skills, whereas personnel in a shipping department may look at how easy a company's products are to pack and distribute, while accounting personnel will look for accuracy in invoicing and other financial administrative matters. A small company may rate the service it receives in terms of time-saving, rather than how competitive a bank loan is or the range of services provided by a travel company. The reason is that time is a finite element, whereas most companies can readily find an organization to lend them money or to provide them with travel services.

How to check if the questionnaire is addressing the critical customer satisfaction issues

How can one ensure that the questionnaire focuses on the critical issues? One obvious answer is to include the customer in the design stage. This can be done if there is time to run a small-scale qualitative survey. It can also be done by running a 'pilot' – that is, conducting a few interviews at the start of the survey to which questions are added at the end, asking respondents what they considered the main purpose or focus of the survey has been. If the answers are different from those expected, more work is required to clarify the purpose of the survey for the respondent.

Revealing to respondents at the start of an interview who is sponsoring the survey is one of the more contentious issues in questionnaire design. Without a doubt, revealing for whom the survey is being conducted will boost response rates, as it suggests that neither the research agency nor the client has anything to hide. However, it may also bias the answers provided by some respondents. In some cases therefore it is better to reveal the sponsorship at the end of the survey, if required, rather than at the beginning.

QUESTION DESIGN

In his excellent *Questionnaire Design* (2004), Ian Brace describes the function of a questionnaire as being a medium of communication between the researcher and the subject, albeit sometimes administered on the researcher's behalf by an interviewer. Therefore, it is very important that everyone is in accord with the questions that are to be asked of the respondent, because if the wrong questions are asked, or if they are in the wrong place, the respondent will provide misleading information through misunderstanding the question. This could result in meaningless data being collected and the money invested in the project being wasted.

Consider for a moment the question 'Do you still beat your partner?' If asked this question, some people might interpret it as about a sport they play with their partner. Others might think it is asking about physical violence. It is also a misleading question because if someone answers 'No', a possible interpretation is that he or she used to beat his or her partner but no longer does. There is no option for respondents to say they have never beaten their partner.

Why designing customer satisfaction questions can be difficult

Designing questions for a customer satisfaction survey can be particularly difficult. This is because it is probably intended to find out about people's attitudes, and attitudes are very complex to research. The best advice is that all questions should be simple and clear to understand. This sounds easier than it is in practice. Most respondents have a very basic core vocabulary which consists of words that they use on almost a daily basis. They also have a broader vocabulary of words that they recognize, but do not use that often. Often the meaning of these words can be misunderstood. Therefore when designing questions it is important to take great care that the vocabulary matches that of the intended audience. The best way to achieve this is to ask if the meaning of the question would be clear to virtually every respondent, and to use simple, short sentences. Sometimes this means using two or more short sentences rather than one long one.

Beware of local differences

Local variations in the use of vocabulary are another factor to bear in mind when designing questions. For example, in parts of the UK and the United States people eat breakfast, dinner and supper, while in other areas of these two countries people will say they eat breakfast, lunch and dinner. If you were to refer to dinner in a customer satisfaction questionnaire in both countries, some respondents will talk about their midday meal while others will talk about their evening meal.

Grammar

Another question design issue is the use of grammar. Grammatically, the spoken language can be up to 50 years ahead of the written language. Very few people today say 'whilst' or 'amongst', but we still see these words in written questionnaires. It is important therefore not to be too concerned about being grammatically correct in a questionnaire, as long as the meaning of the question is clear.

Comprehension

Comprehension can also be a concern if the question contains two items to be assessed. For example: 'In terms of being clean and tidy, would you rate the store as excellent, very good, good, fair or poor?' Some respondents might perceive the store to be clean and tidy. However others might consider it tidy but not clean, or clean but not tidy. How could these individuals interpret the question? They might answer 'don't know' because they cannot decide on one rating for both cleanliness and tidiness. Alternatively they could choose, say, 'good' as a compromise between an 'excellent' rating on cleanliness and a 'poor' rating on tidiness. As you will see in a later chapter, determining how to interpret what a 'good' response really signifies in this situation is virtually impossible.

Social desirability

Another factor to bear in mind when designing a question is the risk of respondents providing an answer they believe the interviewer wants to hear, or one that is in their mind socially correct. For example, take the question 'How important is it to you that the store provides facilities for people with disabilities?' Respondents who do not have a disability might never have considered this issue before. Consequently, they could arguably be expected to answer the question in a neutral or negative way (choosing 'don't know' or 'not at all important'). However, many people would say it *is* important that the store provide facilities, because they feel it is the 'correct' thing to say.

Personal or sensitive questions

In some situations, it may be necessary to ask questions that people could consider to be personal or sensitive. For example, the company might want to determine whether all customers receive the same level of service regardless of their race or religious beliefs. However, these questions are considered as 'sensitive' and in the UK are categorized as such by the Data Protection Act. It is very important therefore that questions on these subjects are handled professionally and sensitively. Usually this requires providing respondents with an option not to reply to any questions they would feel uncomfortable answering. In addition, the researcher has to consider the method being used for collecting the data. Self-completion questionnaires or those conducted face to face can usually handle such questions by using 'prompt' material such as show cards. This option is not available for a telephone survey.

Order bias

Just as there can be order bias as a result of the positioning of a question in the survey (as mentioned earlier), so there can be order bias as a result of the way a list of service attributes about which the researcher wants customer opinions is presented. When respondents lose interest in the survey they sometimes start answering each question in an identical fashion. So for example, if the scale being used is 'excellent, very good, good, fair, poor' they might rate everything as 'good'. One way to obviate this is to word some of the attributes in a positive manner and others in a negative way. However, this too can introduce a bias, as some customers find it more difficult to rate statements that are phrased negatively than those that are phrased positively.

Another way to tackle this matter is to rotate or randomize the order in which the attributes appear. Then if respondent fatigue occurs, at least each statement will be equally affected. Of course the best solution is to limit the number of attributes to be rated. If the research is being conducted using a self-completion approach, it is not really possible to rotate the order in which the attributes appear. Researchers could of course go to great lengths to produce several different versions of the questionnaire, with each version listing the statements in a different order, but usually the cost for doing this is not felt to be justified. For self-completion surveys the impact of non-rotation can sometimes be lessened by listing the attributes in a way that would be expected by the customer if he or she was contacting the organization. So, for example, the questionnaire might begin with statements about initial contact (ease of finding a number to call, speed of call answering and so on), then move on to attributes about the staff member spoken to, the automated phone menu people were offered, and so on.

Pre-coded answers

Most questionnaires contain questions that are asked in an open-ended way but that require the interviewer to listen to what the respondent is saying and then select the appropriate answer from a list of codes provided. Many clients are more than happy to let the agency develop the list of answer codes to be used in the questionnaire. While this usually is not a problem, sometimes it is more helpful at the questionnaire stage for the client and the agency to discuss and agree an appropriate list. Far too often the client list is too long and detailed for interviewing purposes. If an interviewer has to trawl through a long list of pre-codes, two things could happen. First, interviewers do not bother to read through the code list and just record the response as 'other'. This saves time (which is a critical matter if they feel that the interview is too long and the respondent is getting bored, or if interviewers are paid according to the number of interviews completed). If 'other' does not require any further specification, an added complication appears at the analysis stage: there will be a large percentage of 'other' answers and neither the client nor the agency knows what the 'missing' answers are.

Selecting appropriate response scales in a customer satisfaction survey

One of the most challenging aspects for a researcher is selecting an appropriate response scale for respondents to use. With the exception of the Simalto scale mentioned in Chapter 2, there are basically two types of scale, verbal or numeric. An example of a verbal scale is 'excellent, very good, good, fair or poor', while a numeric scale involves asking respondents to select an answer on a scale of (say) 1 to 10.

Numeric scales

Interestingly, the research method can affect how respondents answer when using a numeric scale. It is usual to label either end of the scale to help respondents understand what they are rating (for example, 1 representing 'poor' and 10 'excellent'). If a self-completion or a face-to-face interview is being conducted, respondents can be shown the 'labelled' numeric scale on a show card, or it can be printed on the questionnaire. However, if they are taking part in a telephone interview, they have to 'visualize' the scale for themselves in addition to deciding how to answer the question.

Furthermore, some respondents find it difficult to determine a point on a 10-point scale, as they cannot distinguish what a '7' or an '8' represents. Other respondents may feel the scale is rather too broad, and so be reluctant to give an answer below a '5' – thus effectively turning the 10-point scale into a six-point scale.

If the survey is international in scope, 10-point scales introduce a range of other difficulties. In some parts of the world (such as European countries bordering the Mediterranean, and parts of Latin America), respondents are prepared to use the full 10-point scale, while in Northern Europe there is more of a tendency to use the upper half of the scale only. This can make drawing cross-country comparisons from the results difficult.

Verbal scales

Verbal scales can also introduce biases. The 'excellent–poor' scale mentioned earlier is skewed in so far as three of the points on it could be considered positive, one could be viewed as positive or negative ('fair'), while only one is really negative ('poor'). However, this is quite a common scale to use in customer satisfaction and loyalty surveys, as most people claim to be relatively satisfied with the service they receive, and so the scale takes this into account by providing more graduation of the positive elements, while keeping the entire scale quite short and easy to administer and understand.

Specific types of scale

Scales are used to help determine graduation in customer opinions about a particular product or service. However there is a range of different types of scales that can be used, the main ones being the Likert scale, verbal frequency scales, paired comparison scales, comparative scales, semantic differential scales, numeric scales, ranking scales and pictorial scales. As each of these different types of scales can be used in customer satisfaction and loyalty research, I provide a brief description of each.

The Likert scale

The Likert scale (named after its creator) is used to determine how much a respondent agrees or disagrees with a particular statement or opinion. For example, the question might be, 'How much do you agree or disagree that your car insurance is good value for money? Would you agree completely, agree a little, neither agree nor disagree, disagree a little, or disagree completely?' The strength of this scale is that if it is being used for a range of attributes, comparisons of customer perceptions can be made across the battery of statements.

There are a couple of things to bear in mind when using a Likert scale for customer satisfaction surveys. First, if some of the attributes are stated negatively rather than positively (for example, 'You never have to queue when you visit this store'), some respondents may get confused when trying to apply an agree–disagree scale. Second, even if the respondents are not confused, it can be difficult to interpret the results. For example, if half the respondents disagree strongly that 'You never have to queue', what does this really mean? Is there actually a queuing problem?

Verbal frequency scales

A verbal frequency scale is used to find out how often something is occurring. So if the company provides a computer support service, the research might want to find out how often customers contact the help desk, how often they use their computers, and so on. Naturally, the scale has to be created with appropriate labels (which might be 'daily, weekly, monthly, less often' or 'always, often, sometimes, rarely, never').

The ordinal scale

A variation of the verbal scale and the Likert scale is the ordinal scale, where respondents are asked to place a list of attributes in a specific order. An example is, 'Here are five things that other travellers have considered important when deciding which destination to choose for their next holiday abroad. Please list them in order of importance to you, starting with the most important.' However, for customer satisfaction surveys ordinal scales can produce misleading answers if they are not used carefully. The data that this type of question produces indicates the order of the items but says nothing at all about the distance between them. For example, perhaps a respondent ranks 'speed of answering the telephone' as the most important item and 'has polite staff' as the second most important. However, the primary concern of that person is the speed of answering the telephone, with all the other aspects being of secondary (or little) importance. Therefore, great care needs to be taken when interpreting ranked data.

Comparative scales

Paired comparison scales are used to offer a straight choice between two alternatives. For example, a company might be interested in knowing how it compares with its main competitors in a variety of dimensions. One way of finding out is to give respondents a list of statements and ask them which company is better (or worse) on each statement. The drawback to this approach is that respondents need to be sufficiently familiar with the two companies to be able to draw distinctions. In addition, the answers do not indicate whether the preferred supplier is a little bit better than its rival or a lot better. This would have to be determined by a follow-up question.

Comparative scales are another popular research device, and are especially useful to help evaluate how service rates today (for example) compared with the same time last year. The question might be, is service much better than a year ago, a little better, about the same, a little worse or much worse?

Semantic differential scale

Semantic differential scales are used to draw out differences between the company or service and that of other organizations across a range of image or service attributes. They are usually either 7 or 10-point scales, with either end of the scale denoted by words that are opposite in meaning. For example, the statement might be 'Speed of answering the telephone' and the scale ends would be labelled 'quickly' and 'slowly'. When this approach is used in a face-to-face or a self-completion survey, the interviewer can pictorially show the series of 'points'

between the ends of the scale to demonstrate the degrees of graduation. In telephone surveys this option is clearly more difficult. Great
care has to be taken both in composing the battery of attributes to be
covered and in the choice of the polar opposites.

Numeric scales

Numeric scales were mentioned earlier in this chapter and so are not
covered in detail here. The one great advantage of using numeric scales,
especially across a range of attribute statements, is that the results can be
used as both an absolute measure and a comparative measure. That is it
can be determined that customers rate staff, on average, at 8.5 out of 10
in terms of politeness, but it can also be noted that this was the highest
(or lowest) average rating of all the attributes covered in the survey.

Pictorial scales

Pictorial scales are a useful device when conducting face-to-face or self-
completion surveys and there is a concern about either the literacy or
the age of respondents. Instead of words, pictures and graphs are used
to depict the degree of gradation on the scale. These might take the
form, for example, of 'smiley' faces or thermometers.

Using attribute statements in customer satisfaction surveys

If attribute statements are used to help measure how customers feel
about particular aspects of a product or service, it is critical that the
attributes chosen are relevant to the respondents. It is very difficult to
gather an overall attitude about a product or service. Normally organizations want to know what underpins this attitude, and this calls for a
battery of attitude statements that enable the researcher to obtain a
detailed understanding. Qualitative research and letters from customers to the company can be very helpful in creating attitude statements with which respondents can identify.

Open-ended questions

One of the most useful forms of question to use in a survey is the 'open-
ended' question, which allows respondents to provide the answer in
their own words (which the interviewer records). An example of this
type of question is 'Why do you say that?' following a rating given by a
respondent to the previous question. Provided the interviewer captures
accurately what is being said (more about this in the next chapter), these
questions can prove very informative. These questions do not normally

work well in self-completion surveys as in these contexts they are totally dependent on respondents being able to articulate their thoughts clearly and succinctly. However in a face-to-face or telephone situation the interviewer can probe for clarity and understanding, and so capture very useful information.

One of the benefits of open-ended questions is that they make it possible to capture information that the research commissioner might not have considered as relevant, but the customer does. For example, the survey might focus on administrative issues such as the handling of address changes or the quality of service received when contacting the company by telephone, but the real issue for customers is the poor performance of the investment product they bought from the company. If the core product is under-performing and your survey does not have any questions about this, customers will still find a way of bringing it into their answers. However, adding one question, such as 'What one thing would you like the chief executive to do to improve the service you receive from company "x"?' makes it possible to gather information on the really important issues facing some, or all, of the customers.

The questionnaire close

The final part of the questionnaire is as important as the opening. Finishing a questionnaire by thanking respondents for their time and opinions is crucial, as is telling them again who has conducted the survey and on behalf of which company (if relevant). In addition, if interviewers give respondents a telephone number or other contact details in case they have any questions or concerns about the survey, this will leave them feeling more positive about the encounter, and it can be hoped they will be just as willing to participate in future surveys.

OTHER MATTERS

International issues

A challenge for all researchers who conduct international surveys is identifying scales and attribute statements that can be translated unambiguously from one language to another. One US-headquartered global organization wanted to check if the company was seen as an 'ethical' company in each of the countries around the globe where it had operations. Therefore it decided to ask customers to rate how 'ethical' the company was. German colleagues immediately said the question could not be translated into German, as the concept of an 'ethical' company would not make sense in that language. However, the client was insistent. When the results revealed that 4 per cent of the respondents rated the company as ethical and 96 per cent answered 'don't know', the client immediately wanted to know why the company was not perceived as 'ethical' in Germany!

Another amusing (in hindsight) incident was when a multinational client insisted that 'delighted' was used as the top box on a satisfaction scale. French colleagues pointed out that the direct translation of 'delighted' ('enchanté') was more appropriate to use when talking about human physical attraction rather than as a point on a satisfaction scale.

Finally it should be borne in mind with international surveys that while people may be able to count to 10, and so the use of a 10-point scale is appealing, in certain countries its use can be a little unsettling for respondents. For example, in schools in Germany pupils are brought up using a six-point scale where 1 is the top point and 6 is the lowest point. So, if a 10-point scale is used in Germany (or a six-point scale for that matter) where 1 is the lowest rating , it runs the risk that some respondents will forget and start awarding 1's thinking they are giving the attribute the highest possible score.

Asking about 'importance' in customer satisfaction surveys

Another issue frequently raised by researchers in regard to customer satisfaction surveys is whether or not interviewers should ask respondents how important a particular aspect of service is to them, and then rate the company on that particular aspect (as is the approach used in the SERVQUAL method described in Chapter 2), or whether it is better to use statistical techniques to derive the importance of the attributes being measured. This can be quite a critical issue, as it is possible to obtain very different conclusions depending upon the approach used.

For example, consider the train service. If customers are asked to rate the importance of a series of attributes about trains, safety will virtually always be rated as being extremely important, and usually ahead of other factors such as comfort, availability of refreshments and so on. There are all kinds of reasons for this. Who, for example, would not consider safety important? But suppose for a moment respondents are not asked to rate the importance of these factors. Suppose they are just asked to rate their supplier, in this case a local train company, for performance on safety, trains arriving on time at their destination, comfort, availability of refreshments, and so on. How can the research determine which attribute is the most important in terms of overall satisfaction? After all, if it were known what aspect customers thought the most important, and how well the company was perceived to be doing on this attribute, it could determine how much to focus on that aspect of its service.

One way of doing this is to use a correlation analysis to determine the strength of the relationship between each of the individual attributes and the overall satisfaction with service. From this it might be discovered that 'arriving punctually' is relatively more important than train safety for most commuters. The reason is that most customers expect rail travel to be safe, and even though each year there are a number of train crashes, the publicity they receive ensures that management keeps on top of safety issues, while the chances of their involving an individual is quite small compared with other modes of transport. So other factors gain in importance as far as most commuters are concerned, and the most important of these is arriving at their destination on time.

Some researchers make the case for asking both importance and satisfaction questions in the same survey, but prefer to ask the satisfaction questions before the importance questions. Nigel Hill and his colleagues at the Leadership Factor have found that when the importance section follows the satisfaction section, they obtain a wider range of importance scores, while ratings for satisfaction vary little whether they are asked before or after the importance questions (Hill, Brierley and MacDougall, 2003: 63).

Where to place 'overall satisfaction' questions

Should one ask 'overall satisfaction' questions at the start or the end of the questionnaire? This is another of the questions clients most frequently ask researchers. Asking the question as close as possible to the start of the survey will capture the opinion that a respondent would give to a friend, relative or a colleague. If the matter arose during a conversation, most people would say how satisfied they were with a particular company, product or service before explaining what it was that made them feel that way.

If the question is asked at the end of the survey, the survey process might unwittingly have put some ideas into the minds of respondents that would not have otherwise occurred to them. As a result, they might start thinking more rationally about their answer than if the question had been asked at the start. Critics of this approach argue that once the interviewer has asked about overall satisfaction, respondents answer the following questions more positively, as they want to 'justify' the overall rating. In my experience this is not the case. I have analysed results where the respondents gave a very positive overall satisfaction rating when asked at the start of the survey but were then critical (sometimes very critical) in their rating of an attribute or brand value that was the subject of the very next question.

Asking about 'loyalty'

Another question that is often asked by clients is how the survey can ask about loyalty. In many respects this depends on the client's business objectives for the survey. For example, if the aim is to measure a respondent's level of commitment to the organization, there might be a question about how likely respondents are to consider the organization for future services or product purchases. This type of question provides an indication whether or not the company is on the 'radar screen'. It is a type of question that can be useful when customers do not make frequent purchases (for example, for many financial services such as loans, mortgages and insurance). However, it would be inappropriate for food retailers, as most people regularly visit stores to buy food. In this case the solution might be a more direct question (such as, 'How likely are you to use this store the next time you go shopping for food?'). However, it is important not to interpret the answers to these questions too literally. Respondents might accurately give their current perceptions about their future behaviour, but when the time comes they will have received many other stimuli to buy elsewhere, and so may act differently.

Impact of changing questions in a customer satisfaction tracking survey

One of the challenges researchers face is the request to make changes to a tracking survey questionnaire. Making the actual change is usually not difficult. What is difficult is determining what impact the change has on the resulting data, and whether or not it will materially affect the trend data from earlier surveys.

Clients normally conduct tracking surveys in order to measure the impact of the actions they have taken on the perceptions of their customers (or the market). Therefore they try to make as few changes as possible to the survey, so any changes in the results will be predominantly due to the actions they have taken and not other factors (such as a change in the economic climate or a change in the research methodology, sample or questionnaire).

However, the market place itself is constantly changing as new companies enter the market, new products and services are introduced that could result in a need for the organization to update its own products or services, changes to economic trading conditions occur, new regulations are introduced, and so on. Therefore, if the questionnaire did not change to reflect the customers' world, very soon the tracking vehicle would be producing potentially misleading or skewed data. This does not solve the problem that adding or changing the wording of a question can alter the way customers respond to later questions. So not only is it necessary to start tracking the results from the new question, there might also be a change in the results for other, unchanged questions. One way to mitigate the effect of this is to run the new and old questions in parallel surveys, which helps to show the impact of the changed questions. However, this is more difficult than it sounds, as it is necessary to keep as many other aspects of the survey as possible constant (such as the profile of respondents, timing, and so on).

Pre-testing customer satisfaction questionnaires

Pre-testing questionnaires is an essential part of any survey, but unfortunately one that some clients feel is a luxury rather than a necessity when it comes to the matter of paying for a pilot survey. The main reason for piloting a questionnaire is to see that the questions work the way in which they were intended, and that respondents do not have any difficulties understanding or answering them. Client researchers should encourage their internal sponsors to attend pre-testing sessions of the questionnaire, as the pre-tests may raise issues that can lead the client to reconsider whether the questionnaire is focusing on the critical issues. Furthermore, a questionnaire that the client sponsor has 'approved' may read very well when viewed in a written format, but when the same question is asked out loud it can appear decidedly pedestrian. One of the best examples of this is when the client insists that the question needs a long preamble to 'explain' what is about to be asked. If the client cannot describe it in a short sentence, usually the customer has difficulties grasping it as well.

CLOSING COMMENT

Readers who wish to gain a deeper and broader understanding of various aspects of questionnaire design are referred to Ian Brace's excellent *Questionnaire Design* (2004).

Part III

'TOUCHING' THE CONSUMER

9 Facing the consumer

This chapter looks at what happens when customer satisfaction surveys are in the field. It covers issues about the recruitment and selection of interviewers, how much briefing and training interviewers should be given, and what ongoing training and coaching should be provided. It also offers some thoughts on what interest and involvement clients should have in this stage of a survey, the value of 'listening-in' sessions for telephone surveys, and the problems that they and other forms of 'accompanied' interviewing can cause. It looks at the administration of fieldwork, including the need for monitoring sample usage and the quality checks that should be used. While the value of piloting surveys was covered in Chapter 8, other aspects about piloting will be covered here.

Three additional topics are covered in this chapter. The first is what should and can be done regarding customers who raise serious service issues during the interview, which ought to be addressed by the client immediately. Second, the matter of client confidentiality concerning fieldwork is covered. Finally the chapter looks at ways of gaining trust and commitment from respondents.

> Thank God, in these days of enlightenment and establishment, everyone has a right to their own opinions, and chiefly to the opinion that nobody else has a right to theirs.
>
> **Ronald Knox**

I would not be surprised if many client and agency-based researchers who design research surveys and questionnaires decide to skip reading this chapter. After all, they probably believe their job has been done. The research requirements have been agreed, the questionnaire has been signed off, and now all they have to do is sit back and wait for the interviewers to get on and complete their task of conducting the interviews. Not only would this be a folly, it would show how little regard and understanding there is of what the interviewing task involves, for both the respondent and the interviewer. In fact, I feel that all researchers should spend some time in their careers actually conducting interviews. If they did so, they would obtain not only a greater appreciation of what an interviewer has to do, but also a clearer understanding of what they can ask from their respondents.

THE SITUATION FROM A POTENTIAL RESPONDENT'S POINT OF VIEW

Market research is often conducted in difficult circumstances. Interviewers stop people on the street when they are going to buy sandwiches for their lunch, or just wanting to get out of a stressful office environment for a bit of piece and quiet or some retail therapy. In the midst of this a stranger approaches and asks if they will take 10 or 15 minutes out of their hour to give their views on a subject that may be of little interest to them, and the last thing they want to talk about at that time.

Alternatively, when people have just got in from work after a hectic day and a crowded train journey (or sitting in a traffic jam for an hour), and are settling down for a few minutes to recharge their batteries before taking the dog out for a walk or putting the children to bed, the telephone rings. It is someone whose name they didn't quite catch, asking if they recently made a call to their bank about extending their overdraft and wanting to know how they felt about the service they received. Or they are on a business trip and when they checked into their hotel room, they notice a leaflet saying that the hotel prides itself on catering to the needs of the business traveller and would welcome their views on its service. However, the card looks like it has been there for 10 years and been used as a coffee mat by a previous guest.

What it is like to be in the front line

In my opinion, the real heroes are those interviewers who go out in all weathers knocking on people's doors to solicit an interview. I have seen what it is like to be out on a cold, wet, windy January Saturday afternoon trying to achieve a target three interviews per hour. Why three? Because a research executive back in head office has calculated that the interview will take eight minutes to conduct, therefore the researcher will spend less than half of every hour interviewing and the rest of the time going from door to door finding the next eligible respondent. Of course, the executive has not actually done any door-to-door interviewing. He or she has not accounted for the time needed to cover the usual niceties of thanking respondents for inviting you into their home, taking off your wet coat and hanging it somewhere, unpacking your laptop computer and powering it up, then waiting while the respondent makes you a cup of tea or coffee and offers you a biscuit. Neither does the calculation take into account the effect on interviewers when potential respondents angrily slam the door in their face for disturbing them while they are watching football on the television, or refusing to let them into their home because it's raining and their coat is wet. In my experience, it is often the more upmarket areas where one finds the least helpful people.

In other words, people are often asked to participate in a survey and to give up their time to provide their thoughts and opinions about particular subjects at quite inconvenient moments. Often they will agree to do so provided the interview does not last too long and the subject matter is something they want to discuss.

The interviewing stage of the project is critical to its success, and the influence an interviewer can have on a project should not be underestimated. It is also an area that the client and agency researchers should be very concerned about.

HOW AGENCIES RECRUIT AND SELECT INTERVIEWERS

The starting point for any agency is the recruitment and selection of interviewers. What kind of people are market research interviewers? Many of them work part-time, either alongside other jobs or because they have other commitments. Many interviewers are students who want to earn money to help fund their education, or actors who are between assignments, or semi-retired people who are supplementing their income or wanting to fill some of their spare time. Other interviewers work full-time, perhaps because they have decided they want work that involves dealing with the general public but does not involve selling. Some interviewers work exclusively for one research agency, while others may work for a number of agencies.

A good interviewer needs to be friendly and polite, well organized with good attention for detail, have good communication and listening skills, and enjoy dealing with people. Those who conduct face-to-face interviews also need good health and stamina, as much of their time could be spent outdoors and on their feet. Perhaps not surprisingly, interviewers need to be numerate and have good oral skills. For international work they should also be fluent in other languages. More and more projects these days involve the use of computers, as computer-assisted personal and telephone interviewing has grown in popularity. Therefore most agencies will also seek people who are not afraid of using technology.

CASE STUDY

Network Research, a UK research agency that specializes in telephone research in the areas of new product development and customer satisfaction, always conducts a telephone screening interview first with potential interviewers. As its business is telephone interviewing, if the candidate cannot make a good impression over the telephone, then the chances are he or she will not be very suitable for telephone interviewing. Therefore great attention is paid to the interviewer's tone of voice and the way he or she answers some simple questions. Network Research also tells prospective interviewers during the initial call about the shift pattern and the rates of pay they can expect. Assuming candidates find these acceptable, they are then asked about their experience in market research or what they think the job entails. Experience is not essential, as like most agencies, Network Research has an extensive training programme that all new interviewers go through, even if they have previous market research experience. This is because the company's reputation (as well as that of its clients) is on the line each time an interviewer makes a call. So it is crucial that interviewers understand the company's culture and values, and approach each market research interview in a consistent and professional manner.

BRIEFING AND TRAINING FOR INTERVIEWERS

In the UK there is an industry requirement that all interviewers are adequately and appropriately trained, and that the training is fully documented. For example, those interviewers who are already trained must still receive a minimum of three hours' training when they join a new agency. Those new to interviewing must have a minimum of six hours' training. In addition, they must be monitored or supervised as close to the start of their first assignment as possible to ensure that they are adequately trained. There must be documentary records confirming the date(s) and amount of training the interviewer has received, and all interviewers have to be appraised at least once every six months.

Besides the obligatory requirement to inform interviewers about health and safety at work and other administrative matters such as how they will be paid and when they can take breaks, the aim for all training must be to ensure that a consistent interviewing standard is achieved and maintained for a project. It should cover how interviewers should introduce themselves and the project to respondents, how to pace and control the interview, how to probe for clarification of respondent's answers in an objective way, and how to record and handle verbatim comments. Verbatim comments are answers that respondents provide to open-ended questions such as 'Why do you say that?' It is crucial that these answers are recorded word for word, or as close to it as possible.

'Controlling' the respondent is an essential skill, especially on customer satisfaction surveys. When conducting consumer interviewing on such subjects as product usage, interviewers often find that respondents have relatively little to say. However, when it comes to customer service or subjects that have a more emotive element (such as interviewing men about cars), they often have a lot to say. As a result, they often try to tell an interviewer more about their experience or opinions than is required from the question. Interviewers need to skilfully bring them back to the subject in hand without alienating them or causing them to become reluctant to continue with the survey, because they think the interviewer is not really interested in what they are saying.

Briefing interviewers for a customer satisfaction project

In addition to more general training, interviewers can expect to be fully briefed about each project they are to work on. This briefing can take many forms. A personal briefing is the most expensive approach, partly because (face-to-face) interviewers have to travel to attend a briefing session. However this is the best method for briefing interviewers, as the researcher can ensure that all interviewers have understood the briefing and what is expected of them. In addition, the researcher can go through the questionnaire with the interviewers to ensure they understand all the questions, the routeing and any quota requirements. The researcher will, of course, be on hand to answer any questions the interviewers have.

If a personal briefing is not possible because the project would not warrant the expense (or because the client does not have the budget for it), the next best type of briefing is one conducted by telephone. However, there are limitations to telephone briefings. If a large number of interviewers are to be used, the agency will probably brief the supervisors for the project and ask them to brief the interviewers. This increases slightly the risk of misunderstandings or miscommunication.

The least preferred method of briefing is by posting interviewing instructions to the interviewers. Naturally the agency expects the interviewers to read and understand the instructions, but it cannot be certain that each interviewer has fully understood them, or that they are fully remembered at the time the fieldwork begins.

ONGOING TRAINING AND COACHING

Keeping interviewers interested and involved can be a challenge on a large-scale tracking survey. This is especially so for a customer satisfaction survey. Customer satisfaction questionnaires can be very repetitive. Often they use a similar set of answer scales throughout the survey (for good reasons). Nevertheless, for an interviewer, it can become very tedious. In addition, once they have conducted a fair number of interviews they will begin to feel that they have 'heard all this before'. There is a risk that attention will drift or standards fall. In this situation interviewer supervision becomes vitally important. In the UK there is a requirement that a degree of validation is conducted on each survey. Validation can be conducted by real-time monitoring (via a remote listening-in device), by listening to taped interviews, or by telephoning respondents after an interview. In the UK at least 10 per cent of all interviews in a survey must be monitored (unless the interview has been done in a telephone centre with remote monitoring, where the minimum requirement is 5 per cent).

Personality

I mentioned earlier that personality is one of the factors that can influence people's suitability for the role of interviewer. However, certain personality types may have difficulties when faced with the requirement for maintaining a consistent approach.

Because a good interview is akin to a conversation between two individuals, even when one of them is adhering to a script, it is important that each respondent is asked the questions in the same way. However, difficulties can arise, particularly when administering open-ended questions that require a verbatim response. Naturally during the interviewer briefing process and in the interviewer training, an agency will have briefed its interviewers on how to probe a respondent's answers for clarification or for gathering more information. However, interviewers are human, and if they have a bubbly personality, they may run the risk of not adhering to the approach required by the agency. The question is whether such interviewers should be allowed to work on the project.

For example, most agencies specify particular questions to be asked when probing, such as 'How interesting, can you tell me more about that?' or 'So why do you say that?' However, some interviewers sound unnatural asking these types of questions because they do not come naturally. Instead, they are more likely to probe by saying in a genuinely interested way, for example 'Oh, really?' or 'Gosh, you don't say?', and in the majority of cases respondents react to this comment by adding much more detail and insight. Should these interviewers be allowed to continue working on the project, or should they be made to 'conform'?

In my opinion they are not introducing a bias because they are not putting ideas into a respondent's mind. Perhaps more importantly, they are getting a far better quality of response from the respondent (and so are of more value to the client) than if they were to be 'forced' to use the standard probing techniques that do not come naturally. However, I am not advocating anarchy. I feel one should consider each situation on its merits. I remember on one occasion a British banker was horrified when he heard an Australian interviewer call one of his customers 'mate'. The banker told me it was not acceptable to speak with one of his customers in that manner, and suggested that this interviewer should no longer be used on his project. Ironically, this interviewer conducted many hundreds of interviews and never once had a customer complaint. He didn't hide his Australian accent and people accepted him for what he was, speaking as he would naturally. He never veered from the script apart from adding the occasional 'mate' or 'OK mate' in response to comments from the respondent.

I feel respondents find participating in interviews far more interesting and rewarding when an interviewer sounds genuinely natural and interested in what they are saying. Nevertheless, care must be taken. If, for example, an interviewer were to answer 'brilliant' every time a respondent gave a 'top box' rating, it would be wise to point out that this is not acceptable because the interviewer is unwittingly providing a psychological reward every time the respondent gives a very positive response.

Maintaining interviewer interest in a customer satisfaction tracking survey

Monitoring is not the only way that standards are maintained. Excellent interviewers never forget that while they may have interviewed hundreds of customers on a particular survey, for most people it is the first time they will have heard the questions. Therefore it is vital that the interviewer shows as much interest in what the first respondent is saying as the 50th or the 100th. To maintain interest, agencies can regularly re-brief their interviewers on tracking surveys to reiterate why they are doing this work and how important it is both to the client and to the agency.

However, in my experience the best long-term motivation comes when the agency researchers show a genuine interest in what is happening to the survey. This includes actively seeking out feedback from the interviewers (and being seen to act on the feedback), and situations when the client shows enough interest in the project to come to see the interviewing while it is in progress. Both these situations are motivating, as well as showing respect for the interviewers' skills and the contribution they are making to the project.

It is, of course, good practice for interviewers to receive regular updates about the surveys on which they are working. This is especially so when there are changes to the questionnaire or to the types of people they will be contacting (or to the products and services that they are calling about).

CLIENT INTEREST AND INVOLVEMENT IN THIS STAGE

Many clients are very particular about the way their own staff deal with customers. Often they have invested heavily in training their sales people, customer service agents or counter staff on how to approach or handle customers in a wide range of situations. This is very apparent in those companies that believe customer service is a strategic differentiator. Consequently, they will want reassurance that the interviewers an agency uses on their projects are good ambassadors for their organization. One way to ensure this is for the client to provide the agency with supporting materials such as details about their products or services and a glossary of common terms that customers may use during their interview. Some clients provide the agencies with additional material such as internal training videos and documents that describe the 'tone of voice' agents should use when talking with customers.

If time permits, the client should attend interviewer briefing sessions. Not only does this get the message across to the interviewers that the client is truly interested in the survey but it also enables any unforeseen issues that may arise to be dealt with there and then. This ensures there are no unnecessary delays to the start of fieldwork because of a need for some last minute clarification from the client.

THE VALUE OF CLIENTS 'LISTENING IN' TO CUSTOMER SATISFACTION INTERVIEWS

It is not uncommon for clients to request that they attend some of the interviewing being conducted on their survey. There are many reasons for wanting to 'listen in' to interviews. Here are just a few:

■ To listen to a few interviews of a newly designed customer satisfaction questionnaire to see if people are having any difficulties understanding the questions, or to see if they are interpreting the questions in a different way from that intended. If conducted at the start of the survey, this is referred to as a 'piloting interview' session.

■ To get a feel for the depth of interest and intensity of respondents' feelings on the subjects covered in the survey. Data from surveys provide clients with the actual numbers of people answering each question, but they cannot convey the emotion with which respondents are answering. Attending a listening-in session provides an indication of the degree of emotion that respondents are showing about the subject under discussion.

■ To listen to the way interviewers handle the calls, in terms of their objectivity, pace and accuracy of recording the answers to the questions. This is critical because clients want to feel assured that interviewers are not influencing the way that respondents answer the questions (which could lead to misleading results). There are many ways that interviewers could influence respondents. Here are just a few examples:

– Stressing certain words in the question or answer scales that are read out. (For example, 'How would you rate the *staff* on doing everything they can to help you?' may elicit a different response than if the question had been read as 'How would you rate the staff on doing *everything they can* to help you?')

– Prompting a respondent with a suggestion for an answer. (For example, 'You have said they were "good". In what way were they good? Was it their friendliness that you spoke of earlier?')

– Speaking too quickly so that the respondent does not fully understand the question.

Types of questions clients raise at listening-in sessions

If clients do attend interviewing sessions, the agency personnel in attendance can expect them to raise questions or observations. The types of question they will raise vary depending upon the reason for the visit, the client's knowledge of market research and his or her job position and responsibilities. For example, if a client is attending a 'piloting session', the types of questions include:

- What questions did your interviewers have during your briefing and training sessions?
- What do your interviewers think about this questionnaire?
- Which questions have your interviewers found difficult to ask, or answer, during their rehearsals?
- Could I see your interviewer briefing notes?
- Why do you think that respondents are misunderstanding question 'x'?
- How long is this interview taking?
- What would happen if ... (followed by various suggestions for changes to questionnaire wording, order of asking questions or the like)?

If a client is not very experienced in market research, the range of questions asked is very varied, such as:

- How do you find people to participate in this survey?
- Do many people refuse to participate in an interview?
- How representative are the views that we get from participants, as I know I always say I haven't got time for an interview?
- Where do you find your interviewers?
- What training do you give your interviewers?
- Are the answers we are hearing in this survey very different from other surveys you have conducted?
- Who are your other clients?
- Can we have the names and addresses of the people who have participated in this survey, as I can tell that many of them would benefit from a call from our customer services department?

More experienced researchers may well ask about strike rates, response rates, sample selection and similar issues.

Certain questions will be determined by the responsibilities that the attendees have in their organization. So, for example marketing people will be very interested in the types of comments that respondents have about their company's image, their attitudes to products, services, advertising and competitors. Customer service and call centre staff will be interested not only in respondents' views on customer service, but also on the way that the interviewers establish rapport and interact with the participants. Operations staff tend to focus on what customers have to say about the way company systems work (or not, as the case may be).

How agencies can demonstrate customer focus at listening-in sessions

If they are not too careful, agency staff can underestimate how even the smallest of details can impress a client on these types of visit. They provide an opportunity for the agency to show how customer-focused it is. For example, before the visit the agency should obtain a list of the attendees and their expected time of arrival. In this way the receptionist or the interviewer (if the visit is to attend some face-to-face interviewing) will be able to greet the visitors and show they are expected. Furthermore, the agency should determine if its guests are likely to have any special requirements (such as disabled access to the facilities, taxis booked to meet them at the local station, or taxis to take them back to a station). Naturally, the interviewers should have been briefed about the visit, and appropriate arrangements made regarding work breaks and the like. In addition, it is essential that the necessary paperwork be on hand before the client's arrival. This includes copies of confidentiality forms, a paper copy of the questionnaire, interviewer briefing materials, and pens and pads of paper for note taking. If the visit is being held in a central venue, it is equally important to ensure that the facilities are up to scratch. After all, if the client has to visit the washrooms and finds they are dirty or lacking in some way, it will suggest that the agency does not care for its staff and their comfort.

These days many companies do not have dress codes. Therefore it is quite common to wear a more casual style of clothing than was the case 10 or 20 years ago. However, it is still good business practice for those hosting a client visit, or likely to be introduced to the client, to dress more formally. In most cases this means smart business clothes. Most clients dress formally in suits or in company uniforms, and so it is important for the agency to project a similar image.

Clients often notice the smallest of gestures. Therefore greeting them with a smile and a firm handshake makes them feel welcome. Clients also give other signals that should be picked up by agency personnel: for example, how they address each other. If they use first names, this is a signal that first names can be used during the session. If they raise questions, they should be answered truthfully and succinctly. Clients understand that agency staff may not have the answers to all questions, and so are usually perfectly happy to receive the information later.

Surprisingly, given the agency has usually done all the preparatory work for these visits, it is important to remember that this is the clients' meeting and they are attending because they want to hear interviews. If a client has been at a listening-in session at a telephone centre, it is polite to ask if he or she would like to meet the interviewers who have worked on the job. Usually he or she will not want to, but if he or she says yes, it is an opportunity for the interviewers to hear how much their work has been appreciated. This normally takes only a few moments, but it demonstrates that the agency is completely open about its working methods and has confidence in the staff it employs.

After the client has departed

Immediately after the client has departed it is good practice to thank the interviewers for their contribution and provide quick feedback about what went well and what could be improved. If any particular interviewers need personal feedback , they should be told their supervisor will discuss the interviews with them individually, either later that day or at the next available opportunity. (This should then be followed up as promised.) In addition it is good practice to create a set of meeting notes. These should be typed up and placed in the job file as a record of the visit. They should contain a list of attendees, a list of all the interviewers who worked on the job, notes of all the key issues that were raised and discussed (including what the agency contact said) and any follow-up action that was agreed. Finally, the agency researcher should make a personal note of any things he or she thought were handled well, and any 'lessons learnt' from things that could be handled better the next time.

THE NEED FOR MONITORING SAMPLE USAGE

While interviewing is progressing it is vitally important that an eye is kept on the way that the sample is being distributed and used, and to identify early on if there are any problems arising from the sample. For example, many customer satisfaction surveys involve interviewing customers who have had a recent contact with the client organization. The client may well tell the agency it is providing a (randomly) selected sample for interviewing. However, what the agency does not know and the client does not realize, is that the people who actually pull the sample may well skew it in a particular way.

For example, the brief may be to interview people who had recent correspondence with a particular company. The client wants to know how satisfied its customers are with the way the company responded to their written enquiries and complaints. However, if the person within the client company who selected the list of customers to be surveyed had not been told the purpose of the research, and selected a sample of customers who had recently been sent a marketing letter, things could go wrong very quickly. However, if the interviewers and the agency researchers are doing their job well, this type of problem should become obvious at the start of interviewing. Unfortunately, this type of situation can lead to the project being delayed while a new sample is drawn.

Quota monitoring

One of the more difficult tasks for an agency is managing any quotas that may have been set for the fieldwork. As mentioned in an earlier chapter, quota sampling is one of the most widely used sampling techniques in quantitative customer satisfaction research. If, as is usually the case, the client or the agency has background knowledge of the market, specific quotas may well be set for the survey to ensure the profile of respondents matches the universe or customer base. These quotas can be based on demographic characteristics such as age or gender, or set on product usage or other characteristics. When the project is in the field, interviewers can be set specific quotas, and it is their job to select the people to be surveyed who fit the quota requirements.

Monitoring sample usage

Another interesting challenge that an agency can face is sample usage. If a client is providing the agency with a sample of its customer base for the survey, normally it will have been agreed beforehand how many names need to be provided to achieve the required number of interviews. There is no magic formula to this. Each situation has to be determined on its own merits. For example, the agency and the client might agree that 10 times as many names are required as the volume of interviews it is hoped to achieve. The client might require that certain categories of customers are not called, such as people who have unlisted numbers or people who have participated in any market research in the past 12 months. The more criteria that are set, the greater the proportion that will be lost from the original pool of names. Assuming the client cannot provide the agency with any more names at short notice, it is very important that the interviewers try to maximize the use of the pool they already have. This could mean, for example, calling every number (if it is a telephone survey) up to 10 times over the period of five days to try to obtain an interview before discarding that potential contact and replacing it with another.

Modern technology allows the interviewers to 'manage' the quota they have to achieve. They can send data back to their head office electronically overnight to report on the progress they have made. If they have achieved their quota, the computer system can block the sample from releasing any more names for the interviewing.

THE VALUE OF PILOTING SURVEYS

'Piloting' surveys is a term that refers to the testing of the questionnaire before full-scale interviewing begins. There are many excellent reasons for piloting a questionnaire. Ian Brace (2004: 164–65) provides 15 excellent reasons for piloting a questionnaire:

- to check if the questions sound right (they might look fine on paper but sound stilted or false when spoken out loud);
- to check that interviewers understand the questions (if they cannot understand the questions there is little chance that interviewees will);
- to check that respondents understand the questions (the questions may contain jargon);
- to check that there are no ambiguous, double-barrelled, loaded or leading questions in the survey;
- to check that respondents can answer the questions (that is, that questions are being asked that respondents are capable of answering);
- to check that the response codes provided in the questionnaire are sufficient (if some are missing it can result in large numbers of 'other' answers which, if captured will require coding at the analysis stage);
- to check that the interview retains the attention of the respondents throughout;
- to ensure that interviewers and respondents understand the routeing instructions in the questionnaire;
- to check the interview flows properly (that is, it has no, or only a minimal number of 'jumps' between apparently unrelated topics);
- to check that the questions and responses answer the brief;
- to check how long the interview will take (which has an impact on the cost of the survey);
- to check for mistakes;
- to check the routeing works;
- to check the technology works in the field.

It is not necessary to conduct many pilot interviews. It would not be unreasonable for between 5 and 10 to be conducted for a business survey, and perhaps 30 or more for a consumer survey containing complex routeing or quotas for a number of different segments, each of which are to be asked different questions.

Some companies believe it is sufficient to pilot a questionnaire among colleagues. While this has obvious cost benefits and can identify a number of issues, it is no substitute for using actual interviewers piloting the survey among actual respondents.

Piloting interviews with respondents

There are a number of ways to pilot interviews with respondents. For example, the researcher might accompany a face-to-face interviewer who is piloting the questionnaire, then at the end of the survey ask the respondent if there were any particular questions he or she found difficult to understand or answer. The researcher could also probe respondents for more information about their underlying thoughts when they provide unexpected answers to questions. This might reveal a flaw in the question, or suggest that an additional element needs to be covered in the survey. If the survey is being conducted by telephone, a similar approach can be undertaken, with the questions being asked at the end of the interview.

It may not be possible to accompany or listen in to pilot interviews in all situations. If it is not possible, it is important to obtain feedback from the interviewers as soon as possible after the completion of the pilot. In these situations it is worthwhile asking interviewers to make notes about anything and everything that arose during the pilot, and for the researcher to review these with them. Often the smallest item can have an impact. For example, the survey might ask customers the reason for their last visit to a company's offices, and the questionnaire allows the interviewer to code just one item. Respondents might say they visited to discuss a number of issues, or to conduct a range of transactions, because it is their habit to 'store up' matters to discuss on their next visit. If the interviewer can only record one, the wrong impression will be gathered. Perhaps even more importantly, if this question is then used for further analysis to see if the reason for the visit is a driver of customer satisfaction, even more misleading information will emerge.

Some companies believe in treating the initial interviews from a survey (that is, the first tranche of actual interviews to be analysed) as 'pilots'. They believe this saves time, and if the pilot does not reveal any flaws, it has saved them the expense of a separate pilot. This can be a false economy, as the research agency has to allow for a 'pause' in the interviewing schedule to allow for questionnaire and other possible changes to be made, and then to rebrief the interviewers before the project recommences. If it is a large-scale survey that involves many interviewers, this 'stop-start' approach is not only very disruptive but can also dent the enthusiasm and interest of the interviewers who work on the project. It also causes disruption to the researchers, who have to discuss with the client the reasons for stopping the survey and agreeing a new timetable, and for the analysts or programmers who have to stop working on other projects to amend this one. In addition, the client may find it too needs to change an internal schedule because of these delays.

Finally, if the subject of the survey is customer satisfaction, it is essential to ask respondents how they felt about participating in the interview. Did they find it enjoyable? Was the topic interesting? Did they feel pleased that they had given up their time to participate? Were there any questions they were expecting to be asked that did not come up? This last point may reveal a 'gap' in the survey that is important to consumers even it is not considered so important within the client organization.

HANDLING SERIOUS SERVICE ISSUES ARISING DURING THE INTERVIEW

Sometimes when customer satisfaction surveys are being conducted, customers discuss matters that have serious implications. For example, they might reveal details of fraudulent or other potentially criminal behaviour. They might express a frustration that the client does not appear to be handling a problem or complaint well, and indicate that the matter is causing them extreme stress or financial loss. Faced with these types of issues, what should an interviewer or research agency do, especially if the introduction to the survey reminds respondents that any data they provide will be treated as confidential?

The actions agencies can take will depend upon the situation. In the UK for example, the industry's code of conduct does not take precedence over national law, and the UK Market Research Society provides an advice service to help its members on any such issues.

If however the issue the respondent raises is one where the agency may be in a position to help, then with the respondent's express permission the agency can send the particulars of the problem to the client. In such cases, the respondent must be clearly told what information will be sent to the client, and his or her express agreement must be gained before the data is handed over. Respondents should also be told, where possible, to whom in the client organization the information is being sent. No other data the respondent has provided in the survey must be sent to the client in an attributable form (see the next section).

THE IMPORTANCE OF CLIENT CONFIDENTIALITY

Market research depends upon the willing cooperation of the public and people in customer organizations to provide their time to participate in surveys. To maintain their trust and confidence, it is essential that all market research is conducted in an open and honest way, that it retains its objectivity and that it does not harm or intrude. In addition, market researchers agree to respect the confidentiality of respondents and not to use any data provided in any way that could harm or embarrass the respondent. Market researchers must also ensure that they do not present any findings in a misleading way, while ensuring that they are reporting the data accurately.

It is a simple fact that without respondents, there would be no market research. Therefore, in most countries where there is a thriving market research industry, there is also a professional industry body with its own code of conduct (see Appendix 2).

GAINING TRUST AND COMMITMENT FROM RESPONDENTS

One of the most common questions that market researchers are asked by people who are invited to participate in a survey is 'Who is it for?' Potential respondents are usually looking not only for reassurance that the survey is not 'sugging' (selling under the guise of research), but to know this because the information could impact on other issues, such as whether they think the sponsor of the survey is likely to take any notice of what they have to say.

In other cases, particularly with customer satisfaction research, it is actually necessary to reveal the connection at the start of the survey. This can arise if, for example, the interviewer is to ask respondents about recent transactions they have made with the client's organization, and the client has provided an appropriate customer list. In other cases clients are willing to have their identity revealed at the end of the survey. However it is not always feasible for the interviewer to tell respondents who is sponsoring the survey, as it may influence what they have to say in ways that affect the validity of the survey results. Therefore it is important that the interviewers gain the trust and commitment of potential respondents through being open and honest with them in those ways that are practicable.

There is also a risk when respondents do know the name of the sponsor that they will forget that they are talking to a market research agency, and not only go into a lot of detail about the product or service (which can provide much useful information) but make comments that are not appropriate in the context. It is in these situations that good interviewers really shine as ambassadors for both the research agency and the client.

CLOSING COMMENT

A director of a market research company was once heard to remark, 'For a researcher to go out and observe interviewing is like a general visiting advanced casualty stations during a war – not to be recommended!' However this chapter has shown the importance of being aware of, and in control of, what actually happens when interviewing takes place.

Part IV

OUTPUTS

10 Analysis

This chapter addresses the basic issues surrounding analysis of data from customer satisfaction and loyalty surveys from both the client and supplier perspective. It has three main sections. The first section looks at how the data from each survey is prepared for analysis. The second section discusses how to prepare the analysis specification for extracting the relevant data for analysis. The final section provides a brief overview of some of the tools and issues that need to be considered when analysing data from customer satisfaction and loyalty surveys.

For client-based researchers the chapter includes suggestions on how to brief an agency about specific analysis requirements, involvement in developing code frames, and whether or not verbatim responses should be edited and coded by the agency. It also suggests how client researchers could enhance the quality of analysis through the provision and use of internal company data.

For the agency researcher it includes issues about data cleaning, how to code, who should build the code frames, interpreting client needs, deciding what the data checking procedures should be and the value of statistical testing.

> He uses statistics as a drunken man uses lampposts – for support rather than illumination.
>
> **Andrew Lang**

Data analysis can be one of the most exciting aspects of market research. Once the fieldwork is complete, the next step in a market research project is to check that the data is 'clean', then to look at what it reveals about the objectives that were set for the project. However, it is not only the agency that should be concerned about this. Clients should pay very close attention too, as the results presented to management are directly derived from the analysis specifications set for the project.

DATA PREPARATION

How the data gets from the field into data analysis

After interviewers have recorded respondents' answers on question-naires (or respondents have completed internet or self-completion surveys), it is necessary to gather all this 'raw' data into one place for analysis. However, before any analysis can be undertaken the data needs to be edited, coded and then processed. Market researchers refer to this process as 'cleaning the data'.

Editing customer satisfaction data

Editing is concerned with the legitimate correcting or removal of obvious errors arising during the interviews. For example, a respondent may not have answered a question in a mail survey. As a result the interview is incomplete. So should the data from this respondent be discarded even though all the other questions have been answered? This could be expensive, as it might then be necessary to either mail out more questionnaires and risk delaying the results from the survey, or base the analysis on fewer interviews than is desirable. But if an editor enters a 'question not answered' code for this question, the researcher can use the interview rather than discard it.

Another situation that arises and requires corrective action after the close of fieldwork is when an extra question is added by the client after interviewing has started. In this situation, there will be a number of early respondents who were not asked the inserted question. The usual course of action is to base the analysis of answers to that question on those respondents answering it.

Editors can also legitimately correct the error that occurs when respondents have been asked questions they should not have been asked (because of a routeing error), without biasing the data analysis. As the questions were in fact asked, data exists in the survey for those questions. The researcher and client should agree whether or not this 'additional' data should be included in the analysis. Usually such data should be excluded, for reasons of consistency.

Regrettably, some respondents lose interest during an interview and do not complete it, while others may provide hypocritical answers to the questions. In both these situations the entire interview should be reviewed on an individual basis, and a decision reached on whether to include the interview as a whole or discard it.

Most editing is done by computer these days. Programs exist that enable the computer to check that the right number of people have been asked each question, that those questions where the respondent is to have provided just one answer are in fact single coded, and so on. Therefore, this part of the process is no longer time-consuming. Before the era of mass computing, 20 or 30 years ago, a lot of editing was done manually by teams of editors. In those days it could take a person up to 100 hours to edit 1,000 20-minute interviews.

While editing is seen as acceptable in certain situations, it is important to keep an eye on what proportion of the original data was edited. If the amount of editing is on the high side, care must be taken with any interpretation arising from the data analysis, as this might suggest that the data has been manipulated to produce certain results, or that there were lots of problems with the questionnaire or the fieldwork.

Coding the data

Coding is another skilful 'back office' task that client researchers often request be done on their survey. It is questionable though whether many of them know what is involved, and have seriously considered whether the expenditure on this task is justified.

Coding refers to the classification and grouping of similar answers. There are two types of questions for which it is usually undertaken. In the first, a list of possible answers to an open question is provided on the questionnaire, and the interviewers select whichever answer most closely fits the actual response and 'code' (mark) it accordingly. In the second type of coding, a fully open-ended question is asked and a verbatim response captured. Rather than provide a list of the verbatim responses, the agency reads and categorizes them.

Coding of 'other (SPECIFY)' responses

It is a common practice in customer satisfaction surveys to use a relatively high proportion of open-ended questions in the questionnaire, then provide the interviewer with a list of probable answers. This saves time and money for the client, as the interviewer does not record the answer word for word, and there is no need to spend time after the interview editing and coding the responses. However, sometimes the answers do not readily fit the predetermined classification. To enable interviewers to capture these responses, most researchers add an 'other, please specify' response code. The interviewer then records the reply verbatim in these situations.

Sometimes the 'other' category is heavily used because a response that was predicable with hindsight had not been anticipated. For example, take this question:

Question: 'Why do you recommend company x to your friends and colleagues?'
    Answer codes: Staff
                        Convenient location
                        Opening hours
                        Services
                        Other (Please specify)

The 'other' category might contain a lot of answers specifying 'competitive prices' because there was no specific option that mentioned price.

With (for example) a mail survey, the coder normally takes a sample batch of between 50 and 100 questionnaires, and makes a list of responses in the 'other' category. The list of the most common types of 'other' response can be shared with the client if time permits (or if the client wishes), and agreement reached about whether specific codes to cover them should be used.

One of the challenges facing the agency researcher is whether the coding should be done by one person or by a team. Consistency in coding responses is the key, and if one person can do the task, so much the better. However, if it is a large-scale survey this may not be a viable option.

If CAPI or CATI software has been used (as is usual for telephone or face-to-face interviewing these days), it is customary to print out a full list of 'other' answers. Software exists to count these and make the coding task less onerous.

Coding verbatim responses

One of the most valuable elements in a customer satisfaction survey is the use of open-ended questions to capture customer opinions about a particular element of service, or to identify aspects not otherwise covered in the survey that contribute to customers' satisfaction or dissatisfaction. Recording a customer's actual response can provide a huge amount of valuable and insightful data. For example, the question might be, 'What one thing would you like the chief executive of [client's company] to do to improve the company's service for you?' One possible reply is, 'For a start they could stop putting all calls though to a call centre where they keep you on hold and assume your time is less valuable than theirs, and let us call their offices directly, as we used to be able to do.'

The manner in which such a response is treated can reveal a lot about both the client and the agency's approach to customer satisfaction measurement. All too often, the client asks the agency to code such responses in order for them to be more easily assessed and understood. After all, if each respondent provided a single verbatim comment in a survey of 300 people, this would mean 300 comments needed reading and analysing. Imagine a survey of 10,000 customers where each one provides two verbatim comments – a common enough occurrence – and the scale of the problem is obvious.

However, some researchers argue that coding verbatim responses does a disservice to the client. Assume for the moment that the client has asked the agency to code the sample reply above. The coding might be 'call centres' or 'do not use call centres' – the degree of categorization varies from the very general to the more specific. However, another coder might feel the main point the customer is making is about having his or her time wasted, and code this as 'do not waste customers' time'. A third coder might opt for a double coding, once as 'do not like call centres' and again under 'wasting customers' time'.

Clients might respond to the coding in a number of ways. First, they might legitimately point out that double coding leads to more responses than answers, when the question was for the respondent to mention 'the one thing the chief executive could do'. Furthermore, they might feel that the coding categories the agency has developed are not very useful to them. Perhaps their way of categorizing the answers would focus on issues such as how many of the comments related to existing company policies or procedures, how many were people-related, and how many product-related. A lot of time can be wasted trying to agree how to code these types of responses and then ensuring that all the people conducting the coding are applying the codes in a consistent manner.

Even when this sort of coding is carried out well, it can still be argued that it provides only a very superficial analysis. In the sample answer, there are quite a few clues about this customer's depth of feeling over the company's use of call centres. Any coding of such responses will usually ignore the more 'emotive' aspects (other than to record whether the comments were 'positive' or 'negative'). For example, the answer began with 'for a start'. This immediately signals that there are a number of aspects that could be improved, but as only one has been requested, only one is specifically mentioned. The second emotive aspect is the subtext that the respondent objects to a lack of choice of communication channel. Perhaps he or she feels like a 'captive' customer whose preferences have been ignored.

Enlightened clients should always request a copy of all verbatim comments in their entirety. They are closer to their company's policies and procedures, and will often be able to spot the root causes underlying the customers' comments far more clearly than any research agency. I have known clients to do this and to take corrective action that would have been impossible had they not read the actual comments made.

Editing verbatim responses

'Editing' customer comments refers to taking the comments as provided by the interviewer and converting them into a more readable form. This is sometimes necessary where the interviewer types (or writes) the respondent's comments while the respondent is speaking. When respondents talk about a topic that is emotive or about which they have firm opinions, they often increase their talking speed, and this can make it difficult for the interviewer to keep up. There is an awkward trade-off between trying to slow down the respondent, perhaps interrupting his or her train of thought, and failing to get everything down accurately.

There are various techniques that interviewers use, such as telling respondents they will be writing down the answer word for word before asking the question. This usually works for a large number of respondents. Another technique is for the interviewer to repeat what the respondent has said as he or she types or writes it. This has the effect of causing the respondent to stop talking and check that the interviewer is quoting him or her correctly. The main problem with these techniques is that respondents may decide it is taking too long to get their thoughts down, and truncate their answers as a result.

Some interviewers use shorthand or 'mobile phone texting' language to capture the comments. However the agency may not feel it appropriate to provide a client with comments that read '4 a strt, thy cld ...' Therefore it 'edits' the comments by turning them into standard written English.

If comments are to be edited, it is essential that the editors do not change their meaning. This can be difficult if the quality of writing or spelling is poor. Editors need to refer back to the interviewers for clarity whenever such situations arise.

Digital recording of verbatim comments

The latest development in the 'capture' of verbatim comments is digital recording (provided the appropriate confidentiality safeguards have been offered and accepted by the respondent at the start of the survey). This has a number of advantages. It enables interviewers to concentrate on the discussion and to probe ambiguous comments more thoroughly, as they are not worried about typing fast enough to capture the comments. It also can be used to improve the probing of verbatim comments during interviewer training and coaching sessions. The data files can be edited to take out any elements that could lead to the respondent being identified, and provided to the client as part of an 'interactive' verbatim comments database. In this way, the client can listen to what respondents say first-hand, taking in their intonation and speed. These types of database can provide very insightful information when analysed with other data from the survey.

PREPARING THE CUSTOMER SATISFACTION ANALYSIS SPECIFICATION

How to brief the agency about specific analysis requirements

Once the data has been cleaned and edited, it is ready for analysis. As mentioned in an earlier chapter, the very best research briefs often include a list of questions or information requirements that the client is seeking from the project. These are the starting point for the research agency when developing the analysis specifications. Correctly specified, the analysis should be able to answer all the questions the client has raised in the brief.

For example, the client may believe customers' willingness to recommend its product or service is based on their perceptions about the service they received on their most recent visit or purchase. This can easily be tested (assuming the relevant questions have been asked) by cross-tabulating a question on recommendation and a question on rating of last visit. If the hypothesis is true, people who rate the service 'excellent' would recommend the company, while those who rate the service 'poor' would criticize rather than recommend it. (This may seem self-evident, but it is not always the case. It is possible for quite loyal customers to be irritated by something in their most recent contact, but not to feel sufficiently strongly about the issue to change their overall opinion of the organization.)

Sometimes clients provide the agency with additional data about their customers (such as length of tenure or customer segment) when supplying the original sample, and request that the results are analysed by these criteria. This requirement should be specified in the brief. If the brief does not make it clear why the extra information has been supplied, it is always a good idea for the agency to ask for clarification.

How to brief the data analysts

The way analysis is specified varies from agency to agency, and also depends on the software program used to process the data. Larger agencies usually have a data processing department which carries out analysis based on a specification prepared by the researchers. In smaller agencies the researcher may carry out the analysis him/herself, or outsource it to a specialist data processing company.

If the company has data programmers or analysts in-house, it is usually a good idea to involve them in the project from the start. If they understand why the research is being undertaken they are more likely to provide relevant, accurate and useful analysis.

What customer satisfaction data tables usually contain

Usually a computer table (or tables) is produced for each question in the survey (excluding any questions where the answer is recorded as a verbatim comment and no coding takes place). Each table has a heading indicating what it refers to. In addition it should give the question number, so the researcher (or client) can refer back to the actual wording of the question and any filters that are being applied. Filters simply report that the table is being created on a subset of respondents rather than on all respondents, for example 'All men', which obviously means that female respondents are excluded from the analysis. In customer satisfaction research it is not uncommon to run filtered tables on respondents who share a common attitude (for example, who agree that company x has 'poor' customer service).

Most tables also contain a 'total' column that shows the total number of respondents who have answered the question. If the question is, 'Overall would you rate the service you received on your last visit as excellent, very good, good, fair or poor?' the side headings on the table would be base size (the total number of respondents covered in this table), and numbers responding excellent, very good, good, fair, poor, don't know and no answer. The latter two are provided to cover those respondents who could not answer the question ('don't know') or who did not provide an answer ('no answer').

Beside a 'total' column, most tables have additional columns that analyse the data from particular groups of customers. For example, there might be a requirement to see if men rate the overall service differently from women, so there would be two columns, one containing just the data for men and the next containing just the data for women. The selection of appropriate cross-breaks (as these additional columns are known) should be based on answering the objectives for the survey or testing any hypotheses. So if the client believes men are more critical of its service than women, this could be confirmed or disproved by comparing these two columns of data.

A good set of data tables should contain just the data required to meet the project's objectives. Otherwise they can become too large and unwieldy and lead to 'analysis paralysis'. Often this situation occurs because whoever specified the tables has been lazy and asked for the same set of cross-breaks to be run against all the data tables. This can lead to the generation of many hundreds, if not thousands, of pages of tables, most of which are of no relevance whatsoever. Furthermore, it can lead to an inexperienced researcher drawing spurious conclusions from the data.

CHECKING PROCEDURES FOR DATA TABLES

It is good practice to carry out checking procedures on sets of data tables. The first and most obvious one is to check that the number of interviews that have been conducted tallies with the number shown on the data tables. The next round of checking consists of 'reality checks', to use a phrase my American friends are fond of. For these the researcher asks, 'Are these the results I expected?' For example, with a tracking survey, if the average score for customer satisfaction has been hovering around 65 for a number of waves, but the figure for the current wave has fallen to 45, this calls for investigation. First, the researcher will see whether there is an obvious mistake in the calculations. If none is apparent, other obvious reasons for the shift need to be sought. If none can be found, the data fails the reality check, and it is necessary to go back and re-examine the data more closely.

CASE STUDY

Background

A major UK financial institution continuously surveys the users of its internet banking service. The customers are always very positive about the service and ratings are consistently on the high side. However, one day the agency research executive in charge of the project received a call from the call centre manager, who reported

---

that respondents were being more critical of the internet banking service than in the past, and wondered if the client was experiencing some problems. A quick analysis of the interviews conducted over the previous few days showed an apparent sudden deterioration in the ratings on a range of factors covered in the survey. However, ratings on security were higher than in previous waves. How could this be? Was there a mistake in the data?

The analysis

An initial check of the accuracy of the scores, the source of the data, and the profile of respondents using the service against the profile in previous weeks, brought no obvious reason for the change to light. However a call to the client quickly revealed the probable cause. The bank had recently decided to tighten the security of its service, and when customers next logged into their account they had to pass additional security checks. Many customers recognized that the bank was right to improve security from a 'peace of mind' perspective, but they found the way the change had been communicated was less than ideal. Hence they rated the security higher than in the past but rated other factors lower. The data therefore passed the 'reality check'.

Additional information in data tables

Besides a tabulation of the numbers of respondents and their answers, most research agencies supply two additional pieces of information. These are the standard deviation and standard error.

Standard deviation

The standard deviation is a measure of the average distance of the values from the mean value. It can be very useful when interpreting data where the average scores are similar. Simply put, the larger the standard deviation, the greater the spread of answers. For example a question might ask respondents to rate their satisfaction with the level of service on a 10-point scale, and both men and women might give identical mean ratings. However, the standard deviation of the answers is higher for the men: that is, men show a greater variation in their answers than women. The next step would be to find out why. It could be, for example, that ratings vary considerably by age and the survey interviewed a wider age range of men.

Standard error

The standard error provides an indication of how accurately the results from the sample for the survey are likely to reflect the results for overall population from which it is drawn. The degree of error is based on two elements, the sample size (in relation to the size of the population as a whole) and the degree of variability within the population. (As the latter is rarely available, the survey results are used to estimate it.) The larger the sample, and the smaller the variation in its answers, the closer the result is likely to be to the true population value.

The standard error is usually referred to in conjunction with another statistical term, the 'confidence level'. For example, the report might say, 'This figure is accurate to within plus or minus 2.5 per cent at the 95 per cent confidence level.' What researchers are referring to here is that with only one sample and no other information about the population from which it was selected, there is a 95 per cent chance that the true population figure lies within 5 per cent (that is, plus or minus 2.5 per cent) of the resulting figure from the survey. So, for example, if the survey data showed 20 per cent of the sample rated the service excellent, then had a census been taken (rather than a sample of the population) there is a 95 per cent chance that the true proportion of the population who would rate the service as excellent would lie between 17.5 per cent and 22.5 per cent.

Normally, the research agency will provide guidance on how to interpret the standard error figure and the related confidence level.

SOME USEFUL TOOLS FOR ANALYSING CUSTOMER SATISFACTION DATA

Properly conducted, survey analysis will provide valuable diagnostic information that enables management to improve customer service where this appears necessary. However, interpreting the results and judging what action they call for is not always as easy as it sounds.

For example, suppose the survey indicates that 20 per cent of customers are dissatisfied with the service they receive from a company. This equates to one in five customers. However, perhaps 15 per cent of them should not really be customers of the company. Perhaps some of them were misled by the marketing and bought a product or service that was not designed, and is not suited, for them. Perhaps others are customers from years back, who own outdated products that require constant and expensive service support. It might make no sense for the company to tailor its general customer service offering to meet all the requirements of either of these groups.

This combined group represents 3 per cent (15 per cent of 20 per cent) of the entire customer base. Perhaps the customer service function should concentrate on the other 97 per cent and their requirements. But if it ignores this 3 per cent it will be left with what is possibly a very vocal minority of dissatisfied customers who could be doing a lot of damage to the brand. Therefore it might be better to identify them, to analyse their results separately, and to consider separately how to act on them.

It is common in analysing data to find that the first set of results does not provide all the necessary answers, and raises questions that call for additional analysis. Thus it is crucial that this phase of a project is not rushed. A good client allows sufficient time for the research agency to carry out all the necessary analysis.

In addition to standard computer tables (cross-tabulations) there are several other tools and techniques available to help analyse data. Some of the more common methods are discussed below.

Statistical testing

Management in client organizations needs to be fairly confident that the data It obtains from research surveys is reliable, especially if the data is to be used for business planning or investment purposes. In research surveys where the data has been provided by a sample of the target universe, the reliability of the results will depend on several factors such as the size of the sample and its homogeneity (as noted above). It is important to design the survey so that the *confidence limits* fall within tolerable bounds.

Table 10.1 has been compiled on the assumption that the data has been obtained from a simple random sample, and makes no allowance for any design factor. For most face-to-face in-home consumer surveys the survey design is not based on a simple random sample, so for these surveys the standard error needs to be multiplied by a 'design factor'. These are difficult to calculate and so they are often ignored, but they should be borne in mind when analysing data as the impact of the design can be large (frequently as much as 1.5). In addition, data can be 'weighted' to make it more precisely representative of the population, but weighting the data also reduces its statistical reliability.

Table 10.1 enables one to read off the accuracy of one percentage from one sample at the 95 per cent confidence level.

For example, suppose the sample size is 200 and the figure obtained from the survey is 40 per cent. Table 10.1 shows that the 40 per cent is 'accurate' to plus or minus 7 per cent at the 95 per cent level of confidence. In other words, there is a 95 per cent chance that the true proportion within the population lies between 33 per cent and 47 per cent. If however the sample size had been five times larger (1,000), then there is a 95 per cent chance that the true proportion within the population lies between 37 per cent and 43 per cent.

Table 10.1 Sampling errors on percentages from a simple random sample in survey reports at 95% confidence limit

Percentage	5% or 95%	10% or 90%	20% or 80%	30% or 70%	40% or 60%	50%
Sample size:						
50	±6%	±9%	±11%	±13%	±14%	±14%
100	±5%	±6%	±8%	±9%	±10%	±10%
150	±4%	±5%	±7%	±8%	±8%	±8%
200	±3%	±5%	±6%	±7%	±7%	±7%
300	±3%	±4%	±5%	±6%	±6%	±6%
500	±2%	±3%	±4%	±5%	±5%	±5%
1,000	±2%	±2%	±3%	±3%	±3%	±3%
2,000	±1%	±2%	±2%	±2%	±3%	±3%

Often it is necessary to compare results from two different surveys (for example, two waves of a tracking survey) in order to decide whether the difference is 'real' (or 'significant', as statisticians say, meaning 'not due to chance'). Table 10.2 provides guidance on the size of the differences that can be considered significant at the 95 per cent level of confidence.

Suppose that the first survey has a sample size of 250 and the second survey has a sample of 150. In the first sample 48 per cent is satisfied with service and this figure increases to 52 per cent in the second survey. Is this increase statistically significant? To determine if it is, we use the column closest to the average of the percentages (50 per cent) and the row for the average sample size (200). We can see that the difference

Table 10.2 Differences required between survey percentages for difference to be considered significant at the 95% level of confidence

Average of the two percentages	5% or 95%	10% or 90%	20% or 80%	30% or 70%	40% or 60%	50%
Average sample size						
50	9%	12%	16%	18%	20%	20%
100	7%	9%	11%	13%	14%	14%
200	5%	6%	8%	9%	10%	10%
300	4%	5%	7%	8%	8%	8%
500	3%	4%	5%	6%	7%	7%
1,000	2%	3%	4%	5%	5%	5%
2,000	2%	2%	3%	3%	4%	4%

of 4 per cent is not statistically significant (since this would require a difference of 10 per cent) at the 95 per cent level of confidence.

If the difference is sufficiently large (according to these tables) the researcher can declare the results to be 'significant at the 95 per cent level of confidence' and assume that a real difference exists in the population. However, if the difference is not large enough to be significant, the researcher will indicate that the result is 'not statistically significant'. This means either that a real difference does not exist, or that a real difference does exist but it is too small to be detected at this level of confidence by the sample.

In declaring a result to be significant or not significant, there is a risk of making two possible types of error.

Type 1 error

This is the statistical term for declaring a result to be significant when in fact there is no real difference. The chance of this happening is 5 per cent (that is, 1 in 20) when the confidence limit is 95 per cent.

Type 2 error

This is the statistical term for declaring a result to be not significant when in fact there is a real difference. The chance of this happening becomes increasingly large as the sample size becomes smaller. In practice, small sample sizes identify very few significant differences.

These days statistical programs are available that will provide more accurate statistical testing than can be done using simple manual tools like Tables 10.1 and 10.2.

Advanced analysis techniques for customer satisfaction surveys

In addition to cross-tabulations, researchers often use other, more advanced analysis techniques. Most of these are beyond the scope of this book; however four of the most commonly used are described briefly below. These are factor analysis, cluster analysis, correlation and regression.

Factor analysis

Most customer satisfaction surveys contain a series of questions asking respondents to rate the level of service they have received on a series of attributes or factors such as the politeness of staff and cleanliness of the location. Often there can be 10 or more such attributes in the survey. The aim of a factor analysis is to condense the number of attributes into a smaller set of factors to help understand what impacts on customers' overall perceptions of service. This analysis takes as its starting point the correlations between the variables (see below).

Although usually described as 'factor analysis' in practice, the method usually used is properly known as principal components analysis.

Cluster analysis

While factor analysis looks at the relationship between *attributes*, a cluster analysis is concerned with grouping together *respondents* who have similar attitudes and opinions. Individual respondents are normally categorized as belonging to only one cluster, and it is possible for a survey analysis to generate quite a number of different clusters. Usually each cluster is given a descriptive name based around the dominant attribute that differentiates it from the other clusters ('personal service seekers', 'techno lovers' and so on). A cluster analysis does not have to be limited to attitudinal data. Customers can for example be clustered according to the number of different products they have purchased from an organization, or the number of different suppliers they use in an industry.

Correlation and regression

One of the most common questions that managers raise about a customer satisfaction survey is how it will help them to determine where they should prioritize their actions to improve customer satisfaction, loyalty and profitability. To aid this process two related analysis techniques are widely used: correlation and regression.

Correlation analysis measures the linear relationship between two variables. Imagine three people, one who is 5 ft 6 in tall and weighs 100 lbs, one who is 6 ft tall and weighs 150 lbs, and one who is 6 ft 6 in tall and weighs 200 lbs. It is immediately apparent that there is a relationship between height and weight. The taller the person, the heavier he or she is. In other words, weight and height are highly *correlated*. If the weight of all three individuals were the same, or if (for example) the 6 ft person was the heaviest of the three, there would be no correlation between height and weight.

Correlation is measured by the statistic r, and it can have values between +1 (a perfect positive correlation) and –1 (a perfect negative correlation). A value of 0 means there is no correlation. Negative correlations show an inverse relationship, so that an increase in one variable results in a decrease in the other. This would be true in the example if the taller people were, the lighter they were.

There are two common types of correlation: the Pearson product-moment correlation and Spearman's rank correlation. A useful guide is that Spearman's is used for ranked or ordinal data while Pearson's is used for interval or ratio scaled data.

One point to note, however, a correlation analysis does not show what drives what. That is, the researcher cannot use it to say that weight gain *causes* height gain or that height gain *causes* weight gain. It can only be stated that there appears to be a relationship between weight and height.

As with all statistical techniques, care has to be taken with the application of correlation analyses. Correlation works for data based on numeric scales where the numbers are meaningful. For example, if you are counting money you know that the difference between 1 and 2 is the same as between 2 and 3. But when people are asked in a survey to provide a rating between 1 and 10, it cannot be certain that they consider a rating of 6 to be exactly midway between a 4 and an 8. This is even more so when a verbal scale is used. For example, using a five-point scale such as excellent, very good, good, fair and poor, it cannot be assumed that 'good' is seen as midday between 'excellent' and 'poor'. While many statisticians frown upon the use of correlation analyses with verbal rating scales, many researchers conduct them as they feel they can provide insight as to what is probably happening in the real world.

Regression analysis also looks at the relationship between two or more variables. The term originated from Sir Francis Galton's 19th-century study of the relationship between parent's heights and children's heights. Galton found that the height of the children of very tall or very short parents tended to *regress* towards the average population height, and so this type of analysis became known as regression analysis (Sanders, 1995: 492). Regression analysis differs from correlation analysis insofar as regression analysis looks at the statistical dependence between a dependent variable and one or more independent variables, and tries to forecast the impact of a change in the independent variables on the dependent variable. So a regression analysis examines the *pattern* of an existing relationship, while a correlation analysis looks at the *strength* of the relationship.

A major problem with the use of regression analysis on customer satisfaction data is that often the so-called 'independent' variables are not in fact independent of the variable whose value needs to be predicted. This invalidates the analysis.

Priority analyses

One of the most common outputs from a customer satisfaction survey is data about how a company's service is perceived on a range of variables. For example, imagine the survey has asked respondents to rate the quality of service they received from the staff on the last visit to a company's premises. From earlier qualitative research it has become apparent that the critical service areas for the business are that the staff actively listen to the customer's requirements, that they take personal responsibility for handling the customer's needs, and that the venue is clean. However from the quantitative phase of the survey it is discovered that customers do not rate the venue highly for being clean, but do perceive the staff are very good listeners. In addition, they appear to have mixed feelings about whether the staff take personal responsibility for handling their needs.

Faced with these results, a first reaction might be that the company should prioritize the cleaning of the venues as this factor scored lowest in the survey. Imagine however that the researcher runs a correlation analysis of these variables against the scores for the customers' ratings for overall satisfaction, and comes up with the following results:

Take personal responsibility	0.72
Actively listen	0.55
Venue is clean	0.33

A reasonable conclusion is that a positive overall rating is driven more by taking personal responsibility than by active listening or having a clean venue. However, this is not to say that personal responsibility is more 'important' than the other two attributes. All these attributes are important. It would be better to say that personal responsibility has more impact on overall satisfaction than the other two attributes.

There are several potential problems with correlation analyses:

- As mentioned earlier, a correlation can never prove causality.
- The size of correlations can reflect, in part, the scales on which the questions are based. If for example, overall satisfaction and most aspects of performance are measured on a seven-point scale but one performance attribute is measured on a five-point scale, then this difference will impact the correlation for this attribute.
- There might be a high correlation between an attribute and overall satisfaction because both share a strong correlation with some other aspect of performance, which is the real driver.

If there is information both on how respondents rate each service attribute, and the relative correlation of each attribute against overall service quality, it is possible to suggest possible priorities for attention (urgent, high, whatever) and to suggest some basic 'actions' (improve, maintain and so on), as shown in Figure 10.1.

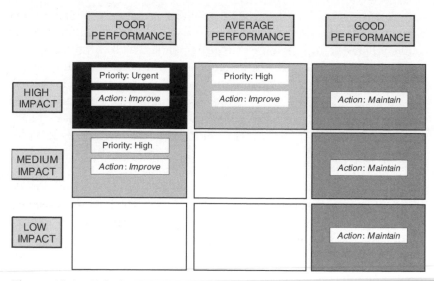

	POOR PERFORMANCE	AVERAGE PERFORMANCE	GOOD PERFORMANCE
HIGH IMPACT	Priority: Urgent Action: Improve	Priority: High Action: Improve	Action: Maintain
MEDIUM IMPACT	Priority: High Action: Improve		Action: Maintain
LOW IMPACT			Action: Maintain

Figure 10.1 *Priority matrix*

As can be seen, this approach suggests that any attribute that has a high correlation (that is, a high impact on overall satisfaction) and a low performance rating should probably be given a high priority and urgent attention. This is because failure to address the issue could lead to a deterioration in overall customer satisfaction. However, care must be taken when interpreting such analyses, because improving the rating on some attributes may not increase satisfaction to the same degree to which a decrease in another attribute would decrease overall satisfaction (or increase dissatisfaction). For example, you may recall the train example I gave in Chapter 1. If a train arrives on time, it may not have a major influence on customers' overall satisfaction with the service, but if it were to consistently arrive late, that would be another matter.

There are a couple of other matters it is important to consider when using matrices to show data. First, one option is to display the data by plotting its actual position on a graph rather than in a matrix as in Figure 10.1. This approach enables clients to see clearly how the various factors are placed in relation to one another. The drawback to this approach is that it can create an impression of spurious 'accuracy' about the data, obfuscating the fact that if another survey is conducted and there are minor differences in the ratings on a few of the factors, the relative positioning of each of the factors could change.

Other matters that need to be considered when suggesting areas to prioritize are the financial and strategic implications of the suggestions. For example, if the cost of implementing the change far exceeds the benefit, it is probably not worth recommending. From a strategic perspective, it is often worth considering prioritizing a few actions that can provide 'quick wins', as well as those that require more time and resources. The 'quick wins' will ensure that interest in the programme is maintained, as well as providing some financial benefit while work on the larger or more complex areas prioritized for action is under way.

How much data analysis to do

As was hinted at earlier in the chapter, the rule for data analysis is 'the more, the better', as long as it is contributing to the business objective. For example, the researcher might conduct a priority analysis and stop at that point: after all, this provides management with information that can enable it to take action. However, if the researcher stopped after the first priority matrix, he or she might in fact have produced some potentially misleading information. For example, the perceptions of some groups of customers might differ from others. In order to show this it would be necessary to run separate improvement matrices for each unique customer group.

Some clients provide additional information about their customers to the research agency, and this can be put to good use during the data analysis stage. For example, say the company has developed its own segmentation of its customers, with four segments:

- crown jewels (that is highly profitable);
- potential crown jewels (customers worth developing as they are showing similar signs in the relationship to those the crown jewels segment did at a similar stage of their relationship);
- appreciateds (worth maintaining a relationship, as they are profitable customers, but will never command the high value segments);
- residuals (not profitable and unlikely to become so).

If the data for each of these groups is analysed separately, it might reveal that those in each group have different levels of satisfaction, different priorities for attention and different perceptions about their likelihood to consider purchasing from the company again. Therefore if one of the requirements from the survey was to support advice to management on which segment to invest most resources in, the data analysis of these segments could be vital. Often this type of analysis requires the combined efforts of both the client and supplier researcher as well as others in the client organization (from strategic planning, finance and so on), to help get the most out of the survey data.

Analysing data from customer satisfaction benchmark surveys

Benchmark surveys can trap the unwary analyst when it comes to interpreting data. If the benchmark survey was conducted to evaluate the company's performance relative to its competitors on issues that are important to its customers, it is important to avoid the trap of assuming that what is important to the client organization's customers is also important to its competitors' customers. It may well be that its competitors have very different strategies and types of target customer. For example, First Direct, a UK bank, provides a telephone banking service, with branch banking services being supplied by its parent company HSBC. It is often cited as being innovative, and it usually scores particularly highly in customer satisfaction surveys (Foss and Stone, 2002: 18; Smith and Wheeler, 2002: 28). However, a competing branch-based bank that included First Direct in its competitor benchmarking survey would need to bear in mind that it had targeted customers who preferred a telephone banking relationship. Any analysis of the data pertaining to First Direct's customers could mislead if it was seen through the lens of what was important to branch-oriented customers.

CLOSING COMMENTS

Data analysis should not be left to agency researchers or data analysts alone. It should be an iterative process, and sufficient time should be given to enable it to provide the nuggets of information that could make the difference between 'providing information' and 'making a contribution to the business'.

Many of the statistical concepts and multivariate techniques available to researchers are beyond the scope of this general introduction to researching customer satisfaction and loyalty. Readers who want to gain a more in-depth knowledge are recommended to consult Derek R Allen's *Customer Satisfaction Research Management* (2004).

11 Reporting the findings

In this chapter four aspects of reporting results from customer satisfaction surveys are discussed. The first part covers the physical format of reports, including how to decide what types of reports are required, by whom, how often findings should be reported, and how to decide what to include and what to exclude. The second section looks at issues client researchers face when presenting research data. It includes the benefits and risks of the agency s including commentary about the findings in reports, and presenting the results in person. It also looks at what can be done when the results from the survey contradict internal company data, and ways that client and agency researchers can overcome difficulties associated with not invented here and denial when management are faced with uncomfortable findings from customer satisfaction surveys. The third section addresses some of the more specific reporting issues relating to customer satisfaction and loyalty research, and the final section looks at what should happen after the results have been reported to management.

> [The War Office kept three sets of figures:] one to mislead the public, another to mislead the Cabinet, and a third to mislead itself.
>
> **Herbert Asquith (in *Horne*, 1962)**

Once the analysis phase is complete, the next step in the process is to produce a report of the findings from the survey (or surveys if it is part of a tracking programme). In *Measuring Customer Service Effectiveness* Sarah Cook quotes a study by Customer Champions that shows 65 per cent of the results of customer feedback surveys are not listened to or acted upon. In her opinion this is because in many organizations senior managers do not make an effort to act on the results or monitor whether any action has been taken (Cook, 2004: 4). This may be partly because of a lack of attention when the survey was originally commissioned to how it would link to the business goals. It may result from a lack of planning about how to distribute the findings to all those areas in an organization that could benefit from them.

THE PHYSICAL PRESENTATION OF CUSTOMER SATISFACTION AND LOYALTY RESEARCH REPORTS

Changes in the reporting of market research data

The reporting of market research has changed quite dramatically over the past 20 years. In the 1970s and 1980s it was usual for written reports to be produced. These usually contained highly technical appendices with details of the sampling method, a copy of the questionnaire and any stimulus materials that were used for the fieldwork, response rates, and sometimes even a copy of the client s original briefing document and the corresponding proposal. In addition, the reports contained chapters outlining the background to the survey, the business and research objectives, executive summary, and detailed sections describing the main findings, supported by tables and graphs inserted in appropriate places. These reports often took a couple of weeks to produce. Some clients would also ask for a presentation of the results before the final written report was issued, so that if any matters arose during the presentation they could be incorporated into the final report.

However, these days it is very rare for such reports to be produced. Usually clients require top-line findings as soon as possible after the close of fieldwork, then a presentation-style report a couple of weeks later. In addition, these presentation reports are usually shorter and more incisive than the older-style written reports. If the survey is a continuous one, reporting can take many forms, some of which are described below.

The different types of customer satisfaction report

Whatever style it is produced or presented in, the report is one of the few tangible outputs from the client s investment in the research. As a result it can have a major influence on how management views the survey and the agency that produced the report. It can also have an impact on the credentials of the internal research (or project commissioning) department. The person writing the report has to think very carefully about the intended audience for the document, and adopt an appropriate style for it. For example, if the intended audience is to be senior or board-level management the report needs to be short, to the point and authoritative in style and content.

Management consultancies are very good at producing these kinds of report. They do not dwell on the technical research aspects of the project, preferring to present these as an addendum or in a separate volume. They concisely review the background and objectives, then present their summary and conclusions. If at this time the audience is interested in seeing more, the consultancy presents more detailed findings either there and then if time is available, or in a separate report or presentation. In addition, their reports often allude to past research or projects and other sources of corroborative data. In other words, their reports and presentations are well constructed, authoritative, and concise yet thorough.

However, the more traditional method of reporting is still popular in some areas. For example, some government departments and some industry bodies prefer summary tabular reports with specific references to computer tables.

Market research reports are often quite different from those produced by management consultancies. The professional associations recommend that market research reports should contain, or at least make available, all the information necessary for replicating the survey. This means that they should contain the questionnaire, fieldwork procedures and instructions for interviewers, appropriate field stimulus materials such as show cards (if a face-to-face survey), details of the sampling method, and specific technical details (such as details of any weighting that has been applied, response rates and incentives used). If subcontractors have been used for the project, they too must be mentioned. Finally there must be a clear distinction between the results and any interpretation of the findings.

Deciding what types of reports are required

The client is best placed to determine the types of reports his or her organization will require. Client researchers know whether their senior managers like short one-page summaries, and whether they require a presentation to be made to them, with a leave behind report for their records and for circulating to their colleagues. Often clients need to add further information to an agency s report, either as support or to provide senior management with further pertinent information about the project (such as why it has been undertaken, or what the next steps should be).

If the survey is a wave of a continuous programme of research, it may well be that a simple report is required, showing the key metrics and how they are changing (or not) over the course of the survey. Some clients know their managers prefer a more graphical style of report, while others prefer a more tabular style. Whatever the situation, the agency should be able to produce what is required. Some clients have even provided their agencies with internal data so that it can be reported alongside the external customer data. In this way they can demonstrate how changes in internal performance have an effect on customer perceptions.

Methods of delivering customer satisfaction data

Today there is a huge choice of ways that data can be delivered to clients. They start with the relatively straightforward sets of printed data tables and reports, and continue through to providing data files in various software packages such as Quanvert, SPSS and SAS. In large organizations there are intranet sites where results from the surveys can be posted. This may be seen as a good way to spread the information rapidly across the organization. It is arguably also a rather lazy way of distributing the data. It relies on employees taking the trouble to seek out the information. Is it not far better for the internal client researcher to send details of the key relevant findings to management and others who could benefit from them in the organization, and invite the recipients to get in touch if they would like more details, or to provide them with a more tailored presentation of the findings? This is not to say that an intranet is not worth using, but it should be seen as just one vehicle among many for the dissemination of the research findings.

How to decide what to include and what to exclude from reports

As Lewis Carroll wrote in *Alice s Adventures in Wonderland*, begin at the beginning, the king said gravely, and go on till you come to the end;

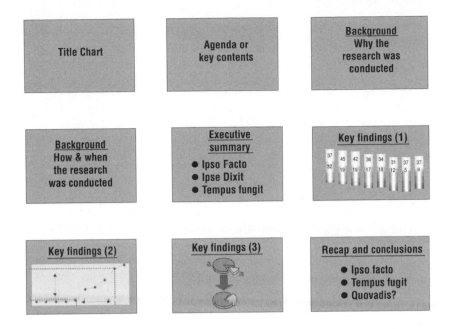

Figure 11.1   *A sample report storyboard outline*

then stop. This is very good advice for any budding report or presentation writer. The aim is to tell a relatively short, succinct story. Researchers new to report writing may find that adopting the method advertising agencies use to present their embryonic ideas for new television commercials is a good starting point. They put together a storyboard, a series of vignettes that describe frame by frame how the commercial will appear. Mapping out the broad outline of a presentation or report in a similar way can make the process much less daunting (see Figure 11.1).

For example, start with a chart showing the main points that will be covered in the presentation/report (the agenda). Then follow this with no more than four charts on the research background, methodology and a glossary of key terms (if required). Next should come no more than two charts showing the executive summary . Deciding what should be in this is very easy. Imagine you get into a lift and the chief executive gets in right behind you. He or she greets you, then says, Tell me the key things I need to know from the latest customer satisfaction survey. You know you have just 30 seconds before the first of you gets out of the lift.

Anything else can follow in the main findings, to which the next 20 or so charts should be devoted. These should be structured around the key objectives set for the research. Finally, the presentation/report should end with a couple of summary charts and then, if required, the researcher s recommendations. Any additional technical details should be made available as appendices.

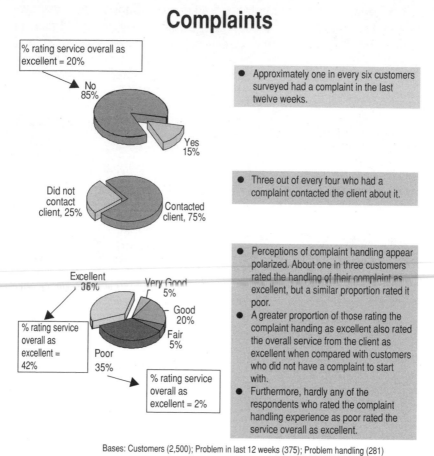

Figure 11.2 *A sample slide with report findings and interpretative comments*

Adding interpretative 'commentary' in reports

Many research presentation reports include a set of charts summarizing the agency s conclusions or interpretation of the data. Some agencies also provide such interpretative commentary on each chart in the report. There are certain advantages to this. The main one is that no matter to whom the report is circulated, the commentary on the key finding for each chart is there for everyone to see. This helps ensure that everyone reading the chart will, at the very least, see what conclusion the agency has drawn from the chart. Figure 11.2 shows a sample of this approach in practice.

However, there are drawbacks to the agency interpreting the data. For example, it might not have been made aware of changes within the client organization that could affect the interpretation. Or, as in the case presented below, the agency might not have been given the full facts of the case, making it very difficult for its staff to reach the correct (and obvious, to those in the know) conclusion.

CASE STUDY

An agency presented the results of its client's marketing promotion, which showed that the sales of the meat it was promoting had risen dramatically during the promotion period. There were smiles and nods all around the management table. Then the results of meat sales through competitive outlets were revealed. All bar one competitor had seen sales remain static. However for one competitor sales had risen even more than they had in the sponsor's company.

The presenter expected to see the mood in the room change. It did, but not in the way expected. The mood became even lighter and brighter. The agency could not determine why the competitor's sales had done so well, and the suggested explanation on the chart was that the competitive offer had been even better than the sponsor's.

In fact the sponsor had supplied the meal for both promotions, so was delighted to see that sales had risen in both its and the 'competitor's' outlets.

Lesson to be learnt

Disclosing to the agency the full facts of the situation enables it to focus its analysis and interpretation on the relevant business aspects of the survey. It also would have eased the concern the agency executives faced in presenting data for which there was no obvious explanation. Finally, if the interpretation had been wildly off the mark, not only would the agency presenter have lost some credibility in the eyes of the audience, but so too would the client researcher (who, after all, had put his or her own reputation on the line by recommending to management that this particular agency was the best one for the job).

The importance of timeliness

Ask any client how important it is for a project to be delivered on time, and he or she will tell you it is very important. However, I wonder whether all agency personnel are equally convinced about this. There are a host of reasons why projects can run late. Maybe the sample is not delivered on time or the client does not approve the final version of the questionnaire on schedule. Perhaps customers had far more to say than expected in their verbatim answers, and so there is a greater volume of comments to be coded or edited (or both). However, when it comes to reporting the findings, clients generally frown upon delays.

Often agencies fail to realize that often the management decision for which the research is intended to contribute guidance simply cannot be delayed. Business involves a degree of risk, and market research is often undertaken to reduce this level of risk, but if the data is not available at the time the business decision has to be made, it will be made without the research. This can reflect poorly on any internal researcher who has promised that the data will be available in time to contribute to the decision.

THE DISSEMINATION OF RESEARCH DATA

How quickly findings should be reported

Usually clients want the data from their customer satisfaction survey as soon as it is available. Often this reflects an understandable wish to see the results. Other factors can bring pressure to see the data as soon as possible after the close of interviewing. The client s internal management might have arranged a meeting where the data could make a valuable contribution to the discussion. The research could be part of an incentive programme, where staff will be rewarded if the level of customer satisfaction has increased. It may even be an impatience to get the project completed. After all, for many clients there is a hiatus while the interviewing is in progress, and a concern that management may lose interest in the findings if there is too long a period without any news or updates.

The 'rush to data'

Richard Bierck, a freelance financial writer based in Princeton, made a couple of very telling observations about this rush to data in a *Harvard Management Communication* article, Are you reaching your customers? (2000). He points out that:

> too often marketing people assume the data s the thing — that it tends to yield up significance on its face. However, often this isn t the case. The data may tell you something is happening, but not necessarily why. Those who make assumptions about why often miss the target.

Having a lot of data does not mean the organization has a deep and clear understanding of its customers. It takes time to extract meaning from the data, and often it is necessary to probe quite deeply into it to find the nuggets that help explain what is going on. Failure to allow time for this data mining will result in superficial analysis, and perhaps worse, misleading interpretations of the data, as seen in the case study.

CASE STUDY

A few years ago a bank introduced a new, enhanced computer system for counter staff to use in its branches. Naturally there were expectations of a few teething troubles, but when the customer satisfaction tracking survey started reporting that customers were becoming increasingly negative about the amount of time they had to queue, management decided it had to take action immediately. It set about trying to come up with innovative solutions to make the queuing situation more palatable during what it saw as a period of transition.

However, further analysis of the data in the survey, coupled with investigations by the client's research team, suggested another factor contributing to the increase in queuing. Around the same time as the introduction of the new computer system, the bank had opened a number of new call centres to handle customer enquiries. These call centres were brought on stream very quickly as part of a strategy to have all calls handled by customer service centres. This was partly in response to customer concerns about branch staff not having the time to answer the telephones when they rang, or not returning calls. Therefore these new call centres had to cope with a volume of customer calls at a time when they were still hiring staff and training them about the bank's policies and procedures, its products and services, and so on. Not surprisingly, the average length of time it took to handle customer enquiries was longer than expected. Customers found it difficult to get through to the centres (as the lines were often busy) or found that the staff were not able to handle all their requirements. As a result, they did something they knew worked: they went to their branches.

These two factors acting in concert had contributed to the increase in queuing. Once this new piece of analysis came to light, management was able to take corrective action in the call centres. This quickly led to more customer calls being handled on first contact, and not long afterwards customer perceptions of queuing started to recover to the levels seen prior to the introduction of the new computer system.

Factors influencing how often research findings should be reported

Sample size

The frequency with which reports should be issued for a customer satisfaction tracking survey depends upon a number of factors. In surveys where sample sizes are relatively low, reporting data on a weekly or monthly basis can be problematical. The data may appear to fluctuate even though the changes are not statistically significant. This can lead to difficulties within the client organization, when client researchers try to explain to their internal sponsors that the changes that appear in the data are not in fact real changes. However, if it is decided to combine monthly data into longer periods (such as three-month rolling periods), while the trend data may appear to be more stable, it runs the risk of becoming a lagged indicator of change, because changes occurring in one month are being diluted (or masked) by the data from the other two months. Obviously, the greater the period being combined, the greater the amount of masking that can take place.

Familiarity

Another problem with issuing frequent reports is that internal clients may well stop reading them after the first few have been issued, and only look for key results. This can result in important findings being overlooked. Here the style of reports can make an important contribution. If the reports are issued on a frequent basis, it is often worthwhile having a special section that reports on particular aspects of the business, with a new aspect being selected for each report. This provides a reason for management to read each report. Another good technique is to provide verbatim comments on each report. I have yet to come across a client who asks for customers comments to be excluded from a report.

Flat trend lines

Even more worrying is that if the results remain stubbornly similar from month to month, management may become disheartened and start to look for faults with the tracking survey — a kind of shoot the messenger situation. Managers might even start to question whether the right questions are being asked, whether the right people are being surveyed, whether the right analysis is being conducted, and so forth. However, flat trend lines are often worthy of very close analysis. They may be flat because the most dissatisfied customers decline to participate in the survey, and not being represented, do not depress the scores. To determine if this is happening, it is necessary to look at the company s overall customer retention levels. Are they rising, stable or falling? If the latter, the chances are that the survey is not completely representative of the company s customer base.

Ways to overcome problems with reporting customer satisfaction trend data

Of course there are a number of ways that researchers can address these types of issues. First and foremost, when the project is set up, they should manage internal sponsors expectations (or for an agency, client expectations). They should query what results managers expect to see, how quickly they expect the results to change, and most importantly, what plans are in place (or being considered) for follow-up actions once the results start to be issued. As the project progresses the researchers should keep in touch with the post research actions, and where possible conduct additional analyses on the data to show how the changes that are taking place within the organization are being reflected by changes in customer opinions. Sometimes there can be a lag between the two, and it is incumbent on the researchers to manage their clients expectations in this regard.

Who should present the key research findings to management

One of the key decisions client researchers have to make is whether to ask the agency to present the findings to management. Having the data directly presented to the client s internal management has many benefits but it also has risks. If the agency is not thoroughly prepared, its staff will not only discredit themselves (and possibly damage their prospects for future business), they can also discredit the client researcher who had entrusted them with the project. Often this situation will not arise because if client researchers have any concerns they will not let the agency present the data, but present it themselves instead. However, on some occasions the agency may be asked to present the results of the data because the client is aware that the findings will not be well received. Having an outside company present can introduce a degree of objectivity that will allow any questions or discussion to be less emotive than if the results had been presented by an internal company member.

Preparing for a presentation of customer satisfaction data

If the decision is to have the data presented by an agency, some simple steps can be taken to ensure the presentation is a success.

■ Before the presentation, the client researcher should send out an invitation to the appropriate management team. The invitation should include an agenda for the meeting and some appropriate background materials to set the scene (such as a condensed version of the research brief, or at the very least details of the business and research objectives). The researchers should also ask whether there are any particular matters that attendees would like to see covered during the course of the presentation.

- The client researcher should also provide the agency with the names of the attendees, their role in the organization and an indication of the types of issues that may be of interest to them.
- The agency researcher should determine what equipment the client will provide and what the agency will need to bring. He or she should also find out how much time is available for the presentation and discussion. In addition he/she should determine what reports or other materials need to be brought to the presentation.
- At the presentation, the agency personnel should arrive early to set up the venue and ensure that all their equipment is working. They should agree with the client on the best room layout. Most presentations are boardroom style, with the attendees sitting around a table. This is not always the best way, as people nearest the screen have an uninterrupted view of what is being presented while those further back may have to bob and weave to get sight of the screen. However, this layout works well if the main emphasis is on the follow-up discussion, as all the people around the table are able to participate in it face to face. If however the purpose of the presentation is to share learning or information, with minimal discussion, a theatre-style layout may be better.
- Once everyone is in the room, the client researcher should provide a succinct introduction, thanking the attendees and providing a brief synopsis of why the research was undertaken. This is important, especially if a few weeks have elapsed since the project was commissioned, as it brings the audience back to the point when the project was first commissioned. It also enables the audience to view the findings in light of the original situation rather than focusing on their current concerns (which could be different from those for which the project was originally designed). The client researcher should introduce the agency staff. It is also good practice for all members of the audience to introduce themselves, and for the presenters to ask what they are hoping to discover from attending the presentation. This last point enables the agency presenter to fix on who to address particular aspects of the presentation to.
- At the start of the presentation the presenter should outline the agenda, how long he or she expects the presentation to last, and whether he/she is willing to take questions during the presentation or at the end. Unless the client has requested it, technical details about the project should be kept to a minimum. Normally audiences accept that the agency is the technical expert and that the technical element of the project has been fully discussed and agreed with their own internal researcher. Therefore they will be

less interested in this aspect of the project. They are there to hear the findings and the agency s interpretation of them.

■ When the presentation ends, the agency should invite questions. Sometimes there are none. If this happens, a good technique to get a conversation started is to ask the attendees if the results were what they expected, and if so, what steps they think they can take to improve them.

Handling results that conflict with internal data

One of the more exciting aspects of presenting customer satisfaction research data is when agency data conflict with the client s internal metrics. Not surprisingly, clients usually conclude that their internal data is correct and that the data being presented is incorrect.

This can happen particularly when presenting data about customer complaints. Most companies track the volume of customer complaints. If the survey research reports that the percentage of customer complaints is increasing, while the internal metrics suggest it is falling, the researchers will need to be able to reconcile the apparent conflict. There are a host of reasons for this situation to arise. They include:

■ The client company defines a complaint in a different way from customers.
■ Time periods may differ. The client may be referring to a complaint received in the present calendar month or in the previous four weeks, while the questionnaire asked respondents if they had made a complaint in the last month.
■ Client staff may be recording customer complaints as enquiries rather than complaints.
■ Client company staff may not consider issues that are resolved on first contact as complaints.

A trickier situation can arise when the results from the survey appear to contradict the results from another survey, particularly when the new results are worse. There are a number of aspects to investigate when this happens. It is also very important not to jump to conclusions before completing the investigation. The critical areas to look at are:

■ The sample: are there any obvious differences in who has been interviewed?
■ The questions: is the wording identical?
■ The position of the questions within the two surveys: is the context the same?

- Timing: have the surveys been conducted at broadly the same time and not affected by any external influences?
- The research methods: any differences?
- The analysis: have the results been calculated in the same manner?

Usually one of these factors will account for the differences.

'Not invented here' and 'denial'

Not everyone who receives the results from a customer satisfaction survey will accept the findings. There can be a number of reasons for this, arising from personal experience of evidence to the contrary, a lack of commitment to the programme because individuals felt there was a better way to conduct the research, and denial because the results are too unpalatable to contemplate. Let us examine each of these situations in more detail.

Personal experience suggests the customer satisfaction survey data is wrong

Some clients run a business where they are in personal contact with customers (such as a small local retailer or restaurateur), or work in a large customer service department where they receive calls daily from customers. In such situations they naturally feel they know their customers and relate to them. If they receive feedback from a customer survey indicating not all the customers are happy with the service from the organization, they may feel that something cannot be right with the survey, so a natural reaction is to reject its findings.

But is this sensible? For example, on occasions people stay in a hotel and the checkout staff ask if everything was all right during their stay. The guests have not been impressed with the service or with the quality of the food in the restaurant, but have decided they will not be staying there again, so they cannot be bothered to make a fuss, and mumble that everything was fine. The staff report to the manager that everyone checking out that morning claimed to be happy with their stay, and the manager relaxes in the knowledge that yet again the hotel has been full of contented customers. However, the manager would have a different opinion if she heard what these customers said to their friends and colleagues on returning home. So it is with customer satisfaction surveys. Respondents often report differently about their experience than they do directly to client staff. What is important, however, is that what they tell the researchers is real . Furthermore, why should respondents be less than honest with the interviewer? While one or two respondents may stretch the truth or embellish their responses, if a majority of respondents report similar experiences, there is a real likelihood that the service experience is as reported.

The research could have been conducted differently ('not invented here')

A more difficult situation is when someone does not want to embrace the research because he or she feels there was a better way to conduct it. If this situation emerges at the reporting stage, the internal client researcher needs to understand why these concerns were not picked up earlier. Of course some people may have been open about their concerns from the start of the project, and in these circumstances it is often worth having personal follow-up meetings with them to see where there is common ground and in what areas differences continue to exist. Rarely have I come across a situation where such differences cannot be overcome through further discussions. Often the reasons for the objections are valid, and future surveys can address the areas of concern.

Facing unpalatable news (or 'denial')

Denial is often the immediate reaction that happens when the results from a survey are very different from those expected. In such circumstances it is important to avoid being confrontational. Often it is best for the researcher to suggest that he or she will review the data to see if there is any more learning to be had from the survey, then reconvene in a few days to discuss the findings further and see what internal data the client has on the subject.

CASE STUDY

The problem

The management of a large company that prided itself on the quality of its customer service received a presentation from a research agency that had just completed its quarterly customer satisfaction tracking survey. The results were disappointing, and the attendees at the presentation became quite aggressive towards the presenter. They could not understand how these results could be representative, as year in and year out the company had won industry awards for the quality of its customer service. It was agreed that the agency would return in a couple of weeks following a rigorous audit of its fieldwork and analysis (to check that no mistakes had occurred) for a further debrief.

The agency was very confident about its findings but nonetheless carried out a thorough check of all its processes and the data from the survey. It could find nothing that changed the initial conclusions.

The senior manager started the second meeting by stating that his fellow managers had dismissed the findings of the survey, but

---

had decided to conduct some personal calls themselves to the company, and also to go unannounced and spend a couple of hours in the call centre listening to the way employees dealt with customers. 'It was an eye-opener,' he said. Everything that had been reported by customers had been subsequently borne out by the investigation. The managers admitted that they had been in denial. The company put in place a raft of training and coaching initiatives, reviewed policies and procedures, and invited the research agency to undertake further waves of research to measure progress.

Reviewing the frequency of customer satisfaction surveys

Sometimes it may be more sensible to conduct customer satisfaction surveys less frequently than originally planned, but on larger samples (for consumer and those business-to-business surveys where this is possible). In this way there is time after the initial wave and before the next wave of the survey for the client to consider the findings, put appropriate actions in place, and allow sufficient time for these actions to filter through to customers. This also allows a research programme to maintain its momentum and the support of its management.

There is no set rule about how large the interval should be between waves of research. It depends on the organization, the size of the task and the funds available. If, for example, customer satisfaction with a change programme that is quite large and complex is being monitored, it is important to be able to measure all aspects of the customer experience in some detail — and many parts of the organization may be affected. Imagine the client has decided to change its refund and returns policies in an effort to save costs. No doubt it will have informed its customers about the change — maybe by letter, possibly by adding messages to the call centre automated welcome and thanks for contacting us greeting, or by putting signs up in its establishments. However, it is also important that the organization has thoroughly briefed all staff about the changes and the reasons for them, then ensured that staff, especially those in direct contact with customers, fully understand the rationale for the change.

If the research programme shows an adverse response to the change (or through the use of verbatim comments, captures growing customer unease about it), management must be counselled not to react immediately to the first signs of negative feedback. If the change programme is still in its early phases, not all the internal communications and training may have been completed. Of course, in some cases the reaction may be so strong and vitriolic that management should sit up and take notice, but if this is the case then there is likely to be supporting evidence of the size of the problem from other sources within the company, such as direct customer complaints or media coverage.

CUSTOMER SATISFACTION AND LOYALTY REPORTING ISSUES

The use of composite scores

Many customer satisfaction and loyalty surveys these days use composite scores for tracking and reporting their results. These composite scores are often based on a combination of results from several questions. Sometimes this score also reflects a particular theory of what drives customer satisfaction or loyalty. For example, a composite score might be based on customers rating of the organization s overall service quality, their willingness to recommend the organization to others, and the likelihood of their considering the organization for future purchases. This composite score therefore contains data about current perceptions of service, advocacy and loyalty (where loyalty is represented as future purchase intention). However there are many other ways to build composite scores (for example, based on overall service quality, or customers ratings of the organization s brand values and advocacy). The key question for researchers is, should they report a composite score (an index) or a straight percentage score?

Benefits of using a simple score rather than a composite score

The advantage of reporting a straight percentage score (for example, 20 per cent of customers rate the overall service from company x as excellent) is clarity. Everyone understands what the score means, and more importantly can relate to it and any targets set based on it. For example, 20 per cent reporting the overall service as excellent means, in straightforward terms, that one in every five customers surveyed rated the overall quality of service as excellent. Furthermore, if the organization wants to set targets for improvement, they too can be easily communicated. For example, Currently one in five customers rate our overall service excellent. Next year I would like to see one in three customers rate us excellent.

Benefits of using a composite score

The advantages of using a composite score for measuring customer satisfaction and loyalty are the stability of composite scores and what they represent. Most individuals have a view of an organization that has been built up over the years through a combination of word-of-mouth recommendations, personal experience, advertising and so on. As a result, a score comprising a range of these elements is more likely to represent how the organization is seen. This is the basis for many of the research models mentioned in Chapter 2 that purport to measure customer satisfaction and loyalty.

Composite scores are also more stable than a single score in so far as each of the elements accounts for only a portion of the total score. So unless customer opinions change for all the elements that comprise the score, the likelihood of the score changing dramatically is less than where a single score is used to report customer satisfaction.

However, the consequence of this is that composite scores are harder to move over time, so the task of maintaining interest in the project over time becomes more difficult, as managers begin to question whether all their programmes and investment in changing customer perceptions of service are having any effect.

Calculating composite scores at an individual respondent or at an aggregated level

Another aspect that researchers need to consider when reporting composite scores is whether to calculate the score at an individual respondent level or at an aggregated level. For example, let us suppose the results on a composite score are based on three questions: overall service quality, advocacy and likelihood to purchase again from the company. The question arises how to handle situations where not every respondent has answered each of these questions. An aggregated approach simply calculates a mean score for each of the three questions based on those respondents answering the question, and applies whatever weighting factor has been chosen for calculating the composite score. However, an alternative approach is to determine a composite score for each individual respondent (thereby representing his or her own view of the organization according to the research parameters), then sum the individual scores to calculate the overall score. In this scenario, if respondents do not answer one of the elements their score is calculated based on the maximum they could have scored from the questions answered.

The problem that arises is that this ends up with a different score from the aggregated approach, and management tend to ask which is the more accurate. In fact, neither is more accurate . They are just different ways of reporting a composite score based on an internal view of how customer satisfaction and loyalty should be reported. Therefore it does not matter which approach is adopted as long as it is applied consistently.

POST REPORTING

Agency responsibilities following client receipt of data

Once the client has been sent the data, the research agency s tasks are not over. There are certain actions that must be taken to safeguard respondents data. All hard copy and electronic address lists that have been provided must be held securely until destruction, and when the time comes for destroying the records, staff must ensure the steps taken are appropriate for the confidentiality of the data being destroyed. It is paramount that the research agency fully complies with local legislation concerning the protection of data. These requirements vary from country to country.

Client responsibilities following receipt of the data

Meanwhile, at the client company there may be demands for various uses to be made of the data from the survey. For example, publication of the findings from the survey may be requested as part of a marketing or PR campaign. If this is the case, then in the UK the client researcher needs to ensure that the technical details about the research are available for scrutiny, and that other findings are made available. The agency researchers must also check any client-prepared materials before publication to ensure that the published results are not misleading. Should the agency consider that the findings published by the client are misleading, the agency must refuse permission for its name to be used further in connection with the misrepresented findings. In addition it needs to publish a statement to the effect that the results have been represented in a misleading way, as well as publish the appropriate technical details to correct any misleading reporting. These safeguards help ensure that market research retains the confidence (and also the willing participation) of the general public. Similar requirements exist in many other countries.

Providing sponsors with the facilities to conduct their own analyses

Most quantitative customer satisfaction tracking surveys create a huge volume of data for analysis and reporting. One aspect therefore that researchers need to consider is whether they should provide their internal sponsors with access to the survey databases, or with software to enable them to conduct their own analyses. After all, the best way to ensure that research data gets used is to encourage ownership of the data, and what better way to encourage ownership than to provide the internal sponsors with the facilities to conduct their own analyses? By encouraging more widespread use of the data, a client organization can learn more about its customers. After all, the intellectual capacity of an organization does not reside solely in the market research department. The whole organization benefits from shared learning.

If client researchers distribute databases or other analysis packages to their internal sponsors, how can they ensure that the same message is being disseminated throughout the organization? The answer of course is that they cannot. But they can take a number of steps to manage the situation. First, they can create a best practices manual in which the principles of data analysis and interpretation are spelt out, together with examples drawn from the project. Second, they can issue accreditations to individuals who have been through a special training programme on how to analyse and interpret data, as well as how to use any software that is distributed for analysis purposes. Third, they can hold forums or workshops where users of the data come to share learning and to pick up ideas for further analyses, either from the research suppliers or from other interested parties. In larger organizations centres of excellence can be developed where different parts of the organization take responsibility for exploring, in depth, specific aspects of customer satisfaction and loyalty.

It has been my experience that the more people who work with the data inside a client organization, the better the return on investment. Not only does it take courage for researchers to allow this to happen, it also requires a change in their role in the organization. They have to become facilitators and enablers rather than information providers. Old-fashioned concepts about knowledge is power need to be squashed, and a climate of shared learning and experience needs to be put in place. This can mean fundamental cultural changes for many large organizations.

Determining whether the investment has provided value for money

Market research is like any other investment in so far as at some time a researcher in a client organization will be asked to justify the investment in a survey. Because many customer satisfaction and loyalty surveys tend to be quantitative and repeated on a fairly regular basis, the likelihood of the finance department or other senior management requesting an audit of the programme and a justification of the investment is high. How can a client researcher provide a response to this type of request? After all, it is no different (except perhaps in scale) from a request to justify investment in customer service departments, customer relationship management programmes and the like.

Faced with such a request, I believe the client researcher needs to be able to demonstrate the following:

- The project followed established practices for commissioning any large-scale project: namely, three competitive quotes were obtained. In addition, the quote selection process was shown to be fair and unbiased. Ongoing checks have been taken to ensure that the programme remains competitively priced.
- Post research actions have been taken by internal sponsors and the results of these actions can be determined financially. This almost certainly will involve the researcher knowing (or finding out) what sponsors have done with the data and what added value has resulted from their actions. Sometimes these actions have clear direct costs and benefits (such as re-engineering processes resulting in head count savings or improved efficiencies). Sometimes they are more nebulous (as with re-evaluating the training programmes given to front-line staff).
- Some client companies fuse internal data with the data from the survey and produce models to predict future customer behaviour (such as willingness to purchase additional products or the risk of losing customers). Where permitted by law, companies can then track what the customers who were surveyed actually did in the months following their participation in the survey, and therefore can validate the findings. When this occurs, management often has more faith in the findings from the survey and so is more likely to take action on the results of the survey.
- Where the customer satisfaction and loyalty survey has an element of competitive benchmarking, any perceived gain or loss in market share can be given a financial perspective. Here data modelling provides

useful support. For example, if the organization knows the average customer spend on its product and can determine from the survey its share of wallet, it is possible to determine how much additional customer business would be obtained from increasing the share of wallet by a certain percentage. Naturally this incremental business will come at a cost, but as it is from existing customers, the cost should be lower than if the organization was trying to acquire new customers. The cost of the research programme needs to be included in this calculation.

Other contributions that customer satisfaction research can provide

Strategic planning

Strategic planning is one of the major beneficiaries from a well-planned customer satisfaction and loyalty research programme. Most strategic planners have an external perspective of the business, usually focused on political, regulatory, social and economic factors as well as competitive information. Customer satisfaction and loyalty research provides an additional dimension — that of the perceptions that customers and potential customers have of the organization. If, for example, internal data shows there is an ageing customer base, and customer satisfaction surveys show that customers have very traditional values, any major change in strategic direction taken by the organization may result in a loss of existing customers (as seen in the case study).

CASE STUDY

A multinational organization that had a very profitable business in Switzerland discovered through its market research that there was a segment of the market that was not attracted to its products or services. This segment saw the company as being old-fashioned and out of touch with the needs of younger business people. In response the marketing and strategic planners decided that what was required was a change of image. The organization's advertising agency came up with a new campaign that would directly appeal to the younger business person.

Not long after the launch of this campaign, the number of new customers increased dramatically, with most coming from the targeted segment. However, the number of customers defecting to competitive organizations also rose, and perceptions of the company as reported in its customer satisfaction survey became more negative. When asked why this was, the defectors said that the

---

company had obviously changed direction, and from what they had seen in the advertisements, it was obvious that the company was no longer interested in them. As a result, customer loyalty was badly hurt by this campaign (which was subsequently withdrawn).

Training

Many large client organizations have education programmes. Some even have internal academies of excellence. Usually these academies are there to provide training for on-the-job business skills or to provide services to employees (such as pre-retirement counselling or retraining programmes). Customer satisfaction and loyalty research can often provide much useful information to support these internal training academies, and so they should not be overlooked when data from the surveys are being disseminated.

Employee incentive programmes

As has been mentioned elsewhere in this book, data from many customer satisfaction surveys are used as part of employee commitment (reward) programmes. The idea is that employees can be encouraged to be customer focused by rewarding or incentivizing them based on how customers perceive the service received from them. Naturally the data for the incentive programme has to focus on those aspects that can be directly attributed to the actions of the employees concerned, or the programme runs the risk of becoming a disincentive. If customer-facing employees feel that matters are outside their control (for example, that the overall perception that customers have of the company as a whole are influenced by company policy), they may become embittered because they feel nothing they can do will result in their receiving the suggested rewards.

There are other risks associated with such programmes. For example, it is important to be careful about the choice of incentive. Some employees react better to recognition programmes than reward programmes. In addition, if staff are rewarded with extra payments for something they should be doing as a natural part of their job responsibilities, does it suggest the organization was not paying them enough to begin with? Another matter management needs to consider is how other employees not on the programme will react to it. For example, if front-line staff rely on support from colleagues in the computer department to keep the computers running trouble-free, and on colleagues in finance to pay invoices or credit accounts in a timely manner, why should staff in these departments not be incentivized as well? After all, if they are not doing their job properly, the volume of customer contacts will be greater.

CLOSING COMMENTS

Reporting is an important issue because it is one of the few tangibles that clients have to show for their investment. Therefore time and money spent on getting this part of the research process right is important. However, it is the content and insight provided in the reports and the follow-up actions that clients take that differentiate the best from the rest.

For agency researchers this requires that they continually strive to keep abreast of developments in research as well as in the markets in which their clients operate. For client researchers it means that they have to continually communicate with their sponsors and others in the organization to ensure that the best return on the company s investment is achieved. In addition, as the only really independent voice of the consumer within the organization, client researchers have to rise above issues such as company politics and learn how to overcome resistance to bad news or other efforts to sabotage the voice of customers from being heard loudly and clearly where it matters.

Part V

WHAT LIES AHEAD?

12 What lies ahead?

This chapter briefly recaps the key themes in the book and asks the question: what does the future hold for researching customer satisfaction and loyalty?

> I have been in this business 36 years. I've learned a lot – and most of it doesn't apply any more.
> **Charles Exley, CEO, NCR Corporation (Clemmer, 1993: 76)**

RECAP

This book has been written as an introduction to researching customer satisfaction and loyalty. Its aim has been to demonstrate that while there are many theories and models to help organizations become more customer-centric, there is no simple management model or research technique that will provide a definitive answer to the question: what drives customer satisfaction and loyalty? What can be said is that customer-centric organizations inherently believe that a link exists between customer satisfaction, loyalty and profits. They use market research to provide them with consumer insights into possible underlying causes of satisfaction and dissatisfaction. However, they recognize that there are a number of aspects that need to be carefully considered when designing, conducting and interpreting market research.

In addition, the book has demonstrated that market researchers can provide a valuable service to companies in the measurement of customer satisfaction and loyalty. However, market researchers themselves, both within client organizations and as suppliers, need to broaden their knowledge in the other disciplines of business, from finance to operations, from marketing to strategic planning, and from employee relations to customer service. It is no longer acceptable for market researchers to be information providers. Management has many other sources of information and other knowledge workers on their staff they can consult. So unless market researchers become business 'enablers' they may find themselves being sidelined, with their role shrinking to that of data gatherers and processors.

WHAT THE FUTURE MIGHT HOLD FOR CUSTOMER SATISFACTION AND LOYALTY

Albert Einstein said, 'I never think of the future, it comes soon enough'[1] Researching customer satisfaction and loyalty is a little like looking at both the past and the future. But measuring satisfaction based on customers' perceptions of the experiences they have had, and asking consumers about their future intentions as measures of advocacy and loyalty, may not be enough in the future. Changes in population composition, demographics, legislation, technology and science are already reshaping the way organizations and individuals think and act.

The macro level changes occurring today

Following the Second World War there was a population explosion in the United States and Western European countries. The women of this post-war baby-boomer generation have had fewer children than either their mothers or grandmothers. As a result, the populations of most West European countries are now ageing. Furthermore, because of advancements in pharmaceuticals and changes in lifestyles, people are living on average much longer and healthier lives. As a result, it has been predicted that within the next 25 years there will be more people of retirement age than there are in employment. Perhaps not surprisingly, the burden this could have on taxation and living standards is a growing concern, particularly to politicians.

Moreover, unlike their parents and grandparents, many of this post-war generation have not been saving enough to see them through to a comfortable retirement. This was not considered a problem during the 1990s as the world's economies enjoyed a sustained period of economic growth. Everyone felt better off as their investments and values of their homes continued to rise year on year, and so they looked forward to a healthy and happy retirement. However, the collapse of the dot.com stocks was to herald the end of the good times, as a bear market took hold and people saw the values of their stocks and shares decline rapidly. This, together with actions taken by various governments (such as the introduction of the mandatory 35-hour working week in France, the stagnation of European economies as they try to get their member state economies to converge, huge increases in indirect taxation and other fiscal changes in the UK by its Labour government) has seen a major change in people's perceptions about work and their future prosperity.

Governments have reacted to these changes in a number of ways. They have stopped discouraging immigration, especially by younger people who will, it is hoped, ensure that sufficient people will remain in work to help fund the retired population. To some extent in Europe this has been 'enabled' by the advent of the single market, which allows the free movement of peoples across the region, as well as by the expansion of the Union itself through the addition of their east European neighbours. However, it has generally been recognized that immigration will not be enough on its own, and so governments are also looking at alternatives such as raising the retirement age, introducing legislation against age discrimination, and offering incentives to those people who do not take up their pension rights immediately on retirement.

In addition, there have been major changes in the shape of the economies of the United States and Western European countries. Now there are more jobs in the service industries and government than there are in manufacturing. Job growth has therefore been in either low-skilled service areas (such as serving in fast food outlets) or more highly skilled areas such as computer programming, software design, systems analysts, and in the professions, such as lawyers. In fact the legal profession has seen a huge expansion over the past decade, with the growth in what is termed the 'compensation culture' as more and more people resort to the law courts for compensation over breaches of their 'rights'.

Companies have reacted to all these changes in various ways. To bolster their share prices some have invested in new technology to reduce costs or gain a competitive advantage. Others have sought efficiencies by moving jobs abroad to countries where labour costs are lower. Some have created strategic alliances with other organizations, while others have become truly global in their operations. Some have recognized the value of older employees and actively developed programmes to enable them to stay at work past their normal retirement age. Others have changed their employee pension schemes to less lucrative ones or even ceased providing them altogether.

Many organizations have developed internet sites to provide a new channel through which to sell their products or services. Others have used the internet to encourage customers to take more responsibility for the management of their products and services (such as in internet banking, online share trading and online shopping). In this way organizations have been able to maintain or lower their cost base (and in some cases open up new revenue streams). Many have outsourced parts of their operations to reduce their cost base or to take advantage of the expertise offered by more specialist operations (such as call centres, many of which are now run by companies that have invested in such modern, high-tech equipment that only a few of the largest organizations could afford to match their investment levels if they wanted to keep their customer service operations in-house).

Impact of these macro-level changes

What impact have these changes had on consumers, particularly with regard to customer satisfaction and loyalty? On the positive side, many of the technological developments of the past 30 years or so have transformed our lives. These include e-mail (1971), mobile cellular phones (1973), home computers (1975), the Sony Walkman (1979), portable laptop computers (1981), MTV (1981), the World Wide Web/internet protocol HTTP and HTML language (1990), digital cameras for the consumer market (1994) and DVDs (1996).

While some of these developments are in the field of personal entertainment, two have had far-reaching implications for businesses. E-mail and the internet in particular have provided people with access to much more information than they have ever had in the past. Organizations recognized that the internet offered them opportunities to reduce costs while appearing to offer customers more choice and ability to manage their own affairs (such as self-service internet banking). But in taking advantage of these opportunities, consumers have discovered how very easy it is to become more independent. It has enabled them to discover, for example, how relatively easy it is to move their business from one supplier to another. So companies now have to work much harder to retain their customers' loyalty. New customer segments have emerged, and some organizations have reacted rather like spoilt children who have seen things not work out the way they were intended, by using more negative 'names' for some of these new customer segments (such as 'rate-chasers' or 'rate tarts' to describe those customers who give a company business only for a short period, then when the time comes to renew their contract, will happily move it to a new supplier if it offers a cheaper alternative).

Preferred styles of people management have also evolved over the last decade. The 1990s saw a shift in management thinking, to one that viewed employees no longer as costs to control, but rather as human resources to coach and get the best out of. With this change came the challenges of managing an increasingly diverse workforce in terms of gender, age, culture and so on. The Investors In People standard in the UK, which focuses on the management and development of an organization's workforce, was introduced and has become a well-respected business improvement tool, which establishes the link between employee and customer satisfaction. It follows therefore that research into external customer satisfaction and loyalty cannot be carried out in isolation from employee satisfaction and loyalty.

Markets and technologies are changing so fast these days that management needs to be continually testing new hypotheses and opportunities. It needs to recognize that many people are uncomfortable coping with change, and need encouragement and nurturing, and constant communication of the benefits of change – not just employees, but customers as well. New hypotheses need testing not only against what has gone before but also against reality. Is it relevant to the world as seen by the consumer? For example, the current trend towards off-shoring, and in some cases outsourcing, customer service-related positions may turn out to be more damaging in the longer term than was initially realized. Many customers have not welcomed this development as they realize the impact it will have on jobs and the local economy. This in turn affects employee perceptions of loyalty, as they question how 'safe' their jobs are. Many people still can recall how their or their parents', neighbours' or friends' careers and lives were affected by the ways companies enthusiastically embraced business process re-engineering less than a generation ago, and fear a re-run of those days.

It is interesting to observe the way companies react to new ideas, and how reluctant some are to take a contrary position. There was a saying in the 1970s that no one ever got fired for buying IBM computers, even though there were cheaper and sometimes better alternatives. Why? Because IBM produced reliable mainframe computers that were used by large, successful corporations around the world. In the case of adopting a customer-centric approach to organizational structure, I am reminded of the company that decided to locate its marketing, operations, finance and market research teams on the same floor of its building, and then to locate in the centre of the floor a mini customer service centre. The call centre agents in this centre spent 70 per cent of their time fielding customer calls and the other 30 per cent of their time working with the various departments to improve their customer focus. In addition, each member of the other departments had to spend one hour every three months listening to customer calls, then produce an action plan on what he or she was going to do differently as a result. The impact was immediate. Operations staff saw the effect that buying too cost-effectively ('cheaply' in customer terms) had in terms of customer anger, resentment and product returns. Marketing felt the reaction from the organization making promises that could not be delivered post sale, and so on.

Anyone who actively listens to what customers are actually saying in market research (and other forums) will know that customers no longer accept all change as for the better. They will find ways around what they see as 'barriers' to the service they want. Increasing numbers of customers are no longer prepared to put up with substandard service or poorly manufactured goods. They are more willing to complain, and expect organizations to listen and react to what they have to say. Changes in their perceptions of service are quick to feed through to companies and to the media. Through the internet, consumer pressure groups are emerging to highlight poor examples of customer service, or service that is no longer considered acceptable. From this could emerge a seed change where consumers set the agenda and companies become the 'suppliers' seeking their endorsement. For example, customers might only give their loyalty to those companies that have earned the right and have displayed loyalty to them. Related to this, there is some interesting work being conducted in the area of 'trust' and its link to customer satisfaction and relationship management. Work done by Elena Delgado-Ballester, Jose Luis Munuera-Alemán and María Jesús Yagüe-Guillén has shown for example that brand trust has had a significant influence on brand loyalty.[2]

Other changes could also be on the way. For example, the days of being able to charge fees for customers to access their own money or services may be limited. Customers in the future may demand fees for providing their opinions or for giving up their time to help an organization with its information needs.

Data protection legislation is providing consumers with more rights of access to information held about them, as well as stopping the less ethical companies from using customer data for purposes other than that for which it was originally collected.

But perhaps the biggest change that is emerging has not really received much publicity. This is a result of the developments in knowledge in neurology and the cognitive sciences about how our unconscious minds process data and evaluate products and services. Gerald Zaltman, Dan Hill and others are using the developments in these sciences to show the importance of emotions and memory on our reasoning processes. As Zaltman says:

> People who manage customer relationships must grasp how consumers store, retrieve and reconstruct memories of every interaction with a firm. These interactions may be direct, as when customers deal with a global account manager. They may also be indirect, as through word of mouth. And every new encounter alters a customer's recall of a prior encounter – often in trivial ways, but sometimes in significant ways. Thus every consumer interaction can make – or break – a brand.[3]

In 1997 Ken Parker and Trish Stuart investigated the intense loyalty achieved by football clubs, and posed the question why other products did not achieve the same degree of loyalty. Commenting upon how football clubs are scrutinized in a very public way each week during the playing season, and at the end of the season may experience the joy and elation of promotion or winning the championship (or the despair of relegation to a lower league), they point out:

> Indeed, whereas a lad might regret having 'Sharon' tattooed on his right arm following ten pints and a curry, he would be extremely unlikely to request the removal of 'West Ham United' from his other arm. In the USA, it is said that Harley Davidson is the most frequently requested tattoo, but what other brands could possibly engender such passion in this way?
>
> **(Parker and Stuart, 1997: 510)**

They also point out that choosing a football team to support is often undertaken at an early age 'before the brain has been sufficiently developed to understand rational alternatives' (ibid.) And in the UK, it is very uncommon to find people who have changed their allegiance once they have 'adopted' a football team to support.

Developments in these areas of science therefore have potentially enormous implications for the future developments of CRM, understanding customer loyalty – and also for market research.

THE CHALLENGES FACING RESEARCHERS OF CUSTOMER SATISFACTION AND LOYALTY

Neurological research has revealed that people do not think in linear hierarchical ways. As Zaltman says, 'they don't experience a cake by sampling a sequence of raw ingredients, they experience a fully baked cake' (2003: 5). So the challenge for market researchers is to re-examine the content of many customer satisfaction questionnaires and ask, are we focusing too much on asking customers about the ingredients (staff being polite, knowledgeable and so on) and not enough about the fully baked cake?

In addition, will researchers need to take more risks and start breaking the rules that have guided their profession to date, as suggested by Ian Brace, Clive Nancarrow and Julie Tinson in their paper at the 2004 Market Research Society conference (2004). For example, these eminent researchers point out that nearly all research results considered as 'significant' are those that achieve statistical significance at the 95 per cent level of confidence. But they offer the suggestion, why not let the sponsor or research buyer make the decision about the level of confidence on which it is prepared to have findings reported? After all, what is wrong about reporting that there is a 25 per cent risk a particular result does not represent the population? In most situations market research is just one contributor to a business decision, and so providing a high degree of precision in one area that is not matched in others may not be the best use of a company's investment.

It is probably fair to say that qualitative researchers are more used to experimenting with new ideas than quantitative researchers. So, for example, as broadband services continue to gain in popularity, online video groups should become more viable – thus providing researchers with the facility to observe body language and the like without arranging focus groups requiring personal attendance. However, in addition this will enable clients to see how consumers live in their own homes, how clean and tidy or messy client offices are, and so on. In this way researchers will be able to provide marketers and others within their organization with a clearer picture of how their products and services are consumed in the home and workplace. No doubt a by-product of this will be the attention of legislators and data privacy lawyers to find new ways to earn fees!

Another challenge that researchers are facing is the growing 'threat' that technology offers for companies to do their own research and to bypass the research department altogether. For example, automated surveying systems now exist, which enable a call centre agent to pass customers who are willing to answer a few short questions about their call over to an automated system, where the computer asks the questions and respondents use their telephone key pad to key in their answers. If customers wish to talk with a supervisor at any time during this 'survey', they can do so.

What makes this system different from others is that if a customer provides low ratings in response to the questions, the system can send a signal to the client to call him or her back to 'clarify' the situation. No doubt such 'instant' responses can be seen as being exceedingly beneficial to the organization. However, in some countries this type of call could not be positioned as market research. In addition, one has to ask who is championing the voice of the customer in organizations that are willing to experiment in this way? Who is ensuring that the questions being formulated for the survey are relevant and meaningful to customers? Who has considered the impact of such call monitoring on employees? Who has asked what will happen when everyone jumps on the bandwagon and starts offering an 'after the call' survey? How irritating will it become to consumers? Will they move their business elsewhere? Will they decide not to participate in any market research in future because of the intrusive nature of this 'service'?

Quantitative research is also facing its own challenges. Response rates are falling and costs are rising. In the longer term this could mean that companies will have to consider recruiting panels of customers or consumers who are willing to participate in a number of surveys each year. Technology also offers new developments for quantitative surveys. Juluwun and Gustafsson (2000; 76) refer to the development of kiosks that can be placed in high-traffic areas in malls to encourage people to come in and give their views about services. They can also be located in places of employment to capture customer opinions. Of course this data would need to be analysed, and there could be concerns about how representative the participants are, but the thought of seeing and hearing customer opinions at first hand is very appealing to management these days.

New, more powerful computers are enabling the development of 'knowledge extraction engines' that can 'fuse' and manipulate large volumes of data from consumer surveys and internal operational databases to produce, through regression and other statistical tools, 'models' of customer behaviour and loyalty. The sophistication of these programs enables analysts to create and test numerous hypotheses in short periods of time. Client researchers need to be able to not only understand how these programs work, but also to be on hand with advice on their strengths and limitations to ensure that their organizations get the best value for money from them.

CLOSING COMMENTS

I end this book with three thoughts for the reader to consider. In the future client researchers will have to work even more closely with other departments than they have to date. Researchers face new challenges to their traditional role through the blurring of customer satisfaction and loyalty surveys with 'customer insights', and the implications that arise as companies move towards being 'knowledge based' organizations where insights about customers are endemic throughout the organization, from the boardroom to the shop floor. In addition, technological developments have meant researchers can no longer be seen as the only 'eyes and ears' of the company. Listening posts are cropping up throughout organizations. Client-based researchers will therefore need to spend considerably less time behind their desks and far more out there with their internal sponsors and other people in their organizations, enhancing their ability to interpret data and draw meaningful analyses from it. This is not to say they should abdicate their position as the 'objective' eyes and ears of the organization. Rather it is saying that they need to ensure the voice of the consumer is not being misinterpreted, and that it reaches the boardroom as well as the shop floor.

Second, companies must continually remain vigilant in a world where, thanks to the improvements in communication via the internet, now ideas and advice are much more widely available. As James Heskett and his co-authors report:

> Too much anecdote-peppered advice is given by many service gurus today without a context. We're not told that what worked in one organization may not be appropriate for another. The advice is so overly simplistic that it leads us as managers to seek the elusive 'one big idea' that can help us improve performance.
>
> **(Heskett, Sasser and Schlesinger, 1997: 4)**

My final thought to those of you have travelled on this journey with me is that each new customer satisfaction and loyalty project provides new stimulating gateways to engage the mind, and opportunities for new learning and insights. I feel there are still many new avenues to explore, especially in light of the progress that science is making in respect to how the human mind works. I trust this book has stimulated interest in the subject, and that you will go on to explore more about the fascinating subject of customer satisfaction and loyalty.

Appendix 1:
Market Research Associations

AUSTRALIA
Association of Market Research Organizations
PO Box 658
Glebe
New South Wales 2037
Website: www.amro.com.au

Australian Market and Social Research Society
Level 1
3 Queen Street
Glebe
New South Wales 2037
Website: www.mrsa.com.au

AUSTRIA
Verband der Marktforscher Österreichs
Anastasius-Grün-Gasse
32,1180 Vienna
Website: www.vmoe.at

BELGIUM
Federation of Belgium Market Research Institutes
Avenue de la Couronne 159-165
1050 Brussels
Website: www.febelmar.be

CANADA
The Marketing Research and Intelligence Association
2175 Sheppard Avenue East
Suite 310

North York
Ontario M2J 1W8
Website: www.mria-arim.ca

DENMARK
Dansk Marketing Forum
Nordre Fasansvej 113-115
Postboks 40
2000 Frederiksberg C
Website: www.d-m-f.dk

EUROPE
European Society for Opinion and Marketing Research (ESOMAR)
Vondelstraat 172
1054 GV Amsterdam
The Netherlands
Website: www.esomar.org

FINLAND
Marketing Research Section of the Finnish Marketing Association
Fabianinkatu 4 B
PL 119
00131 Helsinki
Website: www.mark.fi

FRANCE
ADETEM
Pîle Universitaire Léonard de Vinci
92916 Paris La Defénse Cedex
Website: www.adetem.org

GERMANY
Berufsverband Deutscher Markt - und Sozialforscher e.V.
Beite Strasse 24
13187 Berlin
Website: www.bvm.org

GREECE
Association of Greek Market & Opinion Research Companies
99 Michalakopoulou Str
115 27 Athens
Website: www.sedea.gr

ITALY
Associazione Italiana Marketing
Via Olmetto 3
20123 Milan
Website: www.aism.org

JAPAN
Japan Marketing Research Association
1 Magami Building
1-5 Koraku
1-chome Bunkyo-ku
Tokyo 112-0004
Website: www.jmra-net.or.jp

THE NETHERLANDS
MarktOnderzoekAssociatie
Secretariat
MarktOnderzoekAssociatie
Herengracht 138
1015 BW Amsterdam
Website: www.marktonderzoekassociatie.nl

NEW ZEALAND
Market Research Society of New Zealand
PO Box 300-215
Albany
Auckland
Website: www.mrsnz.org.nz

Association of Market Research Organisations
PO 506
Paihia
Bay of Islands
Website: www.mrsnz.org.nz

PORTUGAL
Associação Portuguesa dos Profissionais de Marketing
Av Elias Garcia
172-2ºEsq
1050-103 Lisbon
Website: www.appm.pt

SPAIN
Asociación Espanola de Estudios de Mercado, Marketing y Opinión
Entença
332-334 8º 5ª 08029 Barcelona
Website: www.aedemo.es

Asociación Nacional de Empresas de Investigación de Mercados y Opinión Pública
Velázquez
146, 3º-2 28002
Madrid
Website: www.aneimo.com

SWEDEN
Association of Swedish Market Research Institutes
FSM
c/o Norstat
S:t Larsgatan 32B
S-582 24 Linköping
Website: www.fsm.a.se

SWITZERLAND
Swiss Association of Marketing and Social Research Professionals
Monsieur Primin Schallberger
Dr Gewerbestrasse 5
CH-6330 Cham
Website: www.swissresearch.org

TURKEY
Turkish Association of Marketing and Opinion Researchers
İstiklal Caddesi
İmam Adnan Sok.
No:1 K:3 Beyoğlu - İSTANBUL
Website: www.arastirmacilar.org

UK
British Market Research Association
Devonshire House
60 Goswell Road
London
EC1M 7AD
Website: www.bmra.org.uk

MRS
15 Northburgh Street
London EC1V 0JR
Website: www.mrs.org.uk

USA
Council of American Survey Research Organisations
170 North Country Road
Suite 4
Port Jefferson
New York 11777
Website: www.casro.org

Marketing Research Association
1344 Silas Deane Highway
Suite 306
Rocky Hill
Connecticut 06067-13042
Website: www.mra-net.org

Appendix 2:
The Market Research Society Code of Conduct

INTRODUCTION

The Market Research Society

With over 8,000 members in more than 50 countries, The Market Research Society (MRS) is the world's largest international membership organisation for professional researchers and others engaged in (or interested in) marketing, social or opinion research.

It has a diverse membership of individual researchers within agencies, independent consultancies, client-side organisations, and the academic community, and from all levels of seniority and job functions.

All members agree to comply with the MRS Code of Conduct, which is supported by the Codeline advisory service and a range of specialist guidelines on best practice.

MRS offers various qualifications and membership grades, as well as training and professional development resources to support these. It is the official awarding body in the UK for vocational qualifications in market research.

MRS is a major supplier of publications and information services, conferences and seminars and many other meeting and networking opportunities for researchers.

MRS is 'the voice of the profession' in its media relations and public affairs activities on behalf of professional research practitioners, and aims to achieve the most favourable climate of opinions and legislative environment for research.

The purpose of the Code of Conduct

This edition of the Code of Conduct was agreed by The Market Research Society to be operative from July 1999. It is a fully revised version of a self-regulatory code which has been in existence since 1954. This Code is based upon and fully compatible with the ICC/ESOMAR International Code of Marketing and Social Research Practice. The Code of Conduct is designed to support all those engaged in marketing or social research in maintaining professional standards. It applies to all members of The Market Research Society, whether they are engaged in consumer, business to business, social, opinion or any other type of confidential survey research. It applies to all quantitative and qualitative methods for data gathering. Assurance that research is conducted in an ethical manner is needed to create confidence in, and to encourage co-operation among, the business community, the general public, regulators and others.

The Code of Conduct does not take precedence over national law. Members responsible for international research shall take its provisions as a minimum requirement and fulfil any other responsibilities set down in law or by nationally agreed standards.

The purpose of guidelines

MRS Guidelines exist or are being developed in many of these areas in order to provide a more comprehensive framework of interpretation. These guidelines have been written in recognition of the increasingly diverse activities of the Society's members, some of which are not covered in detail by the Code of Conduct. A full list of guidelines appears on the Society's Web site, and is also available from the Society's Standards Manager.

One particular guideline covers the use of databases containing personal details of respondents or potential respondents, both for purposes associated with confidential survey research and in cases where respondent details are passed to a third party for marketing or other purposes. This guideline has been formally accepted by the Society, following extensive consultation with members and with the Data Protection Registrar/Commissioner.

Relationship with data protection legislation

Adherence to the Code of Conduct and the database Guidelines will help to ensure that research is conducted in accordance with the principles of data protection legislation. In the UK this is encompassed by the Data Protection Act 1998.

Data protection definitions

Personal Data means data which relates to a living individual who can be identified

- from the data, or
- from the data and other information in the possession of, or likely to come into the possession of, the data controller

and includes any expression of opinion about the individual and any indication of the intentions of the data controller or any other person in respect of the individual.

Processing means obtaining, recording or holding the information or data or carrying out any operation or set of operations on the information or data, including

- organisation, adaptation or alteration
- retrieval, consultation or use
- disclosure by transmission, dissemination or otherwise making available
- alignment, combination, blocking, erasure or destruction.

It is a requirement of membership that researchers must ensure that their conduct follows the letter and spirit of the principles of Data Protection legislation from the Act. In the UK the eight data protection principles are.

- **The First Principle**
  Personal data shall be processed fairly and lawfully.[1]
- **The Second Principle**
  Personal data shall be obtained only for one or more specified and lawful purposes, and shall not be further processed in any manner incompatible with that purpose or those purposes.
- **The Third Principle**
  Personal data shall be adequate, relevant and not excessive in relation to the purpose or purposes for which they are processed.
- **The Fourth Principle**
  Personal data shall be accurate and, where necessary, kept up to date.
- **The Fifth Principle**
  Personal data processed for any purpose or purposes shall not be kept longer than is necessary for that purpose or those purposes.
- **The Sixth Principle**
  Personal data shall be processed in accordance with the rights of data subjects under this Act.
- **The Seventh Principle**
  Appropriate technical and organisational measures shall be taken against unauthorised or unlawful processing of personal data and against accidental loss or destruction of, or damage to, personal data.

- **The Eighth Principle**

  Personal data shall not be transferred to a country or territory out-side the European Economic Area, unless that country or territory ensures an adequate level of protection for the rights and freedoms of data subjects in relation to the processing of personal data.

Exemption for research purposes

Where personal data processed for research, statistical or historical pur-poses are not processed to support decisions affecting particular indi-viduals, or in such a way as likely to cause substantial damage or distress to any data subject, such processing will not breach the Second Principle and the data may be retained indefinitely despite the Fifth Principle.

As long as the results of the research are not published in a form, which identifies any data subject, there is no right of subject access to the data.

Code definitions

- **Research**

  Research is the collection and analysis of data from a sample of individuals or organisations relating to their characteristics, behaviour, attitudes, opinions or possessions. It includes all forms of marketing and social research such as consumer and industrial sur-veys, psychological investigations, observational and panel studies.

- **Respondent**

  A respondent is any individual or organisation from whom any infor-mation is sought by the researcher for the purpose of a marketing or social research project. The term covers cases where information is to be obtained by verbal interviewing techniques, postal and other self-completion questionnaires, mechanical or electronic equipment, observation and any other method where the identity of the provider of the information may be recorded or otherwise traceable. This includes those approached for research purposes whether or not sub-stantive information is obtained from them and includes those who decline to participate or withdraw at any stage from the research.

- **Interview**

  An interview is any form of contact intended to provide information from a respondent.

- **Identity**

  The identity of a respondent includes, as well as his/her name and/or address, any other information which offers a reasonable chance that he/she can be identified by any of the recipients of the information.

- **Children**

  For the Purpose of the Code, children and young people are defined as those aged under 18. The intention of the provisions regarding age is to protect potentially vulnerable members of society, whatever the source of their vulnerability, and to strengthen the principle of public trust. Consent of a parent or responsible adult should be obtained for interviews with children under 16. Consent must be obtained under the following circumstances:

- In home/at home (face-to-face and telephone interviewing)
- Group discussions/depth interviews
- Where interviewer and child are alone together.

Interviews being conducted in public places, such as in-street/in-store/central locations, with 14 and 15 years olds may take place without consent if a parent or responsible adult is not accompanying the child. In these situations an explanatory thank you note must be given to the child.

Under special circumstances, a survey may waive parental consent but only with the prior approval of the Professional Standards Committee.

- **Records**
  The term records includes anything containing information relating to a research project and covers all data collection and data processing documents, audio and visual recordings. Primary records are the most comprehensive record of information on which a project is based; they include not only the original data records themselves, but also anything needed to evaluate those records, such as quality control documents. Secondary records are any other records about the Respondent.
- **Client**
  Client includes any individual, organisation, department or division, including any belonging to the same organisation as the research agency which is responsible for commissioning a research project.
- **Agency**
  Agency includes any individual, organisation, department or division, including any belonging to the same organisation as the client which is responsible for, or acts as, a supplier on all or part of a research project.
- **Professional Body**
  Professional body refers to The Market Research Society.
- **Public Place**
  A 'public place' is one to which the public has access (where admission has been gained with or without a charge) and where an individual could reasonably expect to be observed and/or overheard by other people, for example in a shop, in the street or in a place of entertainment.

PRINCIPLES

Research is founded upon the willing co-operation of the public and of business organisations. It depends upon their confidence that it is conducted honestly, objectively, without unwelcome intrusion and without harm to respondents. Its purpose is to collect and analyse information, and not directly to create sales nor to influence the opinions of anyone participating in it. It is in this spirit that the Code of Conduct has been devised.

The general public and other interested parties shall be entitled to complete assurance that every research project is carried out strictly in accordance with this Code, and that their rights of privacy are respected. In particular, they must be assured that no information which could be used to identify them will be made available without their agreement to anyone outside the agency responsible for conducting the research. They must also be assured that the information they supply will not be used for any purposes other than research and that they will not be adversely affected or embarrassed as a direct result of their participation in a research project.

Wherever possible respondents must be informed as to the purpose of the research and the likely length of time necessary for the collection of the information. Finally, the research findings themselves must always be reported accurately and never used to mislead anyone, in any way.

RULES

A. Conditions of membership and professional responsibilities

A.1   Membership of the professional body is granted to individuals who are believed, on the basis of the information they have given, to have such qualifications as are specified from time to time by the professional body and who have undertaken to accept this Code of Conduct. Membership may be withdrawn if this information is found to be inaccurate.

General responsibilities

A.2   Members shall at all times act honestly in dealings with respondents, clients (actual or potential), employers, employees, subcontractors and the general public.

A.3   Members shall at all times seek to avoid conflicts of interest with clients or employers and shall make prior voluntary and full disclosure to all parties concerned of all matters that might give rise to such conflict.

A.4   The use of letters after an individual's name to indicate membership of The Market Research Society is permitted in the case of Fellows (FMRS) and Full Members (MMRS). All members may point out, where relevant, that they belong to the appropriate category of the professional body.

A.5   Members shall not imply in any statement that they are speaking on behalf of the professional body unless they have the written authority of Council or of some duly delegated individual or committee.

Working practices

A.6   Members shall ensure that the people (including clients, colleagues and subcontractors) with whom they work are sufficiently familiar with this Code of Conduct and that working arrangements are such that the Code is unlikely to be breached through ignorance of its provisions.

A.7   Members shall not knowingly take advantage, without permission, of the unpublished work of a fellow member which is the property of that member. Specifically, members shall not carry out or commission work based on proposals prepared by a member in another organisation unless permission has been obtained from that organisation.

A.8   All written or oral assurances made by anyone involved in commissioning of conducting projects must be factually correct and honoured.

Responsibilities to other members

A.9   Members shall not place other members in a position in which they might unwittingly breach any part of this Code of Conduct.

Responsibilities of clients to agencies

A.10 Clients should not normally invite more than four agencies to tender in writing for a project. If they do so, they should disclose how many invitations to tender they are seeking.

A.11 Unless paid for by the client, a specification for a project drawn up by one research agency is the property of that agency and may not be passed on to another agency without the permission of the originating research agency.

Confidential survey research and other activities

(apply B.15 and Notes to B.15)

A.12 Members shall only use the term *confidential survey research* to describe research projects which are based upon respondent anonymity and do not involve the divulgence of identities or personal details of respondents to others except for research purposes.

A.13 If any of the following activities are involved in, or form part of, a project then the project lies outside the scope of confidential survey research and must not be described or presented as such:

(a) enquiries whose objectives include obtaining personal information about private individuals per se, whether for legal, political, supervisory (e.g. job performance), private or other purposes;

(b) the acquisition of information for use by credit-rating or similar purposes;

(c) the compilation, updating or enhancement of lists, registers or databases which are not exclusively for research purpose (e.g. which will be used for direct or relationship marketing);

(d) industrial, commercial or any other form of espionage;

(e) sales or promotional responses to individual respondents;

(f) the collection of debts;

(g) fund raising;

(h) direct or indirect attempts, including the framing of questions, to influence a respondent's opinions or attitudes on any issue other than for experimental purposes which are identified in any report or publication of the results.

A.14 Where any such activities referred to by paragraph A.13 are carried out by a member, the member must clearly differentiate such activities by:

(a) not describing them to anyone as confidential survey research and

(b) making it clear to respondents at the start of any data collection exercise what the purposes of the activity are and that the activity is not confidential survey research.

Scope of Code

A.15 When undertaking confidential survey research based on respondent anonymity, members shall abide by the ICC/ESOMAR International Code of Conduct which constitutes Section B of this Code.

A.16 MRS Guidelines issued, other than those published as consultative drafts, are binding on members where they indicate that actions or procedures *shall or must* be adhered to by members. Breaches of these conditions will be treated as breaches of the Code and may be subject to disciplinary action.

A.17 Recommendations within such guidelines that members should behave in certain ways are advisory only.

A.18 It is the responsibility of members to keep themselves updated on changes or amendments to any part of this Code which are published from time to time and announced in publications and on the Web pages of the Society. If in doubt about the interpretation of the Code, members may consult the Professional Standards Committee or its Codeline Service set up to deal with Code enquiries.

Disciplinary action

A.19 Complaints regarding breaches of the Code of Conduct by those in membership of the MRS must be made to The Market Research Society.

A.20 Membership may be withdrawn, or other disciplinary action taken, if, on investigation of a complaint, it is found that in the opinion of the professional body, any part of the member's research work or behaviour breaches this Code of Conduct.

A.21 Members must make available the necessary information as and when requested by the Professional Standards Committee and Disciplinary Committee in the course of an enquiry.

A.22 Membership may be withdrawn, or other disciplinary action taken, if a member is deemed guilty of unprofessional conduct. This is defined as a member:

(a) being guilty of any act or conduct which in the opinion of a body appointed by Council might bring discredit on the profession, the professional body or its members;

(b) being guilty of any breach of the Code of Conduct set out in this document;

(c) knowingly being in breach of any other regulations laid down from time to time by the Council of the professional body;

(d) failing without good reason to assist the professional body in the investigation of a complaint;

(e) having a receiving order made against him/her or making any arrangement or composition with his/her creditors;

(f) being found to be in breach of the Data Protection Act by the Data Protection Registrar.

A.23 No member will have his/her membership withdrawn, demoted or suspended under this Code without an opportunity of a hearing before a tribunal, of which s/he will have at least one month's notice.

A.24 Normally, the MRS will publish the names of members who have their membership withdrawn, demoted or are suspended or have other disciplinary action taken with the reasons for the decision.

A.25 If a member subject to a complaint resigns his/her membership of the Society whilst the case is unresolved, then such resignation shall be published and in the event of re-admission to membership the member shall be required to co-operate in the completion of any outstanding disciplinary process.

B. ICC/ESOMAR Code of Marketing and Social Research Practice

General

B.1 Marketing research must always be carried out objectively and in accordance with established scientific principles.

B.2 Marketing research must always conform to the national and international legislation which applies in those countries involved in a given research project.

The rights of respondents

B.3 Respondents' co-operation in a marketing research project is entirely voluntary at all stages. They must not be misled when being asked for co-operation.

B.4 Respondents' anonymity must be strictly preserved. If the respondent on request from the Researcher has given permission for data to be passed on in a form which allows that respondent to be identified personally:

(a) the Respondent must first have been told to whom the information would be supplied and the purposes for which it will be used, and also

(b) the Respondent must ensure that the information will not be used for any non-research purpose and that the recipient of the information has agreed to conform to the requirements of the Code.

B.5 The Researcher must take all reasonable precautions to ensure that Respondents are in no way directly harmed or adversely affected as a result of their participation in a marketing research project.

B.6 The Researcher must take special care when interviewing children and young people. The informed consent of the parent or responsible adult must first be obtained for interviews with children.

B.7 Respondents must be told (normally at the beginning of the interview) if observation techniques or recording equipment are used, except where these are used in a public place. If a respondent so wishes, the record or relevant section of it must be destroyed or deleted. Respondents' anonymity must not be infringed by the use of such methods.

B.8 Respondents must be enabled to check without difficulty the identity and bona fides of the Researcher.

The professional responsibilities of researchers

B.9 Researchers must not, whether knowingly or negligently, act in any way which could bring discredit on the marketing research profession or lead to a loss of public confidence in it.

B.10 Researchers must not make false claims about their skills and experience or about those of their organisation.

B.11 Researchers must not unjustifiably criticise or disparage other Researchers.

B.12 Researchers must always strive to design research which is cost-efficient and of adequate quality, and then to carry this out to the specification agreed with the Client.

B.13 Researchers must ensure the security of all research records in their possession.

B.14 Researchers must not knowingly allow the dissemination of conclusions from a marketing research project which are not adequately supported by the data. They must always be prepared to make available the technical information necessary to assess the validity of any published findings.

B.15 When acting in their capacity as Researchers the latter must not undertake any non-research activities, for example database marketing involving data about individuals which will be used for direct marketing and promotional activities. Any such non-research activities must always, in the way they are organised and carried out, be clearly differentiated from marketing research activities.

Mutual rights and responsibilities of researchers and clients

B.16 These rights and responsibilities will normally be governed by a written Contract between the Researcher and the Client. The parties may amend the provisions of rules B.19 – B.23 below if they have agreed this in writing beforehand; but the other requirements of this Code may not be altered in this way. Marketing research must also always be conducted according to the principles of fair competition, as generally understood and accepted.

B.17 The Researcher must inform the Client if the work to be carried out for that Client is to be combined or syndicated in the same project with work for other Clients but must not disclose the identity of such clients without their permission.

B.18 The Researcher must inform the Client as soon as possible in advance when any part of the work for that Client is to be subcontracted outside the Researcher's own organisation (including the use of any outside consultants). On request the Client must be told the identity of any such subcontractor.

B.19 The Client does not have the right, without prior agreement between the parties involved, to exclusive use of the Researcher's services or those of his organisation, whether in whole or in part. In carrying out work for different clients, however, the Researcher must endeavour to avoid possible clashes of interest between the services provided to those clients.

B.20 The following Records remain the property of the Client and must not be disclosed by the Researcher to any third party without the Client's permission:

(a) marketing research briefs, specifications and other information provided by the Client;

(b) the research data and findings from a marketing research project (except in the case of syndicated or multi-client projects or services where the same data are available to more than one client.

The Client has, however, no right to know the names or addresses of Respondents unless the latter's explicit permission for this has first been obtained by the Researcher (this particular requirement cannot be altered under Rule B.16).

B.21 Unless it is specifically agreed to the contrary, the following Records remain the property of the Researcher:

(a) marketing research proposals and cost quotations (unless these have been paid for by the Client). They must not be disclosed by the Client to any third party, other than to a consultant working for the Client on that project (with the exception of any consultant working also for a competitor of the Researcher). In particular, they must not be used by the Client to influence research proposals or cost quotations from other Researchers.

(b) the contents of a report in the case of syndicated research and/or multi-client projects or services when the same data are available to more than one client and where it is clearly understood that the resulting reports are available for general purchase or subscription. The Client may not disclose the findings of such research to any third party (other than his own consultants and advisors for use in connection with his business) without the permission of the Researcher.

(c) all other research Records prepared by the Researcher (with the exception in the case of non-syndicated projects of the report to the Client, and also the research design and questionnaire where the costs of developing these are covered by the charges paid by the Client).

B.22 The Researcher must conform to current agreed professional practice relating to the keeping of such records for an appropriate period of time after the end of the project. On request the Researcher must supply the Client with duplicate copies of such records provided that such duplicates do not breach anonymity and confidentiality requirements (Rule B.4); that the request is made within the agreed time limit for keeping the Records; and that the Client pays the reasonable costs of providing the duplicates.

B.23 The Researcher must not disclose the identity of the Client (provided there is no legal obligation to do so) or any confidential information about the latter's business, to any third party without the Client's permission.

B.24 The Researcher must, on request, allow the Client to arrange for checks on the quality of fieldwork and data preparation provided that the Client pays any additional costs involved in this. Any such checks must conform to the requirements of Rule B.4.

B.25 The Researcher must provide the Client with all appropriate technical details of any research project carried out for that Client.

B.26 When reporting on the results of a marketing research project the Researcher must make a clear distinction between the findings as such, the Researcher's interpretation of these and any recommendations based on them.

B.27 Where any of the findings of a research project are published by the Client, the latter has a responsibility to ensure that these are not misleading. The Researcher must be consulted and agree in advance the form and content of publication, and must take action to correct any misleading statements about the research and its findings.

B.28 Researchers must not allow their names to be used in connection with any research project as an assurance that the latter has been carried out in conformity with this Code unless they are confident that the project has in all respects met the Code's requirements.

B.29 Researchers must ensure that Clients are aware of the existence of this Code and of the need to comply with its requirements.

NOTES

How the ICC/ESOMAR International Code of Marketing and Social Research Practice should be applied

These general notes published by ICC/ESOMAR apply to the interpretation of Section B of this Code in the absence of any specific interpretation which may be found in the MRS Definitions, in Part A of the MRS Code or in Guidelines published by the MRS. MRS members who are also members of ESOMAR will in addition be subject to requirements of the guidelines published by ESOMAR.

These Notes are intended to help users of the Code to interpret and apply it in practice.

The Notes, and the Guidelines referred to in them, will be reviewed and reissued from time to time. Any query or problem about how to apply the Code in a specific situation should be addressed to the Secretariat of MRS.

The rights of respondents

All Respondents entitled to be sure that when they agree to co-operate in any marketing research project they are fully protected by the provisions of this Code and that the Researcher will conform to its requirements. This applies equally to Respondents interviewed as private individuals and to those interviewed as representatives of organisations of different kinds.

Note on Rule B.3

Researcher and those working on their behalf (e.g. interviewers) must not, in order to secure Respondents' co-operation, make statements or promises which are knowingly misleading or incorrect – for example, about the likely length of the interview or about the possibilities of being re-interviewed on a later occasion. Any such statements and assurances given to Respondents must be fully honoured.

Respondents are entitled to withdraw from an interview at any stage and to refuse to co-operate further in the research project. Any or all of the information collected from or about them must be destroyed without delay if the Respondents so request.

Note on Rule B.4

All indications of the identity of Respondents should be physically separated from the records of the information they have provided as soon as possible after the completion of any necessary fieldwork quality checks. The Researcher must ensure that any information which might identify Respondents is stored securely, and separately from the other information they have provided; and that access to such material is restricted to authorised research personnel within the Researcher's own organisation for specific research purposes (e.g. field administration, data processing, panel or 'longitudinal' studies or other forms of research involving recall interviews).

To preserve Respondents' anonymity not only their names and addresses but also any other information provided by or about them which could in practice identify them (e.g. their Company and job title) must be safeguarded.

These anonymity requirements may be relaxed only under the following safeguards:

(a) Where the Respondent has given explicit permission for this under the conditions of 'informed consent' summarised in Rule 4 (a) and (b).

(b) where disclosure of names to a third party (e.g. a Subcontractor) is essential for any research purpose such as data processing or further interview (e.g. an independent fieldwork quality check) or for further follow-up research. The original Researcher is responsible for ensuring that any such third party agrees to observe the requirements of this Code, in writing, if the third party has not already formally subscribed to the Code.

It must be noted that even these limited relaxations may not be permissible in certain countries. The definition of 'non-research activity', referred to in Rule 4(b), is dealt with in connection with Rule 15.

Note on Rule B.5

The Researcher must explicitly agree with the Client arrangements regarding the responsibilities for product safety and for dealing with any complaints or damage arising from faulty products or product misuse. Such responsibilities will normally rest with the Client, but the Researcher must ensure that products are correctly stored and handled while in the Researcher's charge and that Respondents are given appropriate instructions for their use. More generally, Researchers should avoid interviewing at inappropriate or inconvenient times. They should also avoid the use of unnecessarily long interviews; and the asking of personal questions which may worry or annoy Respondents, unless the information is essential to the purposes of the study and the reasons for needing it are explained to the Respondent.

Note on Rule B.6

The definitions of 'children' and 'young people' may vary by country but if not otherwise specified locally should be taken as 'under 14 years' and '14–17 years' (under 16, and 16–17 respectively in the UK).

Note on Rule B.7

The Respondent should be told at the beginning of the interview that recording techniques are to be used unless this knowledge might bias the Respondent's subsequent behaviour: in such cases the Respondent must be told about the recording at the end of the interview and be given the opportunity to see or hear the relevant section of the record and, if they so wish, to have this destroyed. A 'public place' is defined as one to which the public has free access and where an individual could reasonably expect to be observed and/or overheard by other people present, for example in a shop or in the street.

Note on Rule B.8

The name and address/telephone number of the Researcher must normally be made available to the Respondent at the time of interview.

In cases where an accommodation address or 'cover name' are used for data collection purposes arrangements must be made to enable Respondents subsequently to find without difficulty or avoidable expense the name and address of the Researcher. Wherever possible 'Freephone' or similar facilities should be provided so that Respondents can check the Researcher's bona fides without cost to themselves.

The professional responsibilities of researchers

This Code is not intended to restrict the rights of Researchers to undertake any legitimate marketing research activity and to operate competitively in so doing. However, it is essential that in pursuing these objectives the general public's confidence in the integrity of marketing research is not undermined in any way. This Section sets out the responsibilities which the Researcher has towards the public at large and towards the marketing research profession and other members of this.

Note on Rule B.14

The kinds of technical information which should on request be made available include those listed in the Notes to Rule B.25. The Researcher must not however disclose information which is confidential to the Client's business, nor need he/she disclose information relating to parts of the survey which were not published.

Note on Rule B.15

The kinds of non-research activity which must not be associated in any way with the carrying out of marketing research include: enquiries whose objectives are to obtain personal information about private individuals per se, whether for legal, political, supervisory (e.g. job performance), private or other purposes; the acquisition of information for use for credit-rating or similar purposes; the compilation, updating or enhancement of lists, registers or databases which are not exclusively for research purposes (e.g. which will be used for direct marketing); industrial, commercial or any other form of espionage; sales or promotional attempts to individual Respondents; the collection of debts; fund-raising; direct or indirect attempts, including by the design of the questionnaire, to influence a Respondent's opinions, attitudes or behaviour on any issue.

Certain of these activities – in particular the collection of information for databases for subsequent use in direct marketing and similar operations – are legitimate marketing activities in their own right. Researchers (especially those working within a client company) may often be involved with such activities, directly or indirectly. In such cases it is essential that a clear distinction is made between these activities and marketing research since by definition marketing research anonymity rules cannot be applied to them.

Situations may arise where a Researcher wishes, quite legitimately, to become involved with marketing database work for direct marketing (as distinct from marketing research) purposes: such work must not be carried out under the name of marketing research or of a marketing research Organisation as such.

The mutual rights and responsibilities of researchers and clients

This Code is not intended to regulate the details of business relationships between Researchers and Clients except in so far as these may involve principles of general interest and concern. Most such matters should be regulated by the individual business. It is clearly vital that such Contracts are based on an adequate understanding and consideration of the issues involved.

Note on Rule B.18

Although it is usually known in advance what subcontractors will be used, occasions do arise during the project where subcontractors need to be brought in, or changed, at very short notice. In such cases, rather than cause delays to the project in order to inform the Client it will usually be sensible and acceptable to let the Client know as quickly as possible after the decision has been taken.

Note on Rule B.22

The period of time for which research Records should be kept by the Researcher will vary with the nature of the project (e.g. ad hoc, panel, repetitive) and the possible requirements for follow-up research or further analysis. It will normally be longer for the stored research data resulting from a survey (tabulations, discs, tapes etc.) than for primary field records (the original completed questionnaires and similar basic records). The period must be disclosed to, and agreed by, the Client in advance. In default of any agreement to the contrary, in the case of ad hoc surveys the normal period for which the primary field records should be retained is one year after completion of the fieldwork while the research data should be stored for possible further analysis for at least two years. The Researcher should take suitable precautions to guard against any accidental loss of the information, whether stored physically or electronically, during the agreed storage period.

Note on Rule B.24

On request the Client, or his mutually acceptable representative, may observe a limited number of interviews for this purpose. In certain cases, such as panels or in situations where a Respondent might be known to (or be in subsequent contact with) the Client, this may require the previous agreement of the Respondent. Any such observer must agree to be bound by the provisions of this Code, especially Rule B.4.

The Researcher is entitled to be recompensed for any delays and increased fieldwork costs which may result from such a request. The Client must be informed if the observation of interviews may mean that the results of such interviews will need to be excluded from the overall survey analysis because they are no longer methodologically comparable.

In the case of multi-client studies the Researcher may require that any such observer is independent of any of the Clients.

Where an independent check on the quality of the fieldwork is to be carried out by a different research agency the latter must conform in all respects to the requirements of this Code. In particular, the anonymity of the original Respondents must be fully safeguarded and their names and addresses used exclusively for the purposes of back-checks, not being disclosed to the Client. Similar considerations apply where the Client wishes to carry out checks on the quality of data preparation work.

Notes on Rule B.25

The Client is entitled to the following information about any marketing research project to which he has subscribed:

(1) **Background**
   - for whom the study was conducted
   - the purpose of the study
   - names of subcontractors and consultants performing any substantial part of the work

(2) **Sample**
   - a description of the intended and actual universe covered
   - the size, nature and geographical distribution of the sample (both planned and achieved); and where relevant, the extent to which any of the data collected were obtained from only part of the sample
   - details of the sampling method and any weighting methods used
   - where technically relevant, a statement of response rates and a discussion of any possible bias due to non-response

(3) **Data collection**
   - a description of the method by which the information was collected
   - a description of the field staff, briefing and field quality control methods used
   - the method of recruiting Respondents; and the general nature of any incentives offered to secure their co-operation
   - when the fieldwork was carried out
   - (in the case of 'desk research') a clear statement of the sources of the information and their likely reliability

(4) **Presentation of results**

- the relevant factual findings obtained
- bases of percentages (both weighted and unweighted)
- general indications of the probable statistical margins of error to be attached to the main findings, and the levels of statistical significance of differences between key figures
- the questionnaire and other relevant documents and materials used (or, in the case of a shared project, that portion relating to the matter reported on).

The Report on a project should normally cover the above points or provide a reference to a readily available document which contains the information.

Note on Rule B.27

If the Client does not consult and agree in advance the form of publication with the Researcher the latter is entitled to:

(a) refuse permission for his name to be used in connection with the published findings and
(b) publish the appropriate technical details of the project (as listed in the Notes to B.25).

Note on Rule B.29

It is recommended that Researchers specify in their research proposals that they follow the requirements of this Code and that they make a copy available to the Client if the latter does not already have one.

CODELINE

Codeline is a free, confidential answer service to Market Research Society Code of Conduct related queries raised by market researchers, clients, respondents and other interested parties. The aim of Codeline is to provide an immediate, personal and practical interpretation and advice service.

Codeline is directly responsible to the MRS Professional Standards Committee (PSC) to which each query and its response is reported at PSC's next meeting. Queries from enquirers are handled by an individual member of the Codeline panel, drawn from past members of the PSC. As long as contact can be made with the enquirer, queries will be dealt with by Codeline generally within 24 hours. Where necessary, the responding Codeline member can seek further specialist advice.

Codeline's response to enquirers is not intended to be definitive but is the personal interpretation of the individual Codeline member, based on personal Code-related experience. PSC and Codeline panellists may highlight some of the queries and responses for examination and ratification by the PSC, the ultimate arbiter of the Code, at its next meeting. In the event that an individual Codeline response is not accepted by the PSC the enquirer will be notified immediately.

Enquirer details are treated as totally confidential outside the PSC but should 'Research' or any other MRS journal wish to refer to a particularly interesting or relevant query in 'Problem Page' or similar, permission is sought and obtained from the enquirer before anonymous publication and after that query's examination by PSC.

Codeline operates in the firm belief that a wide discussion of the issues arising from queries or anomalies in applying the Code and its associated guidelines within the profession will lead both to better understanding, awareness and application of the Code among members and to a better public appreciation of the ethical standards the market research industry professes and to which it aspires.

How to use Codeline

Codeline deals with any market research ethical issues. To contact Codeline please phone or fax the MRS Secretariat who will then allocate your query to a Codeline panellist.

If you choose to contact MRS by phone, the MRS Secretariat will ask you to confirm by fax the nature of your query, whether or not the caller is an MRS member or works for an organisation which employs an MRS member and a phone number at which you can be contacted. This fax will then be sent to the allocated panellist who will discuss your query directly with you by phone as soon as possible after receipt of your enquiry.

Please forward any queries about the MRS Code of Conduct and Guidelines, in writing to the:

MRS Secretariat, 15 Northburgh Street, London EC1V OJR

Tel: 020 7490 4911; Fax: 020 7490 0608

NOTES

1. In particular shall not be processed unless at least one of the conditions in Schedule 2 is met, and in the case of sensitive data, at least one of the conditions of Schedule 3 is also met. (These schedules provide that in determining whether personal data has been processed fairly, consideration must be given to the basis on which it was obtained.)

Notes

CHAPTER 1

1 Rothschild (1984: 124). Some of the historical examples mentioned in this chapter are summarized from the more detailed coverage of them in this book.

CHAPTER 2

1 Quoted in Mingo (1994: 111).
2 Summarized from a case reported in more detail by Heskett, Sasser and Schlesinger (1997: 18–29).
3 More details about the ASCI can be found at www.theacsi.org/model. This brief summary was produced from data on the site on 10 December 2004.
4 Details about the conversion model have been based on information available on www.conversionmodel.com.

CHAPTER 3

1 The main points in the case study are taken from the booklet 'Menu and deliveries and other quite interesting stuff' issued by Pret A Manger in 2004.

CHAPTER 12

1   In an interview given on the Belgenland, December 1930, quoted in the *Oxford Dictionary of 20th Century Quotations*, Oxford University Press, 1999, p 96.

2   Delgado-Ballester, Munuera-Alemán and Yagüe-Guillén (2003: 46). See also paper by Walter, Mueller and Helfert (2004) and Costabile (2004).

3   Zaltman (2003: 197). Also writing on this subject is Dan Hill (2003).

Bibliography

Allen, Derek R (2004) *Customer Satisfaction Research Management*, ASQ Quality Press, Wisconsin

Alreck, Pamela L and Settle, Robert B (1995) *The Survey Research Handbook*, 2nd edn, Irwin Professional Publishing, Burr Ridge, Illinois

Anderson, Kristin and Kerr, Carol (2002) *Customer Relationship Management*, McGraw-Hill, New York

Bacon, Donald R (2003) A comparison of approaches to importance-performance analysis, *Journal of the Market Research Society*, **45** (1), pp 55–71

Bagozzi, Richard P, Gürhan-Canli, Zeynep and Priester, Joseph R (2002) *The Social Psychology of Consumer Behaviour*, Open University Press, Buckingham

Baker, Michael J (1991) *Research for Marketing*, Macmillan Education, Basingstoke

Beerli, Asunción, Martín, Josefa D and Quintana, Agustín (2004) A model of customer loyalty in the retail banking market, *European Journal of Marketing*, **38** (1/2), pp 253–75

Bierck, Richard (2000) Are you reaching your customers? *Harvard Management Communication Letter* (December)

Birn, Robin J (2004) *The Effective Use of Market Research*, 4th edn, Kogan Page, London

Blanchard, Ken and Bowles, Sheldon (1998) *Raving Fans!* HarperCollinsBusiness, London

Brace, Ian (2004) *Questionnaire Design*, Kogan Page, London

Brace, Ian, Nancarrow, Clive and Tinson, Julie (2004) Breaking the rules: greater insight and greater value? Conference Paper 15, Market Research Society Annual Conference

Bradley, Mark (2004) *Inconvenience Stores: One year in UK customer service*, Ardra Press, Cottingham

Buttle, Francis (1996) SERVQUAL: Review, critique, research agenda, *European Journal of Marketing*, **30** (1), pp 8–32

Callingham, Martin (2004) *Market Intelligence*, Kogan Page, London

Carroll, Lewis (1865) *Alice's Adventures in Wonderland* (children's edition 1954), Macmillan, London

Choi, Byounggu, Lee, Choongseok, Lee, Heeseok and Subramani (2004) Effects of web retail service quality and product categories on consumer behaviour: a research model and empirical exploration, *Proceedings of the 37th Hawaii International Conference on System Sciences*

Clemmer, Jim (1993) *Firing On All Cylinders*, Piatkus, London

Cook, Sarah (2004) *Measuring Customer Service Effectiveness*, Gower, Aldershot

Costabile, Michele (Dec 2004) *A Dynamic Model of Customer Loyalty* [online] www.bath.ac.uk (accessed April 2005)

Customer Service, CRM & Call Centre Management (2004) [online] www.eCustomerServiceWorld.com (accessed April 2005)

Davidow, William and Uttal, Bro (1989), *Total Customer Service*, HarperCollins, New York

Delgado-Ballester, Elena, Munuera-Alemán, Jose Luis and Yagüe-Guillén, María Jesús (2003) Development and validation of a brand trust scale, *Journal of the Market Research Society*, **45** (1), p 46

Dholakia, Paul M and Morwitz, Vicki G (2002) How surveys influence customers, *Harvard Business Review*, reprint F0205A

Ereault, Gill, Imms, Mike and Callingham, Martin (eds) (2002) *Qualitative Market Research: Principles and Practice*, 7 vols, Sage, London

European Foundation for Quality Management (EFQM) (1999) *The EFQM Excellence Model*, EFQM, Brussels

European Society for Opinion and Marketing Research (ESOMAR) (1999) *Mystery Shopping Guidelines*, ESOMAR, Amsterdam

Foss, Brian and Stone, Merlin (2002) *CRM in Financial Services*, Kogan Page, London

Foxall, Gordon R and Goldsmith, Ronald E (1994) *Consumer Psychology for Marketing*, Routledge, London

Goode, Mark M H, Moutinho, Luiz and Chien, Charles (1996) Structural equation modelling of overall satisfaction and full use of services for ATMs, *International Journal of Bank Marketing*, **14** (7), pp 4–11

Grapentine, Terry (nd) *Practical theory: the best research practitioners are the best theorists* [online] www.grapetine.com (accessed April 2005)

Hague, Paul, Hague, Nick and Morgan, Carol-Ann (2004) *Market Research in Practice*, Kogan Page, London

Hart, Mike (nd) *The Quantification of Patient Satisfaction* [online] www.business-kac.co.uk (accessed April 2005)

Harvard Business Review (1998) *Measuring Corporate Performance*, Harvard Business School Publishing, Boston, Mass

Heath, Robert (1999) 'Just popping down to the shops for a package of image statements': a new theory of how consumers perceive brands, *Journal of the Market Research Society*, **41** (2), April, pp 153–69

Herrington, Guy and Lomax, Wendy (1999) Do satisfied employees make customers satisfied? Kingston Business School Occasional Paper Series no 34, Kingston University, January

Heskett, James L (1986) *Managing In The Service Economy*, Harvard Business School Press, Boston, Mass

Heskett, James L, Sasser, W Earl Jr and Schlesinger, Leonard A (1997) *The Service Profit Chain*, Free Press, New York

Hill, Dan (2003) *Body of Truth: Leveraging what consumers can't or won't say*, Wiley, New Jersey

Hill, Nigel and Alexander, Jim (2000) *Handbook of Customer Satisfaction and Loyalty Measurement*, 2nd edn, Gower, Aldershot

Hill, Nigel, Brierley, John and MacDougall, Rob (2003) *How to Measure Customer Satisfaction*, 2nd edn, Gower, Aldershot

Hofmeyr, J (2004) *The Conversion Model*, December [online] www.conversion-model.com (accessed April 2005)

Hofmeyr, Jan and Rice, Butch (2000) *Commitment-Led Marketing: The key to brand profits is in the customer's mind*, Wiley, Chichester

Horne, A (1962) *Price of Glory*, quoted in *The Little Oxford Dictionary of Quotations*, Oxford University Press, Oxford (2001)

Horovitz, Jacques (1990) *How to Win Customers: Using customer service for a competitive edge*, Pitman, London

Humby, Clive and Hunt, Terry, with Phillips, Tim (2003) *Scoring Points: How Tesco is winning customer loyalty*, Kogan Page, London

Johnson, Michael D and Gustafsson, Anders (2000) *Improving Customer Satisfaction, Loyalty and Profit*, Jossey-Bass, San Francisco

Jones, Thomas O and Sasser, W Earl Jr (2001) Why satisfied customers defect (originally published 1995), product number 6838, HBR OnPoint

Kaplan, Robert S and Norton, David P (1991) The balanced scorecard: measures that drive performance, *Harvard Business Review*, Jan–Feb, pp 71–79

Kaplan, Robert S and Norton, David P (1996) *The Balanced Scorecard: Translating strategy into action*, Harvard Business School Press, Boston, Mass

Kon, Martin (2004) Stop customer churn before it starts, *Harvard Management Update*, Article reprint no U0407D, July

Lam, Simon S K and Woo, Ka Shing (1997) Measuring service quality: a test-retest reliability investigation of SERVQUAL, *Journal of the Market Research Society*, **39** (2), pp 381–96

McCarthy, Dennis G (1997) *The Loyalty Link: How loyal employees create loyal customers*, Wiley, New York

McDonald, Colin and Vangelder, Phyllis (eds) (1998) *ESOMAR Handbook of Market and Opinion Research*, 4th edn, ESOMAR, Amsterdam

McGivern, Yvonne (2003) *The Practice of Market and Social Research*, Pearson Education, Harlow

Mingo, Jack (1994) *How the Cadillac Got its Fins and other Tales from the Annals of Business and Marketing*, HarperCollins, New York

Mitchell, Jack (2003) *Hug Your Customers, Love the Results*, Penguin, London

MORI (2004) Qualitative research in the 21st century, *MORI Qualitative Hothouse*, November [online] http://www.mori.com/qualitative/qual-res2.shtml (accessed April 2005)

Morrison Coulthard, Lisa J (2004) Measuring service quality: a review and critique of research using SERVQUAL, *Journal of the Market Research Society*, **46** (4), pp 479–97

Morrison, Lisa J, Colman, Andrew M and Preston, Carolyn, C (1997) Mystery customer research: cognitive processes affecting accuracy, *Journal of the Market Research Society*, **39** (2), pp 349–61

Moutinho, Luiz and Smith, Anne (2000) Modelling bank customer satisfaction through mediation of attitudes towards human and automated banking, *International Journal of Bank Marketing*, **18** (3), pp 124–34

Murphy, John A (2001) *The Lifebelt: The definitive guide to managing customer retention*, Wiley, Chichester

National Institute of Standards and Technology (NIST) (2003) Frequently asked questions, fact sheet, 25 November, NIST

Olve, Nils-Göran, Roy, Jan and Wetter, Magnus (1999) *Performance Drivers: A practical guide to using the balanced scorecard*, Wiley, Chichester

Paine, André (2004) Stuff yourself in like sardines – what tube drivers told commuters, *Evening Standard*, Friday 9 July, p 21

Parasuraman, A, Zeithaml, V A and Berry, L L (1985) A conceptual model of service quality and its implications for future research, *Journal of Marketing*, **49**, pp 41–50

Parasuraman, A, Zeithaml, V A and Berry, L L (1991) Refinement and reassessment of the SERVQUAL scale, *Journal of Retailing*, **67** (4), pp 420–50

Parker, Ken and Stuart, Trish (1997) The West Ham syndrome, *Journal of the Market Research Society*, **39** (3), July, p 510

Peel, Malcolm (1987) *Customer Service: How to achieve total customer satisfaction*, Kogan Page, London

Pret A Manger (2004) Menu and deliveries and other quite interesting stuff, Pret A Manger, London

Prime Minister's Office of Public Services Reform (2002) *Measuring and Understanding Customer Satisfaction: A MORI review for the Office of Public Services Reform*, MORI Social Research Institute (April)

Raymond, Martin (2003), *The Tomorrow People: Future consumers and how to read them today*, FT Prentice Hall, Harlow

Reichheld, Frederick F (1993) Loyalty based management, *Harvard Business Review*, March–April, pp 64–73

Reichheld, Frederick F (1996) *The Loyalty Effect*, Harvard Business School Press, Boston, Mass

Reichheld, Frederick F (2001) *Loyalty Rules*, Harvard Business School Press, Boston, Mass

Reichheld, Frederick F (2003) The one number you need to grow (December), product number 5534, HBR OnPoint

Robbins, Stephen P and Decenzo, David A (2001) *Fundamentals of Management: Essential concepts and applications*, Prentice-Hall, New Jersey

Robertson, Ivan T, Lewis, Barbara, Bardzil, Philip J and Nikolaou, Ioannis (2004) *The Influence of Personality on Customers' Assessments of Service Quality*, Manchester University School of Management, [online] www.sm.umist.ac.uk (accessed December 2004)

Rothschild, William E (1984) *How to Gain (and Maintain) the Competitive Advantage in Business*, McGraw-Hill, New York

Sanders, Donald H (1995) *Statistics: A first course*, 5th international edn, McGraw-Hill, New York

Six Sigma (2004) *What is Six Sigma?* [online] www.isixsigma.com (accessed December 2004)

Smith, Shaun and Wheeler, Joe (2002) *Managing the Customer Experience*, Pearson Education, Harlow

Stone, Merlin, Bond, Alison and Foss, Bryan (with Woodcock, N and Kirby, J) (2004) *Consumer Insight: How to use data and market research to get closer to your customer*, Kogan Page, London

Van Nuys, David (1999) Online focus groups: market research in web time, *San Jose Business Journal*, November [Online] www.e-focusgroups.com/press/online-article.html (accessed April 2005)

Walter, Achim, Mueller, Tjhilo A and Helfert, Gabriele (2004) *The Impact of Satisfaction, Trust and Relationship Value on Commitment: Theoretical considerations and empirical results* [online] www.bath.ac.uk (accessed December 2004)

Ward, Didy (1998) 'Quantitative research', in Colin McDonald and Phyllis Vangelder (eds), *ESOMAR Handbook of Market and Opinion Research*, 4th edn, ESOMAR, Amsterdam

Wilson, Alan (2002) Attitudes towards customer satisfaction measurement in the retail sector, *Journal of the Market Research Society*, **44** (2), pp 213–22

Zaltman, Gerald (2003) *How Customers Think*, Harvard Business School Press, Boston, Mass

Zeithaml, Valerie A, Berry, Leonard L and Parasuraman, A (1996) The behavioural consequences of service quality, *Journal of Marketing*, **60** (April), pp 31–46

WEBSITES

Clark, Robin (ed): www.thewisemarketer.com

EFQM: www.efqm.org

Malcolm Baldrige National Quality Award: www.nist.gov/public_affairs/factsheet

Simalto: www.simalto.co.uk

Index

DATE DUE

GAYLORD   #3522PI   Printed in USA